THE ONE YEAR®
Did You Know
DEVOTIONS 2

Nancy S. Hill

Tyndale House Publishers, Inc.
Carol Stream, Illinois

Visit Tyndale's exciting Web site for kids at www.tyndale.com/kids

TYNDALE is a registered trademark of Tyndale House Publishers, Inc.

Tyndale Kids logo is a trademark of Tyndale House Publishers, Inc.

The One Year is a registered trademark of Tyndale House Publishers, Inc.

The One Year Did You Know Devotions, Volume 2

Designed by Ron Kaufmann and Jessie McGrath

Cover designed by Julie Chen

Edited by Stephanie Voiland

Library of Congress Cataloging-in-Publication Data

Hill, Nancy S., date.
  The one year book of did you know devotions for kids / Nancy S. Hill.
     p. cm.
  Includes bibliographical references and index.
  ISBN 978-1-4143-2014-4
  1. Devotional calendars—Juvenile literature.   2. Christian children—Prayer-books and devotions—English.
3. Curiosities and wonders—Juvenile literature. I. Title.

BV4870 .H43 2002
242'.62—dc21   2002006747

Printed in the United States of America

15 14 13 12 11 10 09
 7   6   5   4   3   2   1

For Zack, my encourager.
For Wendy and Andrew, who are inspiring.
And for little "Alexander the Great" Gentry, whose life touched us all.

Contents

September

October

January 1

Where did the first calendar come from?

This is the day the LORD has made.
We will rejoice and be glad in it.
PSALM 118:24

Thousands of years ago, nothing about the days or months was written down. Farmers paid special attention to the seasons of the year and the nights and days because they needed to know when to plant their crops and harvest them. But everyone was interested in how many days were going by and what time of year it was. An excellent way of keeping track was to look at the night skies, watching when the moon grew full and seeing how the planets changed position among the stars. Eventually people began to see a pattern. It was the Egyptians who first made a calendar that people could use, more than seven thousand years ago. It had twelve months that each had thirty days. Through the years, five special feast days or holidays were added, and then the calendar included 365 days. Today our months are a little different from the Egyptian calendar, but we still use their idea of a 365-day year.

No matter how we count the days or try to figure out what will happen in each one of them, the Bible reminds us what really counts: "This is the day the LORD has made. We will rejoice and be glad in it" (Psalm 118:24). God wants us to appreciate and enjoy each day, and be thankful to him for the gift of life he gives us every day we are here on earth. That is the best way to keep track of what will happen to our hearts and spirits through the months and years, no matter what other things may happen.

January 2

When were ducks in the Olympics?

Be kind to each other, tenderhearted, forgiving one
another, just as God through Christ has forgiven you.
EPHESIANS 4:32

It was the rowing competition in the 1928 summer Olympic Games. An Australian athlete, Henry "Bobby" Pearce, was ahead of everyone else in the single scull, an event in which each athlete rows his own small boat. Suddenly a line of ducks paddled across the water right in front of where Bobby was heading. Without seeming the least bit worried about the race, Bobby lifted his oars out of the water, which slowed his tiny boat and allowed all the ducks to swim away. Then Bobby began rowing again, and he still reached the finish line in time to win the gold medal.

Sometimes it's hard to be kind or forgiving when someone is in our way or is ruining our big plans, or when we're doing something much too important to be stopped. But those are the times we most need to follow the Bible when it says, "Be kind to each other, tenderhearted, forgiving one another, just as God through Christ has forgiven you" (Ephesians 4:32).

January

How did a three-year-old inspire the invention of a camera?

I tell you the truth, anyone who doesn't receive the Kingdom of God like a child will never enter it.
MARK 10:15

Little Jennifer Land simply asked her father a question after he took pictures of her in 1943 while on vacation. Her question was, "Why can't I see the pictures now?" It just so happened that her father was a distinguished inventor in the camera business, and Jennifer's question made Edwin Herbert Land begin to wonder, *Why not?* Five years later, Edwin began to sell his new invention: the Polaroid Land Camera. This camera was the first to develop a picture that came rolling out of the camera only six minutes later. Jennifer now had a way to see a picture of herself on vacation very soon after it had been snapped!

Sometimes little children don't realize that some things just aren't possible. For example, Jennifer was expecting to see something that hadn't even been invented yet. She trusted and believed that everything is possible. Jesus said, "I tell you the truth, anyone who doesn't receive the Kingdom of God like a child will never enter it" (Mark 10:15). Sometimes as we grow up, we forget how to believe in amazing things like little children do. Jesus is just asking us to trust that what seems too good to be true really is true!

January

Why would you need a big boat to help build a road?

Mark out a straight path for your feet so that those who
are weak and lame will not fall but become strong.
HEBREWS 12:13

Long ago, there was one place in the world where people knew they could find that brownish-black sticky tar, called asphalt, to make a road smooth. On an island called Trinidad, across the ocean in the West Indies, there is a lake. This lake does not hold water—it holds asphalt, because there is so much of the gooey stuff in the ground around it. The only way to get asphalt to America in the late 1800s was to scoop the asphalt out of the lake, drop it into a large boat, and sail it to the United States. Because the asphalt got very hard inside the boat on the way over, it had to be chipped out of the boat little by little when it arrived. Then it was mixed with a solution to make it soft and spreadable so it could cover the tops of dirt roads. What a lot of work and trouble just to have a smoother road!

It was worth the extra work, because nobody likes to travel over holes or bumps where they might get hurt. God wants us to work even harder on the steps we take when following him so we will not get hurt. The Bible tells us to "mark out a straight path for your feet so that those who are weak and lame will not fall but become strong" (Hebrews 12:13). Try to show others that you are walking smoothly where God wants you to instead of tripping on "bumps" in the road, like lying or cheating or talking back to your parents. Then others can follow carefully and safely behind you and walk where God wants them to go.

January

Why won't your ballpoint pen write, even when it has plenty of ink?

I will open the windows of heaven for you. I will pour out a blessing so great you won't have enough room to take it in!
MALACHI 3:10

Is it because of some mysterious law of gravity or because the temperature is too hot or cold? Not at all. It's all about age and air. The trick to pens is the thickness of the ink. If the ink is too thin, the pen leaks. But if the ink is too thick, it can't ooze out of the pen and onto the paper. The older the pen is, the more chance that air has been in contact with the liquid ink. The longer the ink is exposed to air, the thicker the ink gets. Have a pen that skips? That means it's getting old. When the pen is ancient and might as well be thrown away, you will know it. No ink will move at all, because it has thickened too much to flow. That's when your pen still looks full, but your paper stays totally blank.

When you want to write, a pen that leaves an empty page is useless to you. It is not what you need. If you allow the Lord to work in your life, you will never end up needing something you do not have. God knows what is best for you and will give you plenty of it. He has said, "I will open the windows of heaven for you. I will pour out a blessing so great you won't have enough room to take it in!" (Malachi 3:10). Like a pen that always flows with ink, God's love will always keep your soul full of what you need, when you need it.

January

What's in your kitchen that used to be locked in a safe?

Keep on seeking, and you will find.
LUKE 11:9

It's the clear plastic wrap that is used to cover food! It was actually invented by mistake. In 1908 a chemist named Jacques Brandenberger was trying to make a tablecloth that could be wiped clean and not show ugly stains. His idea was to cover an ordinary tablecloth with a clear sheet. It turned out that his invention—cellophane—didn't work for the tablecloths, but it was useful for wrapping food. At first, cellophane was so expensive that only the fanciest stores could wrap their products in it. At night, the cellophane was locked up in the store's safe so that no one would steal it. Later, cellophane was made waterproof, and people discovered that ordinary food could be covered in it and kept fresh. Then everyone began using cellophane to wrap just about every kind of food they could think of.

Because cellophane is clear, people like how they can see what is inside. If you want to know more about God, just imagine that the answers are wrapped in cellophane and you can see them easily. It's a promise from the Bible—"keep on seeking, and you will find" (Luke 11:9). God does not want to hide himself from you. He loves to show you more and more about himself every time you look for him.

January

Take a toothpick, some cotton, and a baby's ear, and what do you get?

Purify me from my sins, and I will be clean; wash me,
and I will be whiter than snow.
PSALM 51:7

A Q-tip, of course. Leonard Gerstenzang noticed that his wife put cotton on the ends of a toothpick to clean their baby's ears. He thought that this homemade tool might be helpful to all parents. In 1923, he began manufacturing his new invention. These swabs were made by a machine and were advertised as being "untouched by human hands." Three years later, the name officially became "Q-tips." The Q was for quality, and *tips* referred to the tiny pieces of cotton that were attached to the ends of the stick to make them soft. Later the wooden sticks were replaced with rolled-up paper ones, and that's how one mom's idea became a product that every mother could use.

Did you know that God washes you every day, just like mothers wash their babies? The bad things you do make you look dirty in God's eyes. But because Jesus died on the cross and rose again, he forgives you today for the bad things you may have done yesterday—and that makes you clean. The Bible tells us to ask the Lord to "purify me from my sins, and I will be clean; wash me, and I will be whiter than snow" (Psalm 51:7). You are clean again every day, and God doesn't need a Q-tip to make it happen. The forgiveness of Jesus is the most powerful cleaner in the world.

January

How do iguanas skydive?

You can ask for anything in my name, and I will do it.
JOHN 14:13

Pretend you are out walking one day on the cliffs in southern Mexico. You spot a shy iguana sunning itself on the edge of a towering cliff by the ocean. The iguana is as startled to see you as you are to see it, and without a moment's hesitation, it hurls itself right off the edge of the cliff into nothing but air. Oh no! But there is no need for you to worry. The iguana has one of the most sturdy bodies of any living creature. For an iguana, falling off a cliff is about the same thing as falling out of bed would be to you. Iguanas have been known to land straight down from a sixty-foot drop, right onto jagged rocks at the bottom of a cliff. There is no crashing or smashing. The iguana doesn't even seem to notice the impact when it hits the ground. It lands and immediately starts running away—probably to another high and sunny spot—to try again.

When you can see examples of little miracles all around you, like the iguana just getting up as if it had never fallen, it serves as a reminder that God is so powerful and can make anything happen. The Bible tells us that Jesus said, "You can ask for anything in my name, and I will do it" (John 14:13). Examples of amazing things we have seen with our own eyes make us believe all the more that Jesus is Lord over all the earth—and Lord of our lives too.

January

When did a mirror take the place of a person?

Anyone who belongs to Christ has become a new person.
The old life is gone; a new life has begun!
2 CORINTHIANS 5:17

In 1911, Ray Harroun's race car was registered to compete in the first Indianapolis 500 race. His car started out pretty much like the others, minus one very important addition. All the other drivers had a mechanic who rode with them and kept looking backward to keep track of the other cars. But Ray didn't have a mechanic to be his lookout. Instead, he attached a mirror over the dashboard of his car so he could look backward himself. Ray was the only driver to race alone, and his was the only car to win the race! Later, thanks to a man named Elmer Berger, rearview mirrors became available in all cars.

When driving a car, it's necessary to be aware of what is behind you. But an amazing thing happens when you are a child of God. God promises that your past has been erased, so you don't always need to look behind you and be worried about what you did yesterday and the days before that. The Bible says, "Anyone who belongs to Christ has become a new person. The old life is gone; a new life has begun!" (2 Corinthians 5:17). The only reason for a "rearview mirror" for your soul is to look back and rejoice that you have been forgiven!

January

When did a president play a joke on his guests?

Imitate God, therefore, in everything you do,
because you are his dear children. Live a life filled
with love, following the example of Christ.
EPHESIANS 5:1-2

Soon after he was elected, President Calvin Coolidge was having dinner in the White House with some old friends. Since his guests had never been to the White House and weren't sure what was polite or correct to do at mealtime, they decided to copy President Coolidge's every move. That plan worked well for them until the after-dinner cup of coffee. When they saw the president pour some of his coffee into the saucer under his cup and add milk and sugar, his guests did the same, guessing that at the White House, you drank from the saucer. President Coolidge had fun with what he did next—he put his saucer on the floor for his cat to drink from, knowing that all his guests couldn't do the same thing!

The president's guests thought that he was so important that they needed to follow him exactly. That's the way God's children should feel about Christ. He is the most important person to follow, and when you copy him very carefully, only good can come from it. The Bible says it this way: "Imitate God, therefore, in everything you do, because you are his dear children. Live a life filled with love, following the example of Christ" (Ephesians 5:1-2). God wants you to follow him, but not so he can play a trick on you. When you follow him, you will get a reward that lasts forever. It's no joke!

January

Which food product tasted much better the older it got?

Gray hair is a crown of glory.
PROVERBS 16:31

In 1835, chemists William Perrins and John Lea were asked to re-create, as best they could from the recipe, a sauce a customer had enjoyed while in India. They accomplished the task and hoped to sell it in their drugstore, since it was supposedly so memorable. But it smelled strongly of fish and didn't seem edible, so they gave up and just put it in the cellar. Two years later, when they were cleaning out the basement, they found containers of the sauce and sampled it again before throwing it out. This time it was delicious! In 1837 they began selling it as "Lea and Perrins Worcestershire sauce" (pronounced WOOS-tuh-shur sauce), because they lived in Worcester, England. Not many people could pronounce it, but lots of people enjoyed it anyway.

Not everything that's new and young and fresh is the most valuable. God finds lots of importance in the wisdom and experience that comes as people live their lives. People who are older often know more, can give good advice, and have wonderful solutions for problems. Just like the Worcestershire sauce, the longer people live, the more complete and flavorful their lives are. The Bible says it this way: "Gray hair is a crown of glory" (Proverbs 16:31).

January

What do we eat that has a smile on it?

Search for the LORD and for his strength; continually seek him.
1 CHRONICLES 16:11

That's what the Portuguese explorers who saw this food in the 1400s first noticed about it. It was growing on trees on islands in the middle of the Pacific and Indian Oceans. It was round like a head, with hairy strands hanging on it and dents that looked like two eyes and a smile. The explorers named it "grinning face," which was the word *coco* in Portgugese, and that's how it became known as the coconut. But the coconut isn't actually a nut at all. It's the fruit from the coconut palm tree. Coconuts are very efficiently designed. Each one has a hard shell that doesn't weigh a lot, and there is extra air carried inside, along with a seed, coconut milk, and some chewy white fruit. The shell is then wrapped with a husky, hairy coat that helps everything stay moist inside, while keeping damaging salt water out. Now you have a fruit that can float along on the ocean until a wave drops it off on the shore, where it begins to germinate, or sprout. What a perfect traveling plan for this tasty tropical treat!

Coconuts were a special treat for sailors. Imagine how carefully they searched for coconuts when their ships reached the shore of an island. Sailors would look for the face of a coconut in the trees and on the sand because they wanted a sweet reward. The Bible tells us how much we should want to search for Jesus. "Search for the LORD and for his strength; continually seek him" (1 Chronicles 16:11). If you keep looking until you can sense the smile of Jesus, you will get a sweet reward too—the reward of a closer relationship with him.

January

Why do cows seem sloppy and slow?

He causes the grass to grow for the cattle.
PSALM 104:14, NKJV

Because they are! Cows can produce over four ounces of saliva a minute, which makes a lot of slobber! Cows spend thirteen hours a day lying down and eight hours just chewing food. Cows chew their food, swallow it, and then spit it out again. They chew it all over again to help it digest. In only one day, just one cow can eat twenty pounds of grain and one hundred pounds of feed, and drink a bathtub full of water. A cow burps (and worse, releases gas) all day long—up to two hundred pounds of it per year. A cow would not be your first choice as a roommate!

God cares for even the cow, and he throws in a bonus for us—the cow gives us milk after chewing all its grass. The Bible says, "He causes the grass to grow for the cattle" (Psalm 104:14, NKJV). There is no step in his plans that God forgot about. He takes care of every animal, and us, every single day.

January

Why did people suddenly want a mouse in their homes?

He will be called: Wonderful Counselor, Mighty God, Everlasting Father, Prince of Peace.
ISAIAH 9:6

At one time, people couldn't wait to buy a mouse, bring it into their homes, and keep it on a desk. Why would they behave so strangely? Actually, this mouse was not alive. It was the kind of mouse that can be plugged into a computer and is used to point and click at things on the screen. People were excited about this new computer part, because before the mouse was invented, everything on a computer had to be done using the keyboard. But why such an odd name? The original computer piece had two buttons like eyes near its pointed front and a slim cord at the back that looked like a wiggling tail. The inventor, Dr. Douglas Engelbart, said, "One of the members of the team nick-named the device a mouse and it caught on. We thought that when it had escaped out into the world it would have a more dignified name, but it didn't."

Names often describe something or someone. We can learn what something looks like or what kind of a person to expect when we hear the name. Before Jesus was born, the Bible told people what they could look forward to from his names. We read, "He will be called: Wonderful Counselor, Mighty God, Everlasting Father, Prince of Peace" (Isaiah 9:6). The Bible encourages us to expect a lot from Jesus, and Jesus is true to every name he has been given by his Father.

January

Which sea creature couldn't survive without its powerful eyes?

Open my eyes to see the wonderful truths in your instructions.
PSALM 119:18

Unlike most sea animals, this creature doesn't have a hard shell to protect its skin. So it needs powerful eyes to keep from getting badly injured by bumping into rocks or sharp objects underwater and to see attackers coming. The eyes of this animal are five times more powerful than human eyes, which allows it to see through muddy water, the glare from the sun, and even its own inky cloud that it releases to hide itself from danger. What is this sharp-eyed creature? An octopus! Nothing in the sea can escape a hungry octopus by blending in or moving quickly. The eyes of the octopus are so powerful that they have even been studied to make improvements for camera lenses.

God has provided the octopus with wonderful tools to help it survive. But he has taken even better care of us. If we follow what God teaches us, we can see beyond our earthly lives to the rewards he has waiting for us in heaven. The Bible says, "Open my eyes to see the wonderful truths in your instructions" (Psalm 119:18). Ask God to help you see even more clearly than the octopus can.

January 16

What tricks can a crow perform?

The LORD is good to everyone.
He showers compassion on all his creation.
PSALM 145:9

Crows are smart and like to work as a team to create mischief. A crow will find two other crows to play a game of snatching another animal's food. Imagine that there is a rabbit on the ground, with a bit of lettuce it has found and intends to eat. Two crows will land nearby, one on each side of the rabbit. Both crows pretend they are about to steal the lettuce and fly away with it. While all the confusion is going on, the third crow dives in and swoops for the food, grabbing it and taking off into the sky. Then the other crows leave also, and they all share the lettuce somewhere else. Crows have other tricks too. When a predator or a person approaches a whole flock of crows, one will caw the signal for danger, and they all take off in flight immediately. Crows like shiny things. They collect them. They have been known to take buttons, coins, jewelry, and even silverware—it doesn't matter what it is. They just know they like shiny things, and they will fly off with the shiny objects in their mouths and tuck them away in secret hiding places. Crows also like to amuse themselves just for fun. Sometimes a crow will spot a sleeping animal, dive down silently, and peck it on the head just to see it jump up as the crow caws and flies away.

Watching a crow is sometimes like watching a cartoon. Crows seem to be at the center of lots of mischief. Maybe you get into mischief at times too, and you wonder how God feels about that. At times like that, remember that the Bible says, "The LORD is good to everyone. He showers compassion on all his creation" (Psalm 145:9). You can trust God to always be good to you, even if you've gotten into mischief.

January

Who would want to go where the burglars are?

I am the way, the truth, and the life.
No one can come to the Father except through me.
JOHN 14:6

His name was Edwin Holmes. The year was 1852, and Edwin had just figured out a way to wire a home so that a bell rang when a door or window was opened. He had just invented the first burglar alarm. Edwin installed an alarm system in his own home in Boston, Massachusetts, so people could see how it worked. But his neighbors were not interested in buying one. The problem? People thought they didn't need an alarm for their houses. After all, hardly anyone ever got robbed in Boston in those days. To become more successful, Edwin decided to move to New York City, where burglary was a bigger problem. By moving to a city with more crime, Edwin was able to get more customers.

People go to a great deal of trouble to try to protect their possessions, and even their lives, on earth. But many people don't realize that the most important thing is the protection of their souls so that they can one day go to heaven. How do you make sure you can spend forever in God's Kingdom? Believe in and follow Jesus Christ, who says, "I am the way, the truth, and the life. No one can come to the Father except through me" (John 14:6). You do not need a burglar alarm to keep your soul safe—Jesus will do that job for you.

January

What invention did a kindergartener think of and build?

You have made a wide path for my feet
to keep them from slipping.
PSALM 18:36

Five-year-old Jeanie Low needed to use a stepping stool in her family's small bathroom, but it often got in the way. The clutter had to be pushed aside by family members, and because it was plastic, it broke. Jeanie knew she needed a new stool that she could use but be able to put away somewhere when she didn't need it. So she came up with the Kiddie Stool. The idea was that there would be a platform she could stand on that would be attached to the cabinet door under the sink, and she would be able to fold it up to stick to the cabinet with magnets when she wasn't using it. Her parents took her to the store to buy supplies, but the salespeople told her that her idea wouldn't work. Jeanie tried it anyway, and it was very successful. What did Jeanie work on next? An alarm that goes off when the bathtub is being filled up and is about to overflow.

The Kiddie Stool that Jeanie thought of as a little girl was helpful to everyone in her family. In the same way, God takes care of all his children when they need help. The Bible tells us what God does for us. It says, "You have made a wide path for my feet to keep them from slipping" (Psalm 18:36). It is a good feeling to know that God will be there to lift you up when you cannot climb by yourself.

January

Why does the woodpecker hit its own head?

Your children and your crops will be blessed. The offspring of your herds and flocks will be blessed.
DEUTERONOMY 28:4

Woodpeckers eat insects hidden underneath or in tree bark. Woodpeckers like to look for damaged wood, where more insects are likely to be. To find a good spot, the woodpecker slams its beak against the sides of trees to find a spot that sounds hollow from insect damage. Then it hammers with its bill 150 times a minute, at a speed of about twelve miles an hour, to get into the wood. The force that a woodpecker feels on its skull is 250 times what an astronaut feels on liftoff. Woodpeckers have a much larger brain case than most birds to make sure their brains are not bashing against their skulls every time they drill. And their muscles and bones at the base of their bills work like shock absorbers to keep the force from being unbearably strong. A woodpecker has the longest tongue of any bird. The tongue can reach out two inches beyond its bill, which allows it to reach far into the hole to snag insects. The tongue also has sticky barbs on it so it can spear or stick to insects and pull them out of the wood. A woodpecker's tail is very strong and acts like the kickstand on a bike to allow the woodpecker to rear back and hammer. Most amazing of all, woodpeckers even have special feathers that cover their nostrils to keep out flying chips of wood.

It truly makes you stop and think about blessings when you see how well God provided for the little woodpecker. He provides creatures not only with the tools they need but also with the food. The Bible says, "Your children and your crops will be blessed. The offspring of your herds and flocks will be blessed" (Deuteronomy 28:4). God made sure to give each creature good ways to survive in the world.

January

What was Blibber-Blubber?

Anyone who welcomes a little child like this
on my behalf welcomes me.
MARK 9:37

Blibber-Blubber was not a big success when Frank Fleer invented it in 1906. The gum was crackly to chew and way too sticky, and it wouldn't roll back into your mouth after you blew a bubble. It stuck to your face after the bubbles kept popping, and you had to rub it with turpentine to get it off. Many years later, in 1928, one of Frank's employees, the candy factory's accountant Walt Diemer, came up with the winning formula completely by accident. He said, "I was doing something else and ended up with something with bubbles." He named his new substance Dubble Bubble. The first batch blew great bubbles the first day but wouldn't blow at all after it sat overnight. The next batch was tasty and blew bubbles, but it was an ugly gray color. The third try worked. It was pink because that was the only color of food coloring in the whole factory. Walt took some lumps of Dubble Bubble into a few grocery stores, gave away free samples, and sold the rest. He never got a patent, or license, to prove he invented the gum, because he was afraid that if he wrote down the recipe other companies would copy his gum. But other companies bought some of his gum, analyzed it, and copied it anyway. So Walt Diemer never got rich, even though people seemed to enjoy his gum the most. But when Walt was ninety, he said he had no regrets. He said, "Bubble gum brought a little happiness to millions of kids. And if I could do that, I'm happy."

Walt loved children, which was why he was happier to have helped them than he would have been to have gotten rich. Jesus tells us why that's so important. The Bible says, "Anyone who welcomes a little child like this on my behalf welcomes me" (Mark 9:37). What a wonderful story Walt had to tell!

January

What can a snake's teeth tell you?

He is so rich in kindness and grace that he purchased our freedom with the blood of his Son and forgave our sins.
EPHESIANS 1:7

The snake has a very unusual set of teeth. The only time a snake needs its teeth is to hold its prey in its mouth so the victim cannot get away. Its main way of eating is to swallow, so it needs to have its food stay in its mouth. This is why a snake's teeth slant backward down its throat. Once its food, let's say a mouse, is caught and tries to struggle, the snake sinks in its teeth, and the animal can't move forward to get out of the grip of the snake's teeth. A snake's teeth are very fragile and break easily. Sometimes when the snake is eating a larger animal, its teeth will break. But the amazing thing about the teeth of a snake is that the snake always has an extra full set of teeth as a spare! These teeth grow in a fold of the snake's mouth lining, where they stay tucked away until the snake needs one. When the snake loses a tooth, the extra tooth behind it moves down into the empty spot. Soon, the new tooth has grown into the snake's jawbone and it is very solid, just like the lost one was.

Everyone likes to know they have the ability to start over. When a snake needs new teeth, they appear. And when we need forgiveness and salvation and a chance to go to heaven, God generously provides it for us. The Bible says, "He is so rich in kindness and grace that he purchased our freedom with the blood of his Son and forgave our sins" (Ephesians 1:7). Ask Jesus to come into your heart, and claim your chance to have a new and better life for all eternity.

January

How did the first artificial snow on a ski slope get there?

[God] directs the snow to fall on the earth and tells the rain to pour down. Then everyone stops working so they can watch his power.

JOB 37:6-7

It was Mohawk Mountain in Connecticut in 1950, and there had been no winter snowfall that year. Walter Schoenknecht, who loved to ski, was the owner of a ski slope he had carved out of the mountain himself. Walter got tired of waiting for real snow, so he hatched a plan. He had seen a nearby ski jump work just fine using crushed ice, and he decided ice could be added to the mountain. Since refrigerators had become popular fairly recently, the icehouses that used to sell big blocks of ice for people's kitchens didn't have much to do. Walter got several of them busy making ice again, and he had nearly thirty trucks bringing ice blocks to the mountain all day and all through the night. At the bottom of the mountain, Walter parked a gigantic ice crusher. Everyone wanted to help, so long lines of men formed between the ice trucks and the crusher, passing hundred-pound blocks of ice from hand to hand until the blocks were dropped into the crusher. From the bottom up, the mountain became white with crushed ice, and when ski season started three days later, Mohawk Mountain was open for business.

This passage from the Bible is a good description of what winter is usually like: "[God] directs the snow to fall on the earth and tells the rain to pour down. Then everyone stops working so they can watch his power" (Job 37:6-7). Walter found a way around it when God didn't send snow that year, but look at the difference in the amount of effort! God's snow falls at his command, and that's all there is to it. For people to even begin to copy God's work, it took an incredible number of people and supplies. Everyone involved that winter must have been truly in awe of the power God can so easily display.

January

Which animal attacks by running backward?

You care for people and animals alike, O LORD.
PSALM 36:6

Why would any animal do that? This one has a very good reason. It has quills, like little sharp spears, on its back. Some people think that when this animal is in danger, it shoots the quills into its enemy like rockets blasting off from its back. But that is not what happens. The only way this animal can use its quills to injure another animal is to turn its back, bring its quills up, tuck its head down, and do one of three things: wait for an attack, swat a predator with its tail, or back up quickly into the animal and poke it with its quills. The quills break off without harming the owner, but the animal that was poked gets wounds that become infected. The brave quill-carrying animal, if you haven't guessed yet, is the porcupine.

God has given protective devices to so many animals in the animal kingdom, yet the porcupine's "weapons" are especially unique. The Bible tells us, "You care for people and animals alike, O LORD" (Psalm 36:6). What a caring and creative God we have! Nothing escapes his notice or his concern.

January

Buffalo don't fly, so what are "buffalo wings"?

Don't brag about tomorrow,
since you don't know what the day will bring.
PROVERBS 27:1

The first time anyone saw buffalo wings, they were being invented by Teressa Bellissimo in 1964 in New York. She was making a snack for her son and his friends one evening. She took chicken wings, added a new sauce she'd created, and served the wings with the dipping sauce to the hungry group, who loved them. The new snack became famous at Teressa and her husband's business, and then throughout their town, and then across America. But how did chicken wings become known as buffalo wings? They were first created in Buffalo, New York.

God delights in giving his children pleasant surprises, and you never know when something wonderful will come your way. Since he is all-powerful, God can make anything happen. The Bible says, "Don't brag about tomorrow, since you don't know what the day will bring" (Proverbs 27:1). We could never imagine by ourselves the good things God has planned. Think about the times that God has worked in your life to surprise and delight you. He is waiting for you to accept his special gifts of love every day.

January 25

How was a teapot responsible for waking people up each morning?

Great is his faithfulness;
his mercies begin afresh each morning.
LAMENTATIONS 3:23

In 1902, Frank Clarke, an inventor, came up with a complicated way to wake people up. He built an alarm clock that moved some of its parts and struck a match, which lit and then touched a miniature stove top, igniting a small flame. The flame heated a kettle full of water that was sitting on the stove burner, which started the water boiling. Then steam power from the boiling water operated a system of levers and springs that lifted the kettle to pour boiling water into a waiting teapot. That's when the clock sent out an alarm, and if you weren't already alarmed enough to be awake, the noise would make sure you were!

Getting up in the morning is not most people's favorite thing to do, but maybe it will help you feel a little better to have this thought about God every morning: "Great is his faithfulness; his mercies begin afresh each morning" (Lamentations 3:23). When you open your eyes, you've got a brand-new day to make something special out of, and your God is filled with love to help you get started.

January

What makes snow crunchy?

The rain and snow come down from the heavens and stay on the
ground to water the earth. They cause the grain to grow, producing
seed for the farmer and bread for the hungry. It is the same
with my word. I send it out, and it always produces fruit. It will
accomplish all I want it to, and it will prosper everywhere I send it.

ISAIAH 55:10-11

All over the earth, on every continent, you can see snow some of the time. It's hard to believe, but there is even snow in Hawaii, on top of the volcanoes, where the air is cold enough. Under your own feet, you can tell how cold the snow is by listening to it. If you walk on snow and it is quiet and slides a little, the snow is not completely frozen, so your foot puts pressure on it that warms and softens the flakes a little bit. But if you hear crunching when you walk, that means the snow is very cold. What you are hearing is the snowflakes breaking under your boots, because they are deeply frozen and are too cold and hard for your steps to warm the flakes even slightly. Each snowflake is made up of about fifty tiny crystals that are too small to see. While each crystal has six sides, none of the crystals match any of the others. When all the crystals stick together, they make each snowflake appear to have the shape of a star. A snowflake might take as long as an hour to land once it is formed in the sky.

There are many things we can learn from studying the weather, because God has created each weather condition to bring certain results each time. But there's something we can learn even more from: God's Word. The Bible says, "The rain and snow come down from the heavens and stay on the ground to water the earth. They cause the grain to grow, producing seed for the farmer and bread for the hungry. It is the same with my word. I send it out, and it always produces fruit. It will accomplish all I want it to, and it will prosper everywhere I send it" (Isaiah 55:10-11). God's plans for your soul are way more prosperous than his plans for the crops of the earth.

January 27

Where did the sports term
first string come from?

Many who are the greatest now will be least
important then, and those who seem least
important now will be the greatest then.
MATTHEW 19:30

If you are on the "first string" of your team, it means you are among the best players your team has. The term actually comes from the sport of archery, from way back in the thirteenth century. Each marksman, who shot the arrow from the bow, had a favorite string that he liked to put on his bow before he used it. It was his best—the one he would choose to use first. It was his first string.

Unfortunately, there are usually many people competing for each first-place prize, and only a few will win. We are usually happy for them but sad for ourselves when we lose. But we get reassurance from the Bible when it says, "Many who are the greatest now will be least important then, and those who seem least important now will be the greatest then" (Matthew 19:30). In God's eyes, we all have talents that are worthy of a first place, and he had a purpose when he gave them to us. There may not be an official first-place award for helping your neighbor take her trash cans to the curb or for visiting people in a nursing home, but God may very well be having a ceremony for you in heaven on the days when you use the gifts he gave you to be helpful and thoughtful.

January 28

Oranges and lemons: to stamp or to sticker?

Just as you can identify a tree by its fruit,
so you can identify people by their actions.
MATTHEW 7:20

At first, Sunkist ink-stamped its lemons and oranges with the company name. But there was a problem. The lemon stamps came out clearly, but the orange peels reacted differently depending on the variety. Sometimes the ink smeared or only half the word was stamped, and some packing plants were careful about stamping while others were not. To make sure all the lemons and oranges had the same type of mark, Sunkist switched to stickers. But there was another problem. Sunkist found that almost all the oranges were sold to individual shoppers, so the stickers worked perfectly for oranges. The lemons, though, were mostly sold to restaurants, where many lemons had to be ready in a hurry. It would have taken way too long to peel a sticker off each lemon, so the stickers were often left on, and pieces of sticker would appear in salads or drinks. Now what? Sunkist decided the first idea was best for lemons, and the company went back to ink-stamping them.

No matter which way they identified their fruit, Sunkist was proud for everyone to know that the fruit was theirs. That's how God wants us to feel about our actions. He wants us to do the right thing—the good thing, the thing we can be proud of. The Bible says, "Just as you can identify a tree by its fruit, so you can identify people by their actions" (Matthew 7:20). When people see how you behave, hopefully they can say, "That must be a Christian over there."

January 29

Is talking easier for men or women?

Let everything you say be good and helpful, so that your words will be an encouragement to those who hear them.
EPHESIANS 4:29

A woman's vocal chords are shorter than a man's, which is why her voice usually has a higher pitch. When a young man enters his teens, his vocal chords quickly double in length, and his voice drops lower. When he has grown into a man, and for the rest of his life, he will always have a harder time talking than a woman. Because a woman's vocal chords are shorter, she needs less air to vibrate the vocal chords, so she uses less energy talking than a man does.

No matter how much you talk, it's what you say that makes a difference. Try to talk to people with encouraging words. Tell them things that God wants them to know. The Bible gives us an example of what people need to hear from him: "Let everything you say be good and helpful, so that your words will be an encouragement to those who hear them" (Ephesians 4:29).

January

How could a mom cuddle her baby without using her hands?

Beware that you don't look down on any of these little ones. For I tell you that in heaven their angels are always in the presence of my heavenly Father.
MATTHEW 18:10

In many African countries, babies are carried on their mothers' backs, wrapped next to their moms with bright pieces of cloth. That's where Ann Moore, a pediatric nurse working for the peace corps in Togo, West Africa, first got an idea that she brought back to America. Ann tried the African method for carrying her baby but couldn't tie the cloths securely enough. So Ann showed her own mother some pictures of the African design, and her mom sewed a different version, with holes for the baby's legs and straps to go over the mom's shoulders. She called it the Snugli, and every mother who saw Ann wearing hers seemed to want one. Ann, her husband, and her mother began making the Snugli by hand. Orders went from two a month to eight thousand a month. Those were made in an updated chicken house on Ann's parents' farm. The manufactured version of the Snugli was packaged in a remodeled dog kennel. Ann even heard from zookeepers because animals like monkeys enjoyed the Snugli too.

Ann's family helped many other families make their little ones feel loved and secure, just as the African women did. This tender care of children is very pleasing to God. The Bible tells us that Jesus said, "Beware that you don't look down on any of these little ones. For I tell you that in heaven their angels are always in the presence of my heavenly Father" (Matthew 18:10). The love of children comes from the very heart of God.

January 31

What car was the first car Henry Ford built?

The one who endures to the end will be saved.
MATTHEW 24:13

Henry Ford began building his first car during his spare time while working for the Edison Illuminating Company in Detroit, Michigan. Henry rented a house with a shed in the back, and that's where he spent three years putting the car together. The car weighed five hundred pounds and had four bicycle-type wheels with spokes. He called it the Quadricycle. It had two speeds—ten miles per hour and twenty miles per hour—and a four-horsepower engine, but it didn't have any brakes. Finally, in 1896, Henry tried to take his first test drive with the Quadricycle, but the car wouldn't fit through the doors of the shed. He axed bricks off the edges of the door until the car could get out of the shed, and then he drove it at two o'clock in the morning, right after he'd finished building it. After that accomplishment, Henry was inspired to stop working for the electric company and start designing and making other automobiles on his own. By the way, Henry Ford never had a driver's license.

Henry Ford never gave up on his dream of driving that first car, and in the end he overcame all obstacles and attained his goal. It's nice to have an experience like that on earth. But imagine what a greater reward you will have if you don't give up on your faith. The Bible promises, "The one who endures to the end will be saved" (Matthew 24:13). Imagine! If you hold on to your dream of being in heaven with God and trust him to help you overcome all obstacles, you will have the best dream fulfilled that anyone could ask for.

February
1

How did a mistake and a teacher inspire the invention of the paper towel?

How can I know all the sins lurking in my heart?
Cleanse me from these hidden faults.
PSALM 19:12

Arthur Scott owned a paper company that made bathroom tissue. One day a large roll of paper arrived that was too thick and had not been cut correctly. Arthur wondered what could be done with it. That's when he heard about a teacher in Philadelphia who had given all her students their own paper squares to wipe their hands on, so everyone wouldn't be using the same towel in the restroom. Arthur used the teacher's idea and made his roll of paper into individual disposable towels. Called the Sani-Towel, it was sold to places with public restrooms and later was marketed for use in kitchens as well.

When your hands are dirty or you've made a mess, you can ask for a paper towel. But there are more important things to keep clean than just what we see. Be aware that your heart and soul need to be cleaned as well. In the Bible we read, "How can I know all the sins lurking in my heart? Cleanse me from these hidden faults" (Psalm 19:12). Each time you use a paper towel, let it remind you to ask God to clean you on the inside at the same time.

February

Which piece of clothing always has a buttonhole without a matching button?

The LORD has anointed me to bring good news to the poor.
ISAIAH 61:1

On every man's dress coat, there are flaps of material called lapels that fold out to make a collar. On every left lapel, there is a buttonhole. When you look on the right side of the lapel, there is no button to fit in the hole. What is the extra hole in the coat for? The first coat to have this hole cut into it belonged to Prince Albert of England. He cut the hole himself. He was attending a party with Queen Victoria, who was going to marry him. Someone gave a bunch of flowers to the queen, and she handed one of her flowers to Albert. Prince Albert had nowhere to put his flower, so he sliced a slit in his coat lapel and slid the flower into it. After that, all suit coats were made with a buttonhole in them, just in case the man might want to wear a flower there.

Every time a coat is made, that empty buttonhole is put there on purpose, even if not everyone knows what that reason is. That's how it is with God's children. He made us for a good reason, and he put us here on earth on purpose to spread the news about Jesus Christ. The Bible says, "The LORD has anointed me to bring good news to the poor" (Isaiah 61:1). Your Father in heaven has a good plan for you here on earth—be ready for it!

February

Why were there so many toothbrushes in the White House?

We do this by keeping our eyes on Jesus, the champion who initiates and perfects our faith. Because of the joy awaiting him, he endured the cross, disregarding its shame. Now he is seated in the place of honor beside God's throne.
HEBREWS 12:2

President Lyndon Johnson found that he had his best ideas while he was getting ready in the morning. He thought it would be a good idea to remind people about him in the same way while they brushed their teeth. So visitors to the White House received toothbrushes as souvenirs when they came to the Oval Office or went by invitation to the president's personal ranch. Each toothbrush, of course, had the presidential seal imprinted on it.

Toothbrushes, and every other souvenir we might collect, are symbols we keep to remind us of something important. There is a symbol that means more than anything else on earth, and when you give your heart to Jesus, this keepsake belongs especially to you. It is the cross. The Bible tells us to "[keep] our eyes on Jesus, the champion who initiates and perfects our faith. Because of the joy awaiting him, he endured the cross, disregarding its shame. Now he is seated in the place of honor beside God's throne" (Hebrews 12:2). Whenever you see a cross, you can remember that it is an important souvenir Jesus has given to you to keep in your heart.

February

What is inside an apple?

A good tree produces good fruit,
and a bad tree produces bad fruit.
MATTHEW 7:17

The part of an apple that is harder to eat is the core—the firm, tube-like, bumpy part found in the middle. Inside the ridges are pips, which is what apple seeds are called. Animals and birds that eat the apples also eat the pips in the core, and they transport them to other places through their droppings. That's how the seeds find dirt and begin to grow apple trees. People do not usually eat the core because it is not the softest, juiciest part. When you take a bite from an apple, you break through its colorful peel layer, which protects the soft flesh inside. When air touches the flesh, the apple begins to turn brown.

Inside every apple is the beginning of another apple. Isn't that a neat plan? God thought of everything! The Bible says, "A good tree produces good fruit, and a bad tree produces bad fruit" (Matthew 7:17). And our Father knows what kind of potential is inside of us. So go ahead—let everyone see that good fruit of yours!

February 5

What was so special about rubber gloves?

Who may climb the mountain of the LORD?
Who may stand in his holy place?
Only those whose hands and hearts are pure.
PSALM 24:3-4

Dr. William Halsted invented rubber gloves to help a nurse who was getting rashes on her hands from washing them so often before surgeries. He made a plaster cast of her hands and then took the casts to a rubber company, which created thin rubber gloves based on the size of the models. Dr. Halsted used the gloves himself during surgery, and he found that they created a much more sterile environment than washed hands could possibly provide. It was a happy ending for patients and doctors when soon all medical professionals were using the gloves. An additional happy ending is that Dr. Halsted and the nurse he helped eventually got married.

Washing hands before surgery was a big improvement, and rubber gloves made cleanliness even more certain. It is an amazing thing to save the life of a patient by keeping infection away. But life here on earth is not the most important thing. The Bible tells us, "Who may climb the mountain of the LORD? Who may stand in his holy place? Only those whose hands and hearts are pure" (Psalm 24:3-4). The clean hands the Bible talks about are hands that try to do what's right and stay away from doing something wrong, like stealing or harming someone. Those are things that matter more, because those things will affect your eternity long after your life on earth is over.

February

Why is bread in the shape it's in?

People do not live by bread alone, but by every
word that comes from the mouth of God.

MATTHEW 4:4

The bakers of factory-made bread like to make their loaves look home-made so that more shoppers will choose their bread. At the factory, when the dough has risen and is very puffy before baking, a stream of water is shot down the middle of each loaf to make a groove. This causes a "hill" to rise on each side of the groove, giving the top of the bread a rounded shape. Often butter is added into the groove to make the top browner and tastier. On these types of loaves, you may see the words *split top* or *butter crust* printed on the wrappers to describe what the bakers hope will be a more appealing loaf of bread than the others on the shelf.

Concentrating on the look, smell, and taste of bread is a good idea when it comes to marketing, but remember the words of Jesus in the Bible: "People do not live by bread alone, but by every word that comes from the mouth of God" (Matthew 4:4). Yes, food is necessary to keep our bodies alive, but what our attention should be focused on most is the nourishment of our spiritual lives. And that always begins by reading and obeying God's Word.

February

How did one man make laughter his life's work?

A cheerful heart is good medicine,
but a broken spirit saps a person's strength.
PROVERBS 17:22

Sam Adams was working at a dye company at the age of twenty-five when he had a great idea. One of the dye powders always made everybody sneeze. Sam offered to buy all the annoying powder from his boss, who was thrilled. Was Sam crazy? No, he just had a lot of imagination. He packaged the powder in small amounts and sold it as the first sneezing powder, called Cachoo. He started a trend in America that lasted for several years as people tricked their friends by making them sneeze. By then, Sam had lots of other tricks for sale. Some of his funny inventions were the plastic bug in the plastic ice cube and the Joy Buzzer, which gave someone an unexpected jolt when they shook his hand. He thought of the squirting nickel, the dribble glass, drool gum, and fake fangs. And to tease his wife, who always asked him if he put the tops of the food jars back on tightly, he created a surprise. She always made sure to check each jar top and retighten it, just in case Sam forgot. One day when she opened a jar, she screamed as a toy snake popped out, and that's how his Snake-in-a-Can was invented.

Have you ever noticed how fun it is to have fun? And how good it feels to laugh? As long as your fun and laughter are not hurting other people or their feelings, the Bible has some words you will like: "A cheerful heart is good medicine, but a broken spirit saps a person's strength" (Proverbs 17:22). Life is not always just about hard work and serious thoughts. God gave us the gift of laughter, and he knows we can be encouraged by a lightness and silliness in our hearts from time to time.

February

What are some things you can count on about money?

Store your treasures in heaven, where moths and rust cannot destroy, and thieves do not break in and steal.
MATTHEW 6:20

Here are three interesting facts about money for you to think about. First, look at coins. No coin says how much it is worth with a number. For example, the nickel doesn't have the number 5 on it. Instead, it has the word *five* spelled out. The penny doesn't have a 1, but it has the word *one* on it. Next, there is something about paper bills that you should know. It is a law that no living person's picture can be printed on United States paper money. Another fun thing to know about paper money has to do with counting it. Let's pretend someone is willing to give you a million dollars but only if you will count each dollar one by one. How long would it take? Suppose you count a dollar bill every second, which means that you cannot stop to sleep or eat or talk . . . not even once. You would not be finished counting until eleven days, thirteen hours, forty-six minutes, and forty seconds have gone by. Keeping track of money and its rules can keep you very busy!

Learning about money can be interesting and fun, but God does not want us to give money all our attention. The Bible says, "Store your treasures in heaven, where moths and rust cannot destroy, and thieves do not break in and steal" (Matthew 6:20). Heaven is the best place to keep the treasure of highest price—your soul.

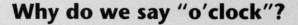

February

Why do we say "o'clock"?

Have I been with you all this time, Philip,
and yet you still don't know who I am?
JOHN 14:9

Hundreds of years ago, when people talked about time, they would say the whole phrase: "it is six of the clock." In the seventeenth and eighteenth centuries, people must have gotten tired of reciting the whole thing. Maybe they realized that everyone knew what they meant. Eventually the word *the* was cut out, so what was said was "six of clock" or "six a clock." Finally, even that phrase must have seemed more than what was needed, and that's how we ended up with the very short "o'clock." The apostrophe stands for the words, and then the letters, that ended up being left out.

Thinking about time reminds us of the years Jesus spent here on earth, trying to help us reach his Father. He loved us very much to give us that much attention. The Bible describes how much Jesus wants us to know him when it says, "Have I been with you all this time, Philip, and yet you still don't know who I am?" (John 14:9). If you haven't yet asked Jesus to be Lord of your life, don't waste another minute. Making that decision right now will be the best possible way to use your time!

February

Why did people put Bubble Wrap on their walls?

Every word of God proves true. He is a shield
to all who come to him for protection.
PROVERBS 30:5

Most people know that Bubble Wrap is a clear plastic sheet made with rows of air-filled circles, which make a fun sound when you pop them. It wraps and cushions things so they won't break when you mail them. But most people don't know how Bubble Wrap started out. In 1957, Alfred Fielding and Marc Chavannes wanted to make wallpaper that had a very modern look and could be easily wiped off. When their product didn't work on walls, they decided to open a company to sell Bubble Wrap for packages, and their company became a big success.

Wanting to protect what's in your packages is a good idea, but it's a much better idea to concentrate on what will protect *you* for eternity. The Bible tells us, "Every word of God proves true. He is a shield to all who come to him for protection" (Proverbs 30:5). Given the choice, who wouldn't choose God over Bubble Wrap as their defender?

February 11

How does sand help eggs hatch?

Don't be selfish; don't try to impress others.
Be humble, thinking of others as better than yourselves.
PHILIPPIANS 2:3

Most mother birds sit on their eggs to keep them warm until they hatch. But for the mallee fowl bird, hatching eggs is a true family project. In the fall, the male mallee fowl digs a hole ten feet wide and three feet deep. He then fills it with leaves he scrapes from the ground nearby. The hole stays there until spring, while the leaves rot inside it. These leaves will turn to compost, which will soon help keep his family of eggs warm. In early spring, the male digs a hole on top of the leaves and adds some new leaves. This is where the female lays the eggs a month later. After the eggs are in the hole, the male covers the hole with sand. For the next ninety days, until the eggs hatch, the male mallee fowl is in charge of keeping them the right temperature. He scratches the sand into a huge mound over the eggs to trap the heat from the compost. Then if the eggs get too warm, he scratches sand off the mound so the layer of sand is thinner. If the eggs are getting too cool, he scratches up more sand on top of the mound to cover the eggs with a thicker layer. The male mallee keeps taking the temperature of the mound so that it always stays at ninety-one degrees.

Maybe there are jobs you are asked to do that you really don't think you should have to do. Try to do them anyway, with a generous heart. The Bible tells you how to be a willing servant like Jesus: "Don't be selfish; don't try to impress others. Be humble, thinking of others as better than yourselves" (Philippians 2:3). God designed the mallee fowl to do its job by instinct, and he designed us to do our jobs with joy.

February

How can you tell a moth
and a butterfly apart?

We live by believing and not by seeing.
2 CORINTHIANS 5:7

Both insects have a dusting on their wings that comes off on your fingers if you pick them up, so those scales won't help you decide which is which. If you see the insect flying around in the daytime, it is probably a butterfly, since moths usually fly at night. Another clue to look for is their shapes: moths are chunky looking, and butterflies are slimmer. You can also notice that a moth's antennae are not as smooth as a butterfly's antennae, which are long and end in knobs.

Sometimes we depend on seeing something to decide what's really true about it. But when it comes to God, we have to decide to believe in him even though we can't see him. The Bible says, "We live by believing and not by seeing" (2 Corinthians 5:7). When Jesus is Lord of your life, he will show you he is never far away from you, even if you can't see him with your eyes.

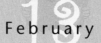

February

How did the spicy sauce
horseradish get its name?

May God give you more and more mercy, peace, and love.
JUDE 1:2

What does a horse have to do with a radish? Do horses like radishes? Are radishes healthy for horses to eat? Are radishes found in fields where horses are kept? No, no, and no. Strangely enough, sometimes words come into our language because of a mistake. This sauce was originally called harshradish—*harsh* meaning strong to the taste, or bitter. That's exactly what happened to the taste of the horseradish root when it was grated, mixed with spices, and turned into a pasty spread to eat with other foods. But as people began to say the name, they didn't pronounce it carefully. After time, the name sounded like "horseradish," and that's what it's been called ever since. Look for a jar in the grocery store, and you'll see that even the label says *horseradish*, and it won't be changing again. The original name and its sensible meaning have disappeared into history, and we are all using a name for this food that really makes no sense.

People use horseradish to add something to the taste of food and to make the flavor stronger. As children of God, there are more important things than food that we hope to add to our lives. The Bible says, "May God give you more and more mercy, peace, and love" (Jude 1:2). Those gifts are much more valuable to our souls than a dose of horseradish is to food—and much less bitter!

February

14

Which finger is closest to the heart?

Let us go right into the presence of God
with sincere hearts fully trusting him.
HEBREWS 10:22

Modern science has proved that no finger is closer to the heart than any other, but that's not what the ancient Egyptians believed. They thought there was a blood vein that ran directly from the ring finger of the left hand to the heart. That is how the finger next to the pinkie on the left hand became known as the ring finger in the first place. The Egyptians chose that finger to be the one that a man's and a woman's wedding rings should be worn on, because it would be the most full of love from the heart. The ring became the symbol of marriage because a ring is a circle, without a beginning or an end. The Egyptians thought that the love in a marriage should go on and on, just like a ring does, without a place for stopping.

We now know medically that the ring finger on the left hand is no closer to the heart than any other finger. But that belief is not what's important about the heart anyway. God wants us to be more concerned with *who* our hearts are close to, and he wants us to be close to him. The Bible tells us, "Let us go right into the presence of God with sincere hearts fully trusting him" (Hebrews 10:22). The important thing is to make sure your heart stays connected to Jesus, and you won't ever have to worry about which finger is closest to your heart. As long as God is, you will always know you're loved.

February

How old was the inventor of the scooter?

The wise inherit honor.
PROVERBS 3:35

The inventor of the scooter was only fifteen years old. In 1897, Walter Lines built a scooter, but his father didn't think the invention would be useful. So they never took out a patent on it to prove that the scooter was Walter's idea. Even so, when Walter grew up, he began his own toy factory, called Triang Toys. The toy that sold the best was . . . the scooter, of course!

Even though Walter was only a teenager when he got the idea for his invention, God gave him the wisdom to see something special in the scooter. And years later, Walter's reward came to him. The Bible says, "The wise inherit honor" (Proverbs 3:35). Think creatively—you never know what honor is in your future. But God does, and he's waiting for you to work toward it.

February

Why was 1908 such a happy year for dogs?

Tell the truth to each other.
ZECHARIAH 8:16

That was when F. H. Bennett, who owned the Bennett bakery, made the very first dog biscuit. He added minerals, milk, and meat products and then baked his invention. He sold the biscuits until 1931, when Nabisco bought the Bennett bakery. Nabisco named the dog biscuit the Milk-Bone. At first, people bought Milk-Bones because they were advertised as a doggy dessert. Later, Nabisco pointed out that the bones worked as a breath freshener for dogs. Owners must have noticed that a dog's breath isn't very pleasant, because the Milk-Bone became very popular, and dog owners bought a huge number of them.

What comes out of the mouth affects people, even if it is just doggy breath. As God's children, we should pay much more attention to what we say than to how our breath smells. The Bible says, "Tell the truth to each other" (Zechariah 8:16). Saying something mean to someone, telling a lie, and spreading gossip are all things that are not pleasant or good to come out of your mouth. Make your words true and kind, and your mouth will always seem sweet to others.

February

When could you talk by telephone to the president of the United States?

The LORD our God has shown us his glory and greatness, and we have heard his voice from the heart of the fire. Today we have seen that God can speak to us humans, and yet we live!
DEUTERONOMY 5:24

You would expect that a place as important as the White House would always have the most current technology and the most elaborate systems for operating it. But with the telephone, the arrangements at the White House were originally quite simple. The first telephone service ever in the United States was not in the nation's capital but in New Haven, Connecticut, in 1878. There were twenty phones in all, so you could only call the other nineteen people who had one. The first telephone in the White House was installed the following year, in 1879, and Rutherford B. Hayes was the first president to use a phone there. But the first president to have a telephone on his desk was Herbert Hoover, who had it installed there in 1929, three weeks after he moved in. Until then, the White House phone was in a phone booth right next to the president's office. President Calvin Coolidge didn't like telephones and refused to ever answer them. On the other hand, President Grover Cleveland didn't even use the help of a secretary or an operator. He answered the White House telephone himself.

Just as we might think the president is too powerful and famous to talk to us personally, many people think the same is true about God. God is a much more important person to talk to than a president, but he still wants to talk to you! And he doesn't need a telephone. He can use anything, even the middle of a fire, to speak. The Bible describes it this way: "The LORD our God has shown us his glory and greatness, and we have heard his voice from the heart of the fire. Today we have seen that God can speak to us humans, and yet we live!" (Deuteronomy 5:24).

February 18

How did LEGOs get their name?

God said, "Let the waters beneath the sky flow together into one place, so dry ground may appear." And that is what happened. God called the dry ground "land" and the waters "seas." And God saw that it was good.
GENESIS 1:9-10

Ole Christiansen lived in Denmark and worked as a carpenter, but he was also talented at making wooden toys in his spare time. He decided to open his own toy company in 1932, which he named LEGO, a combination of two Danish words, *leg godt*, or "play well." Those same words in Latin mean "I put together," which is exactly what kids did with the toys after Ole invented them in 1949. He quickly realized that the blocks would be made better with plastic than with wood, and their first name was Automatic Binding Blocks, which came only in red and white. Soon his son suggested their name should be LEGOs, and the colors green, yellow, and blue were added. In 1961, LEGOs became popular in the United States, and later the company was making over 1,700 pieces each minute.

It is fun to put LEGOs together and create complicated projects, although it may take you lots of hard work. Can you imagine creating the whole earth? That's what God did; in fact, he made the entire universe—everything that exists. Part of the story from the Bible goes like this: "God said, 'Let the waters beneath the sky flow together into one place, so dry ground may appear.' And that is what happened. God called the dry ground 'land' and the waters 'seas.' And God saw that it was good" (Genesis 1:9-10). God didn't need a paper full of directions or a box full of parts, like the ones that come with LEGOs. He created the world and everything in it from his imagination. He made something where nothing had existed before, just by saying it and not even lifting a finger. That's the most terrific example of putting things together you'll ever find!

February

What makes flamingos so pink?

Look at the birds. They don't plant or harvest or store food in barns, for your heavenly Father feeds them.
MATTHEW 6:26

Flamingos are pink because of what they eat—mostly a lot of extremely small animals, tiny water plants, and algae—that contain natural carotenoids, which have a pink pigment. We eat beets and carrots that have carotenoid pigments too, but we could never eat enough of them to turn ourselves pink. To eat, a flamingo sweeps its wide, hook-shaped bill back and forth along the bottom of a pond, sucking up as much gooey scum as it can. Then it forces the water out through its comblike teeth, using its tongue to pump water through its beak four times a minute while trapping the food inside its bill. Flamingos aren't built to defend themselves well, so they live in the middle of water that is so full of salt and soda that predators can't drink it and won't go near it.

God knows the needs of every creature on earth because he created them in the first place. The Bible says, "Look at the birds. They don't plant or harvest or store food in barns, for your heavenly Father feeds them" (Matthew 6:26). When you are worried, remember the brightness of the flamingo—it is proof that God makes sure it has enough food to eat. And he will feed your heart and spirit with his love each day as well.

February

What's in your closet that took the place of a hook?

Your Father knows exactly what you
need even before you ask him!
MATTHEW 6:8

A man went to work one morning in 1903 and found he had no place to hang his coat. The other workers had used every hook available to hang up their things. What could Albert Parkhouse do with his coat? He was employed at a factory that made wire items, like the wire frames that hold up lamp shades, so he used what he could find. Albert took a piece of extra wire and twisted two large loops in it and then twisted a handle on top. What was he holding in his hand now? The first wire coat hanger, which he hung his coat on and calmly began his day's work.

Albert needed a place to hang his coat. Even though that wasn't a big need, like having something to eat or a place to live, it was still important. Just as God gave Albert an idea that would help him, he pays attention to the small things that are on our minds too. The Bible tells us, "Your Father knows exactly what you need even before you ask him!" (Matthew 6:8).

February

What do the keys to the city open?

I will give you the keys of the Kingdom of Heaven.
MATTHEW 16:19

When special guests arrive in your town, it is a custom for the mayor to hand them the key to the city in a public ceremony. But the key really doesn't open anything. So why do we do that? Long ago, the important cities of Europe were each surrounded by a high wall for protection against enemies, and people could only enter or leave the city through a gate that was locked at sundown. If the city was taken over by its enemies, the military commander or mayor would have to turn over the key to the city to the winners of the battle. When we present the key to the city to someone today, we are saying that the person is welcome to enter our town and be an honored citizen.

It is an honor to be welcomed into a city and be given the keys to a place where people want you to feel you belong. But no matter how exciting that might be, God has the greatest honor of all time waiting just for you! Jesus tells us, "I will give you the keys of the Kingdom of Heaven" (Matthew 16:19). Nothing could ever be better than that.

February

How did a bottle turn into a rubber band?

The LORD will hold you in his hand for all to see.
ISAIAH 62:3

Many rubber trees grow in Central and South America, and the native people of those countries were the first to make items from rubber, such as toys, hats, and coats. They also made bottles out of rubber, and one day in 1820, Thomas Hancock of England received one of the rubber bottles as a gift. He took a knife and cut the rubber into many slices, and without even meaning to, he invented the rubber band. But Thomas thought the only thing rubber bands might be used for was to help hold up clothes, possibly as a waistband. Twenty-five years later, another Englishman named Stephen Perry thought of many other things rubber bands could be used for, and after he patented the invention, he opened the first factory that made rubber bands.

We use rubber bands to bunch things together and hold them tightly for us. The Bible shows us that nothing and no one can hold us together and keep us from falling apart except Jesus. The Bible says, "The LORD will hold you in his hand for all to see" (Isaiah 62:3). God will always hold on to you—much more strongly than a little rubber band can.

February 23

What's the story behind the letters *j* and *w* in our alphabet?

Search the book of the LORD, and see what he will do.
ISAIAH 34:16

Our alphabet has undergone many changes since people started using it. After a while, it was decided that we needed more letters to represent sounds. One of the most interesting letters that was added was the letter *j*. The *j* was created by changing the shape of the letter *i* a little bit. That is why *i* and *j* are next to each other in the alphabet and why they are the only two letters with dots above them. Another letter, *w*, was also added later. Its name gives us a clue about how it was created. It was made by putting two letter *u*'s side by side. That's how we came to call it the "double u."

The right letters allow us to have better tools for writing and reading. Of course, the most important book you will ever read is the Bible. The Bible urges us to "search the book of the LORD, and see what he will do" (Isaiah 34:16). But God doesn't want you to worry if you don't understand everything you read. Since God is almighty, he doesn't need to rely only on the right combination of letters. He will make sure that you understand what he wants you to know—he will put the truth into your heart.

February

What was a fly bat, and why was it invented?

Intelligent people are always ready to learn.
Their ears are open for knowledge.
PROVERBS 18:15

In 1905, a Kansas schoolteacher named Frank Rose invented the "fly bat"—at least that's what he called it. If you guessed the fly bat was used for baseball, that's a good guess, but it's not correct. The fly bat was made out of a yardstick handle with a square piece of screen attached to one end. Does that remind you of anything you use in your home? Of course! It was the first flyswatter! It worked better than what had been used previously—a rolled-up newspaper—because the holes in the screen made it move more easily through the air. This created a kind of disguise that didn't alert flies, like the solid newspaper did, that something was coming toward them. Flies didn't move out of the way, and people could hit them more easily. The handle was improved, and Frank changed the name to *flyswatter*. Then everyone knew what it was and what to do with it.

Bothersome flies were a problem for many people, but it took only one person to create a better solution for what to do about them. Maybe someday you will think of an invention that will be helpful to others. The Bible says, "Intelligent people are always ready to learn. Their ears are open for knowledge" (Proverbs 18:15). Good ideas are a gift from God. If he gives you one, try to see if you can make it work.

February

Do mice have anything to do with an athlete's muscles?

Be strong and courageous!
2 CHRONICLES 32:7

In ancient Greek times, when the Greek people watched athletes competing in contests and flexing their muscles, they thought that the rippling motion of the skin around the muscle looked like a mouse running up and down under the skin. Eventually the Greeks told the Romans about this idea, so the ancient Romans started calling this rippling skin *musculus*, which means "little mouse." Much later, *musculus* became our modern word *muscle*!

People who have big muscles are physically strong, but God is more concerned with the fitness of our souls. We are told by the Bible, "Be strong and courageous!" (2 Chronicles 32:7). Staying strong in your spirit and soul and heart is most important, and you can do that by keeping close to God through his Word.

February

Why did babies wear pieces of shower curtains?

I will comfort you . . . as a mother comforts her child.
ISAIAH 66:13

The first idea for a baby diaper had a few problems. Also called a nappy, the diaper was made of cloth, and when it got wet, so did everything else around it. Each dirty diaper had to be washed and dried before it could be worn again. Keeping a baby clean and dry was an all-day job! Then in 1950, Marion Donovan, the mother of a newborn baby, had an idea. She cut a baby-size piece of a shower curtain, added some padding, and wrapped her baby in this new type of diaper that could be thrown away instead of washed. Marion called the diaper a "boater" because, like a boat, it was waterproof. The first disposable diaper had been created!

This mother knew her baby needed to be more comfortable, so she invented a new kind of diaper. Now that you are older, there are other things you need instead of a diaper. Maybe you worry sometimes that God will not give you what you need. But the Bible tells us that God promises, "I will comfort you . . . as a mother comforts her child" (Isaiah 66:13). God made you, he knows all about you and what is best for you, and he loves you more than any human being could. He will take care of you all the days of your life when you trust in him.

February

Can you name that cheese, please?

We know that there is only one God, the Father, who created everything, and we live for him. And there is only one Lord, Jesus Christ, through whom God made everything and through whom we have been given life.

1 CORINTHIANS 8:6

It has been estimated that there are four hundred to five hundred different names for cheeses around the world. But that doesn't mean there are that many different kinds of cheese. When a certain kind of cheese is produced in a certain area, the cheese makers often give their cheese a special name, even though it's the same kind of cheese that people in another area are making. They are hoping you will remember their name and ask for it when you are buying cheese. All in all, there are only eighteen or nineteen separate varieties of cheese worldwide.

Being able to remember the name of something special is important in a small way, but there is only one name you really need to remember. That name is Jesus. He is the only one who could have died for your sins, and he loved you enough to do it. The Bible says, "We know that there is only one God, the Father, who created everything, and we live for him. And there is only one Lord, Jesus Christ, through whom God made everything and through whom we have been given life" (1 Corinthians 8:6).

February
28

What happens to the missing leap year birthdays?

Anyone who does what pleases God will live forever.
1 JOHN 2:17

You are called a leap year baby if you were born on February 29. On many calendars, it looks like your birthday is missing, because February shows only twenty-eight days three years out of four. Is there a big mistake? Not at all. When the earth moves around the sun, it takes a little more than 365 days. So approximately every four years, our calendar loses almost twenty-four hours, so in the fourth year, we add an extra day to catch up. That day is February 29, and that year is called a leap year. If you only counted your leap year birthdays, by the time you were sixteen you would have had only four February 29 birthday parties. Fortunately, people with leap year birthdays can celebrate on February 28 or March 1 instead, so they can have the same number of birthday parties as all their friends.

Whatever day you were born on is important, because that is the day God gave you your first breath. But as God's children, we know that the most important kind of life will not be here on earth. The Bible tells us, "Anyone who does what pleases God will live forever" (1 John 2:17). The most joyous day of new life for you will be the one when your party will be in heaven!

March 1

Why do we call it a Caesar salad?

This same God who takes care of me will supply
all your needs from his glorious riches.
PHILIPPIANS 4:19

Many people think this salad was named after a famous emperor in history, Julius Caesar, but they couldn't really tell you the story. That's because Caesar salad actually has nothing to do with that historical figure. This salad has a much more recent history. It began in Tijuana, Mexico, with an American named Alex Cardini. He was working at his brother's restaurant one night in 1924, when too many customers came in and the restaurant ran out of its usual dishes. So Alex gathered up whatever bits of food he could find in the kitchen and added them all together. He used parmesan cheese, romaine lettuce, eggs, olive oil, garlic, lemon juice, and pepper, with some dried-bread croutons thrown in. Everyone who tried it loved it, so Alex kept making it. The first name for this creation was the aviator salad, since the restaurant was near the airport. But later Alex changed its name to honor the owner of the restaurant—his brother, Caesar.

God cares about everything we do and everything we need, even the smallest details. Before Alex even knew that the hungry people were coming, the parts of the salad were sitting there waiting in his brother's restaurant. The Bible reminds us, "This same God who takes care of me will supply all your needs from his glorious riches" (Philippians 4:19). As you go through your day, look for evidence that God has already been there before you, leaving clues for you to find about how many ways he loves and cares for you.

M a r c h

What happened to all the cars?

You must not steal.
EXODUS 20:15

The Federal Bureau of Investigation (FBI) put out some figures about car theft in the state of Massachusetts in 1976. According to the report for that year, 76,257 cars had been stolen. That meant that out of every 100,000 people who lived in Massachusetts, 1,312.7 cars were being stolen. Picture this: A hundred people gather in a gym. If you look around, it's very likely that at least one of them had their car taken away.

The Bible teaches us about fairness. It tells us that one of God's commandments is "You must not steal" (Exodus 20:15). When someone takes something that doesn't belong to him or her, that person has not earned it. And the person who worked to pay for it is being treated unfairly. When the Lord tells us about stealing, he is reminding us that we should treat other people the way we want them to treat us. Whether it is a movie you snuck into, a song you didn't pay for, or even a pack of gum you pocketed, God will be pleased when you listen to him and choose not to steal.

March

How much salt could you earn in a day?

You are the salt of the earth.
MATTHEW 5:13

More than two thousand years ago, salt was rare and very expensive. The ancient Romans valued salt because it is a mineral our bodies need and it seasons food, and also because salt could preserve food so it could last a long time. Since at that time there were no refrigerators, salt was the best way to keep food from getting spoiled. *Sal* is the Latin word for salt, and Roman soldiers were paid a *salarium*, which means they were given money to be able to buy salt. From that word we get the word used for payment for work in modern times. Even though we don't spend all of it on salt, it's still called our salary.

Salt is something all humans need for their bodies. When Jesus says to God's people, "You are the salt of the earth" (Matthew 5:13), he means that everyone's heart needs to hear about Jesus, and we can be the ones to tell our friends and neighbors about him. When we do, we will be preserving their souls and helping their happiness last a long time—forever!

March

Which American candy was named after someone's daughter?

If you will obey me and keep my covenant, you will be my own special treasure from among all the peoples on earth; for all the earth belongs to me.
EXODUS 19:5

Her name was Clara Hirshfield, but her father used her nickname, "Tootsie," for the candy. The Tootsie Roll was invented in 1896 by Leo Hirshfield, and its unusual name helped people remember it. This candy was rolled up in a tube, and it was the first factory-produced candy to be wrapped in paper. Tootsie Rolls were one of the foods provided for many soldiers through the years. A World War II pilot reported that after his plane was shot down and he parachuted to the ground, he had only Tootsie Rolls to keep him alive in the Sahara Desert. Three days later, he had walked far enough to find friendly people who helped him, but only after he shared his Tootsie Rolls! For many reasons, the Tootsie Roll stood out as being different from other candies, and it became very popular.

Just as Tootsie Rolls were different from other kinds of candy, we who are children of God are different from unbelievers. Our God calls us to listen to him, not to the world. He says, "If you will obey me and keep my covenant, you will be my own special treasure from among all the peoples on earth; for all the earth belongs to me" (Exodus 19:5). Those words should be sweeter to us than any candy. Candy lasts only a few moments, but our relationship with our Creator lasts for eternity.

March

What in the world was a "Dial-a-Fish"?

The LORD gives his people strength.
PSALM 29:11

Young Eric Bunnelle had a problem: his mom wouldn't let him have pet fish unless he could find a way to feed them when it was time for family vacations. Then Eric's teacher asked her students to invent something as an assignment, so he decided to tackle a remote-controlled fish feeder for his project. His first idea was to attach a machine to the telephone that would shake food into the aquarium when Eric called his house and activated the phone. But the power from the phone was too weak to cause the machine to start moving. Eric consulted some experts, who recommended a "Fone Flasher," which was originally designed to turn on a lamp so hearing-impaired people could see that the phone was ringing. Eric attached his Fone Flasher to the shaking machine. It worked! He won a national prize for his invention, and although he hasn't patented it and sold it yet, he did get a reward for his persistence. His mom allowed him to get his pet goldfish!

The problem with Eric's invention at first was that there was not enough power for his creation to work the way it was designed. As God's child, that is something you won't have to worry about. When God has something for you to do, he will also make sure you have all the abilities and support you need to finish the task. The Bible promises, "The LORD gives his people strength" (Psalm 29:11). When you depend on God, he guarantees that you can use his power.

March

When was there a garage sale on the lawn of the White House?

He has removed our sins as far from us
as the east is from the west.

PSALM 103:12

Chester Arthur was the president in 1882, and he decided he didn't like the old furniture in the White House. He had most of the furniture set out on the lawn and sold to whoever came to buy it. President Arthur wanted to make room for new decorations; he admired the work of the interior designer Louis Tiffany, and many of his pieces were used to redecorate. Many valuable and historical pieces were moved to other people's homes, and more than eight thousand dollars was collected at the White House garage sale.

The president wanted all the old furnishings to leave the White House to make room for something grander. God understands that we feel like that sometimes—wanting to start over. God gives us the chance to do that every day. Whenever we've sinned, we can tell him we're sorry and we want something better than the mistakes we've made. Then he'll clean our souls. We are told in the Bible what God does for us: "He has removed our sins as far from us as the east is from the west" (Psalm 103:12). That's a long way. You can't even see that far. And in place of our sin, God gives us a brand-new start.

March 7

What did Vaseline have to do with oil wells?

He heals the brokenhearted and bandages their wounds.
PSALM 147:3

The inventor Robert Chesebrough was told by some oil well workers (known as "riggers") in Pennsylvania that they didn't like a substance called rod wax, the raw material for petroleum jelly. It was gooey and made their machinery stop working. But they did notice something that had been known for many centuries—petroleum jelly was good for putting on cuts and burns. In the past it had been rare and expensive, but oil wells made it available and plentiful. By experimenting, Robert was able to turn the black goo into a clear substance. The name came from the first part of the German word for water, *wasser*, and the Greek word for olive oil, *elaion*. Robert was one of the first salesmen to give away free samples, and he demonstrated his product by giving himself small cuts or burns and then putting Vaseline on the wounds to show how it helped. By 1874 he was selling a jar of Vaseline a minute. He lived to age ninety-six, and he said (although you shouldn't try it) that he had swallowed a spoonful of Vaseline every day.

Amazingly, out of an area covered with dirty, greasy oil came a way to keep wounds clean and help them heal. What a surprise! God can do anything, and he often does so in the most unexpected ways. Everything he does is for a good reason. Turning something unhealthy into something that improves the body is just like God. He is very concerned and involved with your well-being—your soul first, of course. The Bible promises, "He heals the brokenhearted and bandages their wounds" (Psalm 147:3). If you have heartache or hurt feelings or disappointments, take them to God. He is the Great Healer.

March

What's the best way to tell time on a ship?

Let us come boldly to the throne of our gracious God.
There we will receive his mercy, and we will find
grace to help us when we need it most.
HEBREWS 4:16

Long ago, before there were watches and digital clocks, keeping time on a ship was difficult. If there was a pendulum clock on board, the rolling of waves could tip the ship, and with it the pendulum, which would cause the clock to show the wrong time. Then there was the problem of temperature changes, which could make the oil in the clock too thin or too thick to keep the parts moving smoothly. Temperature changes could also make the metal parts contract or expand, so they became too big or too small to help the clock keep accurate time. But in 1735, along came an English clock-maker who thought of a different way to make a clock. His invention was called a chronometer. He built the clock so it would not be affected by the ups and downs of sailing over an ocean, and the metal parts stayed stable. Because of these improvements, it was now possible for sailors to keep track of the two important features of seafaring: latitude and longitude. This in turn saved countless lives, as it made sailing much safer.

Sailors must have been terrified many times when they couldn't figure out where their ship was or what time it was without reliable clocks. The Bible says, "Let us come boldly to the throne of our gracious God. There we will receive his mercy, and we will find grace to help us when we need it most" (Hebrews 4:16). You can ask for God's help and let him take care of the things that give you trouble. Your rescuer has come! The one who cares so much about every detail of your life will turn something bad into something good. And it is an absolute guarantee that the Lord has more power to make you feel safe than a small ticking clock ever could. You can claim this security any time you want to—it's what you've been given as a child of God.

March

Can you imagine a bicycle with ten seats?

[God] knows where I am going. And when he
tests me, I will come out as pure as gold.
JOB 23:10

In 1896 in Massachusetts, there really was one! It was called the Orient Oriten, and it was built as eye-catching advertising for the Orient line of bicycles that Charles Metz was selling. The Oriten weighed 305 pounds, was 23 feet long, and could go up to 45 miles per hour, but it didn't have brakes or gears. As you might think, this bicycle was very difficult to ride, starting with the chore of finding nine other people who want to go to the same place you're going!

If all ten of the riders tried to steer at the same time, it would have been disaster, wouldn't it? Only one person could really make those decisions about where to go—and it should be the person who knows best! It's not so different in our lives. God is the one who knows the best way to go. So instead of trying to go our own ways, we should let him lead. He knows which way we are going and whether or not we are following him. The Bible says, "[God] knows where I am going. And when he tests me, I will come out as pure as gold" (Job 23:10). If you are following right behind Jesus as closely as you can, you, too, will come out like gold in the end.

March

What don't you know about the ladybug?

People who accept discipline are on the pathway to
life, but those who ignore correction will go astray.
PROVERBS 10:17

*L*adybug sounds like such a nice, gentle name, and ladybugs are so tiny and round and cute. But they are not shy, and they don't blend into the background. In fact, ladybugs are bright red or orange with black spots for a good reason. They are flashing warning colors to other insects and birds that they are dangerous and quick to protect themselves. If the colors don't remind predators of their danger, the ladybug will "play dead" when a bird comes nearby. But ladybugs are not fooling, like some insects do, by wearing bright danger colors that are just "costumes" to scare enemies away. If all else fails, the ladybug begins to ooze a terrible-smelling and awful-tasting poison from its legs when attacked. Not very ladylike!

In very direct ways, the ladybug sends out warnings. If other insects pay attention to the warnings, they will be all right. But if they don't pay attention, they might get hurt. All of life is like that. God wants us to pay special attention to the advice he gives us about how to live a life that is pleasing to him. The Bible tells us, "People who accept discipline are on the pathway to life, but those who ignore correction will go astray" (Proverbs 10:17). Other insects might be careful to stay out of trouble with a little ladybug, but we should be much more concerned about how to stay on the right road with Jesus.

March 11

Do large or small hailstones cause the most damage?

> We can make a large horse go wherever we want by means of a small bit in its mouth. And a small rudder makes a huge ship turn wherever the pilot chooses to go, even though the winds are strong. In the same way, the tongue is a small thing that makes grand speeches.
>
> JAMES 3:3-5

The larger the hailstone, the less damage there will be. That seems odd, doesn't it? But imagine that someone is dropping a few baseballs. A few places would be hit. If they dropped many marbles, though, there would be lots more places that the marbles would bounce on and possibly damage. A car might get one dent from one baseball that happened to fall down on it, but if there were multiple marbles hitting it, there would be many damaged places.

Many small things can actually make a bigger difference than you'd guess. Consider these examples from the Bible: "We can make a large horse go wherever we want by means of a small bit in its mouth. And a small rudder makes a huge ship turn wherever the pilot chooses to go, even though the winds are strong. In the same way, the tongue is a small thing that makes grand speeches" (James 3:3-5). Before you assume that a little whisper of gossip from your tongue won't cause any harm, remember the power of little things!

March

What was the first book ever printed?

Even more blessed are all who hear the
word of God and put it into practice.
LUKE 11:28

Johannes Gutenberg invented the first printing press in 1450. His method involved using metal letters that were arranged in words and then put under a press, page by page, where they were covered with ink and stamped onto the page. This made printing multiple copies much faster than the old way of copying books by hand, letter by letter, which was usually the job of monks. Which book did Johannes choose to be the first one ever to be printed with his new, fast invention? It was a copy of the Holy Bible. The version he printed eventually came to be known as the Gutenberg Bible.

What a wonderful gift Johannes Gutenberg gave the world! He provided a way for more people to read and hear of the Word of God. The Bible tells us, "Even more blessed are all who hear the word of God and put it into practice" (Luke 11:28). The Bible is our plan book for how we can live in eternity with Jesus. But it's not just important to read it—we also need to do what it says.

March

What was the one place the bus used to stop?

Those the Father has given me will come
to me, and I will never reject them.
JOHN 6:37

The name *bus* is actually a nickname. The first bus was named an omnibus because it means "everybody vehicle" or "for all" in Latin. The earliest bus appeared in France in 1823. It was a horse-drawn coach with sixteen seats that people could ride from the center of town out to a bathhouse that the bus company owned and then ride back home again.

In some ways, Jesus is like a bus driver. He truly wants the bus going to heaven to be "for all." The Bible tells us that Jesus said, "Those the Father has given me will come to me, and I will never reject them" (John 6:37). Jesus welcomes all who come on board with him, and he rejoices over each person who is saved. Please invite everybody you know to join you on the heavenly bus!

March 14

Why don't spiders get stuck in their own webs?

God is our refuge and strength, always
ready to help in times of trouble.
PSALM 46:1

Spiders know where the sticky sections of their webs are, and they stay away from them. Some spiders make a web with a sticky part that runs around the center in circles, and they use only dry silk for the straight lines that hold the circles together. Then they know to run only on the straight lines to avoid getting stuck. When a part of the spider's body touches a sticky section by mistake, it uses its saliva to get rid of the stickiness.

As God's children, we have a much better way to find help than using our own saliva to get unstuck. The Bible lets us know that we can depend on God: "God is our refuge and strength, always ready to help in times of trouble" (Psalm 46:1). God is always available to you—just call for him, and he will rescue you.

March

15

How did three men change the world of medicine?

Wash your hands, you sinners; purify your hearts, for
your loyalty is divided between God and the world.
JAMES 4:8

It all started with a surprise that Alexander Fleming, a Scottish bacteriologist, found one day in a dish of bacteria he was growing. He had left several dishes of bacteria on his windowsill when he went for a vacation in 1928, and when he came back, he made a discovery. One of the dishes was still growing bacteria, but mold had grown inside the dish too. Where the mold was, there was no longer any bacteria. He was amazed by this mold, which is sometimes found on old bread, and called it penicillin. He cured an eye infection with it and then moved on to other experiments he was more interested in. He thought penicillin might be good for cleaning laboratories of unwanted bacteria, but he couldn't really think of how else to use it. Ten years later, two other scientists, Howard Florey and Ernst Chain, read what Alexander Fleming had written about penicillin. They decided to try getting rid of bacteria inside mice—and it worked. Then they tried penicillin on people, and that's how antibiotics of all kinds got their start. Since then, many people have been cured from strep throat and ear infections, and many lives have been saved.

Our bodies are important, and we want to keep them healthy. But in God's sight, there is something much more precious to keep healthy for eternity, and that is our hearts. The Bible tells us, "Wash your hands, you sinners; purify your hearts, for your loyalty is divided between God and the world" (James 4:8). Try to focus on keeping your soul and heart and mind healthy, and your body next. That way you will stay away from all sorts of sicknesses that could harm you.

March

What odd ideas made
terrible inventions?

It is better to take refuge in the LORD than to trust in people.
PSALM 118:8

Sometimes people's ideas seem strange to us—because they are. Take this invention on how to wake someone up: A device was attached to a bed that lifted up the bed and tilted it. The sleeping person then slid off the bed and down into a tubful of cold water—awake, maybe, but definitely not happy to be! Then there was the invention meant to help a person fly. For this idea, a large hoop was attached to a cage. The person sat in the cage, and eight eagles were supposed to pick up the hoop at the same time and pull it into the air with them. Somebody thought it was a good idea, but it didn't work well at all. Thomas Edison, the inventor of the lightbulb, could have given these inventors some advice. He once said, "Anything that won't sell, I don't want to invent."

If an idea seems wrong to you, it probably is. That goes for inventions, but it also goes for the suggestions of friends. Maybe you know of a group of kids who want to skateboard through the busiest streets of town to get to a movie theater. Or maybe the movie they want to see is full of violence. Whenever you are questioning the wisdom of something, try repeating this Bible verse to yourself, and you should have your answer. "It is better to take refuge in the LORD than to trust in people" (Psalm 118:8).

March

What's one way to catch a criminal?

Those who know your name trust in you, for you,
O LORD, do not abandon those who search for you.
PSALM 9:10

In London in the 1800s, there was a lot of crime, so one inventor decided to tackle the problem. He made a metal collar that people were supposed to wear around their necks under a scarf or tie, and if someone tried to grab them, his hands would be stabbed with big spikes. The problem was that the collars needed to be worn so high up on the wearers' necks that they would be strangled before the criminal could cause them harm.

The best way for us to get protection is to ask God for it. He knows exactly what our needs are, and he wants to provide for us. The Bible tells us, "Those who know your name trust in you, for you, O LORD, do not abandon those who search for you" (Psalm 9:10). You can depend on the Lord when you are worried or afraid.

March 18

What city is home to the most bats?

Praise the LORD! Praise the LORD from the
heavens! Praise him from the skies!

PSALM 148:1

Bats are the only mammals that can fly. They do this by using wings that are like a big hand with webbed skin between the fingers. The people of Austin, Texas, were worried when they saw a huge bat colony settling in under the Congress Avenue Bridge in 1980, but they learned that these bats are gentle and rarely hurt anyone. They are called Mexican free-tailed bats, and 1.5 million of them fly to the bridge from Mexico each March and return to Mexico each November. The Austin colony is the largest known urban bat population in the world. One of the benefits of so many bats is that they eat thirty thousand pounds of insects and mosquitoes *every night*!

Even though the people of Austin were afraid at first of the bats that filled the night sky, they found that the bats could actually be helpful instead of harmful. Bats are just one kind of creature in the sky that shows how God deserves praise. He can turn something that seems bad into his own plan for something good. "Praise the LORD! Praise the LORD from the heavens! Praise him from the skies!" (Psalm 148:1).

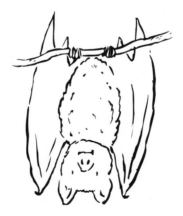

March 19

How did an eleven-year-old help change history?

Don't let anyone think less of you because you are young.
1 TIMOTHY 4:12

Steve Wozniak was eleven years old when he assembled hundreds of electronic pieces, kept on a three-by-four-foot piece of plywood, into a machine that could play tic-tac-toe. Steve had loved electronics from early childhood, and this was his first project using parts that would later become some of the parts in early computers. Steve also got together with other kids in his neighborhood who liked electronics too, and together they figured out how to make an intercom system so they could all talk to each other from their own houses. In high school, when Steve had learned all he could from the electronics classes, he volunteered to work for free at a company that let him see how their computer was put together. He went to college for a year but couldn't afford more, so he kept trying on his own to make a personal computer that people could use at home. He grew up to be a founder of Apple Computer with his friend and business partner, Steve Jobs, and at last he designed the Apple II computer almost all by himself.

Steve was a good example of what the Bible is talking about when it says, "Don't let anyone think less of you because you are young" (1 Timothy 4:12). No one can outguess God on the plans he has for someone. God gave Steve talents far beyond what anyone could have predicted, and he accomplished amazing things at a younger age than anyone thought possible. God gave you talents as well—look for them and use them, no matter how old you are!

March

Which covered wagon was the best in the west?

You have six days each week for your ordinary work, but the seventh day is a Sabbath day of rest dedicated to the LORD your God.

EXODUS 20:9-10

The favorite covered wagon was called the Conestoga wagon, made by Pennsylvania Dutch craftsmen in the Conestoga Valley area of Pennsylvania starting in 1717. Conestoga wagons were very well built and were used to haul many kinds of goods across long distances. They were the only wagons that had brakes during colonial times; all the other wagons had their wheels tied up with a chain that locked them in place, and then the wagon slid down the slopes with locked wheels. The spoked wooden wheels of a Conestoga wagon were six feet tall in the rear and four feet tall on the front of the wagon. Men who drove the wagons were called teamsters because they were in charge of the team of six horses that pulled their wagon. (Much later, men who drove modern trucks called themselves teamsters in honor of the old-time wagon drivers.) By 1850, the locomotive train became the fastest and most popular way to travel long distances, and Conestoga wagons were just used for short hauling trips until the modern truck was invented and took their place.

Moving things from one place to another has always been hard work, but the Conestoga wagon made that duty a little easier. It is understandable that those wagons were busy much of the time. The Bible says, "You have six days each week for your ordinary work, but the seventh day is a Sabbath day of rest dedicated to the LORD your God" (Exodus 20:9-10). Even as we learn how to make work faster and better, we need to remember to rest as well.

March 21

Why is it easier to walk than to stand still?

Just as you accepted Christ Jesus as your Lord,
you must continue to follow him.
COLOSSIANS 2:6

Have you ever noticed that if you have to stand still for a long time, your legs get tired and you feel the need to fidget? The problem is that the longer you stand still, the more gravity pulls the fluid in your body down to your feet and legs, which puts extra pressure on the muscles there. You eventually feel the pooling fluid as pain. But when you move your legs, just by jiggling them or by walking, your leg muscles contract, or get tighter, which pushes the extra fluid back to the upper part of your body again. This allows your veins to get the blood moving back to your heart. Walking is best, and seems easiest, because it sends the blood going faster through your whole body, the way God designed it. All your inner organs, especially your brain, get more refreshed. So the next time you can't seem to stand or even sit still, now you know why—your body is trying to take better care of itself!

When you are getting exercise by walking around, remember to keep your feet headed in the right direction—by following the footsteps of Jesus. The Bible says, "Just as you accepted Christ Jesus as your Lord, you must continue to follow him" (Colossians 2:6). Walking is good for your body, and walking with Christ is good for your soul.

March

Which animal builds its own haystack?

Don't be afraid, you animals of the field.
JOEL 2:22

High up in the Rocky Mountains, a little-known, tiny animal lives an amazingly different life than most other creatures do. The pika (pronounced "peek-a") is a small animal similar to a mouse or a hamster that spends the summer gathering lots of pieces of food from the mountains. It covers the food with dried grass, making what looks like little haystacks that get higher and higher as more food is added. So far, that doesn't sound so unusual. Many animals collect food for the winter, and they either overeat ahead of time or put the food in a safe place—usually where they're planning to hibernate (or sleep) during the winter. But here's the interesting part: the pika does not hibernate. The pika knows that the haystacks will become buried in snow in the winter, which is exactly what the little creature needs. All through the snowy months, the pika goes back and forth from its burrow home to one of the haystacks to get more food. That is why frontiersmen paid careful attention to the height of the pika haystacks. They thought that if the haystacks had been loaded with food and were much higher than usual, a longer, snowier winter was on its way.

The pika uses the instincts God has given it to collect enough food to last through the winter, even if it's a longer season than normal. It is amazing to think of all the little creatures God provides for in so many ways all over the earth, all at the same time, through night and day and winter and summer. The Bible says, "Don't be afraid, you animals of the field" (Joel 2:22). Thinking of all the animals reminds us that God cares even more for you than he does for them, and he loves you and takes care of you at all times too.

March

What if there were bread at the end of your pencil?

Oh, what joy for those whose disobedience is forgiven, whose sin is put out of sight! Yes, what joy for those whose record the LORD has cleared of guilt, whose lives are lived in complete honesty!

PSALM 32:1-2

Ever since people started writing, there have been mistakes in what is written. And ever since pencils were invented, people have been trying to figure out ways to correct their mistakes. For two hundred years, until the eraser was invented, the best way to fix the errors was to scrub the pencil marks away with a small piece of bread. Then, in 1752, the first eraser was made from tree sap. It was also called a rubber because that's exactly what it did—it rubbed out the mistakes. Soon anything made from eraser material was called rubber. Finally, in 1858, American inventor Hymen Lipman thought of the best place to keep an eraser. Of course! He simply slid a slice of eraser into a groove carved on top of the pencil so it would always be handy to make mistakes disappear.

What happens when you make a mistake like lying or losing your temper? You feel terrible about it, but you don't know how you can get rid of the dark mark you have made. God loves you so much that he invites you to come to him and tell him you are sorry, and he will forget whatever it is you've done wrong. The Bible says, "Oh, what joy for those whose disobedience is forgiven, whose sin is put out of sight! Yes, what joy for those whose record the LORD has cleared of guilt, whose lives are lived in complete honesty!" (Psalm 32:1-2). God erases completely the things you wish you had not done, and he never thinks of them again.

24

March

What if you learned your ETAs instead of your ABCs?

Timely advice is lovely, like golden apples in a silver basket.
PROVERBS 25:11

Not a new alphabet, just another way to arrange the letters. The first letter in this rearranged alphabet is there because it is the most frequently used letter in our language. The second letter is the second most common letter. And on the list goes. Which letter is always the last one to get used? *Z*, of course. If someone wants to know how the letters rank, from first to last, based on how often we use them, you can recite the alphabet to them this way: ETAISONHRDLUCMFWYPGVBKJQXZ. Try that one on your teachers!

Letters are powerful tools because they make our words. And words can change someone's day, or even his or her life. The Bible says, "Timely advice is lovely, like golden apples in a silver basket" (Proverbs 25:11). Find someone today who would like to hear that the most powerful being of all time loves him or her, and then tell the story with the words that God gives you.

March

Why was the money on the move?

Remember this and keep it firmly in mind: The LORD is
God both in heaven and on earth, and there is no other.
DEUTERONOMY 4:39

One day Steve Jakubowski, who was in charge of the HyLo Gas Station in Milwaukee, Wisconsin, needed to take some money to the bank. He got a deposit slip and filled it out, putting it in the bank envelope along with five hundred dollars in cash. He went out to his car but realized he had forgotten something else, so he went back into the gas station office. He came right back out after he found what he was looking for, got in his car, and drove to the bank. Meanwhile, David Sellnow and his wife were also driving on the far south side of Milwaukee that day, when they saw dollar bills coming down on their car from the sky. They pulled off the road and began collecting as much of the money as they could. When they had picked up all the bills they could see, they drove to the Greendale Police Station. They handed over the $246, plus the deposit slip they had found. But the slip had no name on it. The police chief then called the Southgate National Bank, where the deposit slip had come from, and the bank could tell by the numbers on the slip that it belonged to Steve. The bank called Steve, and he was able to get his $246 back. But the other $254 never reappeared. Because that money wasn't near the deposit slip, there was no way for any other finders to contact Steve. How did the money fly away in the first place? Steve had put the envelope on top of his car, and he forgot to get it before he drove off. It was a bad day for poor Steve!

Steve must have felt bad that he didn't remember about the money. But there is something even more important for us to remember, and that's who God is. The Bible says, "Remember this and keep it firmly in mind: The LORD is God both in heaven and on earth, and there is no other" (Deuteronomy 4:39).

How did a trail lead to trivia?

Show me the right path, O LORD;
point out the road for me to follow.
PSALM 25:4

Little bits of unimportant information are called trivia. But in Latin, the word *trivia* means "crossroads," or specifically "three (*tri*) streets (*via*)." So now we have a puzzle. How did the word for three streets turn into a word for information? It had to do with the travelers on those three roads in ancient Rome. The place where the roads came together and crossed became a convenient spot for travelers to leave messages for each other about small, interesting things. It's not necessary anymore to go to a place where roads are crossing to find trivia. You can hear or read bits of interesting information almost everywhere, including in books like this one!

Travelers look for directions, like roads or street signs or certain corners, to figure out how to get where they need to go. But as God's children, our destination is heaven, and the only place we need to seek to find the way is in the Bible. We can ask, "Show me the right path, O LORD; point out the road for me to follow" (Psalm 25:4). And the Lord will always provide the way he wants you to go.

March

Why was the hopperdozer invented?

Let's not get tired of doing what is good. At just the right time we will reap a harvest of blessing if we don't give up.
GALATIANS 6:9

Imagine that it's hundreds of years ago and you're traveling through farmland. You look out into a field and see a farmer riding a horse that is dragging a fifteen-foot metal pan along the ground. In the pan is a coating of water and kerosene or tar. What would you guess is going on? The horse is pulling a hopperdozer, and the idea is that when the tray moves across the ground, the crop-chewing insects jump into the pan and become stuck or poisoned. It was a way to get rid of as many of these insects as possible and save the crops. Any idea which insect the farmer hoped to catch with his contraption? That's right—the hopperdozer was for capturing grasshoppers.

In the same way this farmer was dedicated in growing his crops, as God's children, we hope not to give up either as we try to harvest souls for Christ. The Bible says, "Let's not get tired of doing what is good. At just the right time we will reap a harvest of blessing if we don't give up" (Galatians 6:9).

March

Which lizard swims in the sand?

For forty years [God] sustained them in the
wilderness, and they lacked nothing.
NEHEMIAH 9:21

The fringe-footed lizard lives in sand in the desert. Its toes have fringes on them, which makes its feet useful. It is just a tiny lizard—about five inches long—but it can move as fast as fifteen miles an hour. When it gets attacked, the fringe-footed lizard dives headfirst, right under the sand, and "swims" away. It wriggles its body and uses its feet as paddles, and it does the exact same motions another lizard would use underwater. But since there is no water where the fringe-footed lizard lives, it travels through the sand. It also has fringes on its eyelids to protect its eyes, and its nostrils and ears have valves to keep out the sand, so the fringe-footed lizard is just as comfortable in sand as other lizards are in water. In fact, in the heat of the day, the fringe-footed lizard will dive down into the coolness of deeper sand to stay comfortable until the air temperature drops and it can come back up to the top of the sand again.

The Bible reminds us that even though God cares for creatures like the lizard, the creation God loves most is you. We are told, "For forty years [God] sustained them in the wilderness, and they lacked nothing" (Nehemiah 9:21). God is an expert at taking care of his children, no matter where they live.

March

How many times would *you* chew?

Fear of the LORD lengthens one's life.
PROVERBS 10:27

In the early 1900s, Horace Fletcher believed that people should thoroughly chew all their food if they wanted to stay healthy. Horace thought that every bite of food should be chewed thirty-two times or more to help with digestion. His way of thinking was nicknamed Fletcherism, and he came up with a slogan. He said, "Nature will castigate those who don't masticate." It meant that nature won't be kind to your body if you don't chew everything well. People believed Horace because he was very healthy himself. He rode a bicycle for two hundred miles every day when he was fifty years old. Once, he ate nothing but potatoes for fifty-eight days. People heard about what he did and what he thought, and they decided he must be right since it worked so well for him. So they copied him and chewed every bite of food thirty-two times. Meals were very boring for some people for several years, thanks to Horace Fletcher!

Despite what Horace said, God has more important things for you to do with your time than count your chewing. The Bible tells us, "Fear of the LORD lengthens one's life" (Proverbs 10:27). The Lord will let you know how to really count on a longer, more meaningful life.

March

What makes the starfish special?

Christ will be exalted in my body.
PHILIPPIANS 1:20, NIV

The starfish is a sea creature that usually has five arms that grow in the shape of a star from its body, which is in the center. The parts of a starfish all seem to be in mixed-up places. Its eyes are little colored spots—one at the end of each pointed arm. The starfish's arms are also its legs, because underneath each arm at the pointed end is a disk that works like a suction cup. The starfish moves along the ocean floor by gripping with the suction disks. And when it finds food, the starfish pushes its stomach outside of its body to cover its meal and digest it. Then the stomach is pulled back inside the starfish.

We may not have eyes on our arms or suction cups on our feet, but there's something even more special about our bodies: we can use them to serve God. The Bible gives us a goal for our bodies when it says, "Christ will be exalted in my body" (Philippians 1:20, NIV). Try to take good care of yourself, and don't let odd things change your body, like drugs or alcohol or other things that might harm you. God wants us to have all our parts in good working order so we can serve him with our best.

March

Where did the "Happy Birthday" song come from?

Sing a new song of praise to him.
PSALM 33:3

The birthday song started out in a classroom! Two sisters, a teacher named Mildred Hill and a principal named Patty Hill, made up a song to sing to the students. In 1893, the words were, "Good morning to you; good morning to you; good morning, dear children; good morning to all." Some years later, another person added a second verse to their song, changing the words to "Happy birthday to you." Since everyone has a birthday and not everyone is a teacher with students, the song was sung more with its second set of words. In time it became known to everyone as the "Happy Birthday" song.

Singing "Happy birthday to you" makes a person feel happy on his or her birthday, but you can do much more with your singing. The Bible tells us that it is good to honor God with our voices. It says, "Sing a new song of praise to him" (Psalm 33:3). If singing for someone's birthday is special, imagine how pleased God is when you sing for him!

April 1

What's so crooked about croquet?

I will guide you along the best pathway for your life.
I will advise you and watch over you.

PSALM 32:8

The earliest form of croquet was called pall-mall, and it was played in France in the thirteenth century. The whole game simply involved hitting one ball through one hoop with one wooden mallet, which all the players shared. But everything changed when some French people visited Ireland and taught the Irish how to play pall-mall in 1850. The Irish made several improvements. Everyone got an individual mallet and ball, and lots of hoops were added, with stakes to hit once the ball went through each hoop. Finally, the mallet was changed to one that had a crooked head. That's when the game's name changed to croquet—the French word for "crooked stick."

Wouldn't it be wonderful to have someone teach you how to play croquet, especially if you'd never even seen the game before? The news is even better than that—you have God who will guide you through life, especially the new parts. God promises, "I will guide you along the best pathway for your life. I will advise you and watch over you" (Psalm 32:8). You have your own personal Coach who promises to teach you what you need to know. It can't get any better than that!

April

Who was P. T. Barnum?

How joyful are those who fear the LORD—
all who follow his ways!
PSALM 128:1

Phineas Taylor Barnum was a showman. Some would even say his initials stood for "Pretty Tricky." He made his living with a museum and a circus, and he needed to attract a lot of people who would come to see his strange collections and would be willing to buy tickets to his shows. P. T. Barnum tells a story about how he got people's interest and did some advertising in a very unique way. One day an unemployed man came to see P. T. Barnum to ask for a job, and he was hired. The man's job was to take five bricks and lay one down on the road at five different intersections of the city near the Barnum Museum. The new employee was to have a very serious expression on his face, speak to no one, and pretend that he couldn't even hear the questions people were asking him about what he was doing. Once an hour, he was to go into the Barnum Museum and walk through the halls. Then he was to come back outside, pick up a brick, and exchange it for the next brick until he had changed all five bricks and gone back into the museum. Amazingly, about five hundred people started gathering to follow the man as he switched his bricks, and each time he went into the museum, about a dozen people would buy tickets to go in with him, to see if they could figure out the mystery. In that unique way, P. T. Barnum stirred up his own crowd to visit his museum.

Imagine five hundred people following a man they don't know, doing something they don't recognize, for a reason they don't understand! It's a much more exciting journey to follow Jesus, listen to what he says about earthly and heavenly life, and know exactly where we'll end up if we follow him. The Bible says, "How joyful are those who fear the LORD—all who follow his ways!" (Psalm 128:1). Watch carefully which friends you follow, and make sure you know what you're getting into before you do what they're trying to talk you into. You're much better off staying on the path with Jesus instead.

April

What was an electric sink?

He saved us, not because of the righteous things we had done, but because of his mercy. He washed away our sins, giving us a new birth and new life through the Holy Spirit.
TITUS 3:5

The first garbage disposals were called electric sinks. A garbage disposal is really just a high-speed shredder that operates by electricity and attaches to the drain on the sink. Turn on the switch, and the shredder chews the garbage into tiny pieces that wash down the drain in a stream of water. The first garbage disposals were installed in some kitchen sinks in the 1930s, but it was another ten years before they were considered part of the machinery every kitchen should have. The most important rule of using a garbage disposal is never to put your hand into one because it can cause serious injury. And although disposals work well in getting rid of food waste like rinds or peels or eggshells, dropping other objects like bones or metal or plastic into them will cause them to jam and stop working.

When people first started putting their garbage into the "electric sink," it must have made them very happy to watch it disappear. When we have things in our lives that are like garbage, such as when we hurt someone's feelings or treat another person unkindly or make fun of someone, we would feel better if we could wash them away somehow. When you go to God and tell him you're sorry, that's what happens. God will take away your offensive actions just as if you'd put them into a disposal. The Bible says, "He saved us, not because of the righteous things we had done, but because of his mercy. He washed away our sins, giving us a new birth and new life through the Holy Spirit" (Titus 3:5). Try every day to clear your record with God, and happiness will stay in your heart as the things you regret disappear down the drain.

April

Which cure for a disease actually made it worse?

Hope deferred makes the heart sick, but
a dream fulfilled is a tree of life.
PROVERBS 13:12

*M*alaria means "bad air," and long ago that was the name people gave to the sickness they thought was caused by bad air. To make the air—and also the sick person—better, jars full of sweet-smelling flowers were put all around a malaria patient's room. What no one knew then was the reason people got malaria in the first place. It wasn't because of bad air; it was really caused by parasites that were carried from one person to another by the bites of a certain kind of mosquito that lays its eggs in water. Unfortunately the jars of flowers had water in them, and in the water were mosquito eggs that then hatched into mosquitoes and bit the patients. So the sick people kept getting worse instead of better.

It is really discouraging when you hope to get better but you get sicker instead. God understands that feeling. The Bible tells us, "Hope deferred makes the heart sick, but a dream fulfilled is a tree of life" (Proverbs 13:12). We can always have hope as children of God, because God will never disappoint us. His promises to us will always come true.

April

Why are Campbell's soup cans red and white?

There is nothing better than to be happy and enjoy ourselves as long as we can. And people should eat and drink and enjoy the fruits of their labor, for these are gifts from God.
ECCLESIASTES 3:12-13

The company first started out in 1869 as the Joseph A. Campbell Preserve Company, which sold fruits, jams, sauces, canned meats, and soups. When the chemist Dr. John T. Dorrance was hired, he figured out how to condense, or take some of the water out of, the soup. The cans weighed less, and the price dropped from thirty-four cents a can to ten cents a can. Then soup became the company's best-selling item, so the company name changed to the Campbell Soup Company. The colors of red and white were chosen in 1898 because of a football game! That's where a Campbell's executive was when he decided he really liked the color combination of red and white that was used for the uniforms of Cornell University's football team. Alphabet soup is one of the most interesting kinds of Campbell's soup. Each can holds about sixty to sixty-five pasta letters of the alphabet. The same quantity of each letter is made, but the letters are not in order when they are dropped into the cans, so not every can of soup will have a complete set of alphabet letters in it.

Soup is an easy-to-make, easy-to-eat, nutritious meal that allows plenty of extra time for other things you enjoy. This is a good thing, since the Bible says, "There is nothing better than to be happy and enjoy ourselves as long as we can. And people should eat and drink and enjoy the fruits of their labor, for these are gifts from God" (Ecclesiastes 3:12-13). So it's time to eat your soup and get busy!

April

Why count the chirps of crickets?

How great is our Lord! His power is absolute!
His understanding is beyond comprehension!
PSALM 147:5

There is a formula involving cricket chirps that can tell you the approximate temperature outside, near where the crickets are chirping. Crickets are cold-blooded creatures, which means that the warmer the temperature, the faster the cricket will make its chirping sound. To find out what the temperature is, count how many chirps a cricket makes in fifteen seconds. Then add forty to that number. Now you know about how warm it is in Fahrenheit degrees, which is how we usually measure the temperature. Remember, though, that the cricket is telling you how warm it is right next to its own body, not how warm it is next to where you are. Try the experiment and see how close the cricket can get to matching the temperature where you are.

We get excited when we can uncover one of the little mysteries of nature, like using cricket chirps to determine the temperature. It is awe inspiring to think about how God created all the creatures of the earth and their habits and abilities, and how he keeps track of them all every second. The Bible says, "How great is our Lord! His power is absolute! His understanding is beyond comprehension!" (Psalm 147:5). It is a privilege to be able to learn about this creation that God designed for us.

April

Why would a beetle stand on its head?

I thirst for God, the living God.
PSALM 42:2

The Namibian darkling beetle lives in the desert in Africa. Because there is so little water there, the beetle turns itself upside down so that it is standing on its head. Then it uses the shell on its body to capture moisture from the damp breezes that blow. The moisture condenses on its body and forms dewdrops that slide down to the beetle's mouth. Then it drinks the drops.

As human beings, we understand how important it is to get something to drink when we're thirsty. We can't rest until we do! That's why the Bible talks about how much we need to be near the Lord when it says, "I thirst for God, the living God" (Psalm 42:2). He will give you rest and comfort when you are tired, and he will satisfy you with his love. It's a feeling you can't get any other way.

April

Does a bird really "eat like a bird"?

[God] is able, through his mighty power at work within us,
to accomplish infinitely more than we might ask or think.

EPHESIANS 3:20

When you hear someone say that a person eats like a bird, that means that the person isn't eating very much. But the truth is, birds eat a tremendous amount for the size of their bodies. Many birds eat half their weight a day in worms and insects. The American robin is a big eater. It can eat up to seventy worms between sunup and sundown. Baby birds are well known for the way they need to eat all the time. They digest food incredibly fast—some parent birds have to make twenty trips a day to feed their little ones in the nest. One type of baby bird was observed eating 480 times in just one day. Another type of bird, the hummingbird, consumes a lot of food for being so small. If a grown man ate at the same rate the hummingbird does, he would have to eat 285 pounds of meat every day.

God takes care of even the most helpless of creatures in mighty ways, providing for them much more than we might expect that they need. He provides for us in even greater ways. The Bible says that God "is able, through his mighty power at work within us, to accomplish infinitely more than we might ask or think" (Ephesians 3:20). We can't even measure what God does for us every day.

April

How did mirrors help fight a war?

Let all who take refuge in you rejoice; let them sing
joyful praises forever. Spread your protection over them,
that all who love your name may be filled with joy.
PSALM 5:11

A famous Greek inventor named Archimedes was trying to help fight a powerful Roman force that was attacking his city of Syracuse in 212 BC. One of the weapons Archimedes came up with was the catapult, which could send five-hundred boulders flying at the Romans as far as six hundred feet. But according to tradition, one of the more unusual weapons Archimedes designed was an arrangement of simple mirrors. He arranged the mirrors so that they reflected and directed the concentrated rays of the sun right onto the Roman ships, which set the ships on fire.

Sometimes we might think that God has forgotten about us or left us to fend for ourselves. But that is not true. The Lord is watching over his people. The Bible says, "Let all who take refuge in you rejoice; let them sing joyful praises forever. Spread your protection over them, that all who love your name may be filled with joy" (Psalm 5:11).

April

Why don't bones break as easily while you're young?

Let the children come to me. Don't stop
them! For the Kingdom of Heaven belongs
to those who are like these children.
MATTHEW 19:14

There are 206 bones in the human body. The thigh bone, called the femur, is our biggest bone. The smallest bone is the stapes. It is one of the three tiny bones located in each of the middle ear sections of our ears. When we are very young, our bones are mostly made of cartilage, which is flexible and pliable and not usually involved in breaks to the bones. As we grow older, our bones get more minerals in them and become harder. This means adult bones are much more likely to break.

The heavenly Father loves children a lot. One of the ways he shows it is by designing their bones to be flexible when they are little so that their bodies can be protected from harm. Jesus invites you to come to him, no matter how old you are. The Bible tells us what Jesus said to the adults nearby: "Let the children come to me. Don't stop them! For the Kingdom of Heaven belongs to those who are like these children" (Matthew 19:14). Ask Jesus to come into your heart, and that's where he will stay.

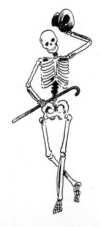

April

When was there a surprise family reunion?

The LORD your God is living among you. He is a mighty savior. He will take delight in you with gladness. With his love, he will calm all your fears. He will rejoice over you with joyful songs.
ZEPHANIAH 3:17

Two brothers, John Patterson and his younger brother, Fred, both worked at the Brewster Aircraft Company in Pennsylvania. When World War II started, Fred enlisted in the army in 1939. Then John joined the air force in 1943. That is when the two brothers lost contact with each other as they helped fight the war. When they returned home after the war, they still had no way to get in touch with each other. About twenty years later, John was working as a cook at a Holiday Inn restaurant in Atlantic City, New Jersey. He happened to see a coworker of his in the restaurant at the exact moment that the man made a familiar facial expression. All of a sudden, John knew! The man he had been watching was not just a new waiter who had been working there for three weeks. He was also John's younger brother, Fred! They were right in the same place at the same time for the first time in twenty-eight years, and neither one realized it until that exciting moment.

You can imagine the excitement of the brothers when they first met again. God is always excited to be with you. He celebrates when you decide to read his Word and pray to him. He delights in you! He loves to be near you. The Bible says, "The LORD your God is living among you. He is a mighty savior. He will take delight in you with gladness. With his love, he will calm all your fears. He will rejoice over you with joyful songs" (Zephaniah 3:17).

April

Which invention was created to pay a debt?

Owe nothing to anyone—except for your
obligation to love one another.
ROMANS 13:8

Even though his invention wasn't a new idea, Walter Hunt modern-ized it by making it stronger, springier, and safer. It was 1825, and Walter had no money. But he owed fifteen dollars to a friend. His friend gave Walter a piece of metal wire and told him to create something useful, which he would accept as payment for the debt. Walter completed his project in three hours and gave it to his friend, who paid him four hun-dred dollars for the idea, canceled the debt, and later made millions from selling the creation. What was it? The modern safety pin.

Some might say that Walter made a mistake to give his safety pin design away for such a small amount of money when in the end, he could have made millions. But Christians understand that there is a more important goal than money—it is receiving the blessings that the Lord will provide when we follow the Bible. We are given this advice about owing someone money: "Owe nothing to anyone—except for your obligation to love one another" (Romans 13:8). The rewards for fol-lowing God's laws are far more valuable than any amount of money.

April 13

What extremely unusual thing happened to President Andrew Jackson—twice?

Put on every piece of God's armor so you will be able to resist the enemy in the time of evil. Then after the battle you will still be standing firm.
EPHESIANS 6:13

President Jackson was shot at twice as he walked through the South Carolina capitol building in 1835 after attending a funeral. With no advance warning, a gun was suddenly only six feet away from him, held by a young man that President Jackson didn't know. The gun was quickly fired, but the bullet didn't come out of it. The gunman pulled out a second pistol and again fired, but the second bullet remained in that gun too. The mentally unstable gunman, Richard Lawrence, was wrestled to the ground. Later the guns were examined, and they appeared to have been loaded correctly and were in excellent condition. No one could explain why the bullets hadn't come out.

People may not threaten your life, but they could be out to threaten your soul. You might be invited to do something you know is wrong, like gossiping, swearing, or making fun of someone. Or you might find that people make fun of your belief in Jesus Christ, trying to weaken your faith. What should you do when you're tempted? The Bible reassures us by saying, "Put on every piece of God's armor so you will be able to resist the enemy in the time of evil. Then after the battle you will still be standing firm" (Ephesians 6:13). Just like President Jackson, you can survive attacks. The evil intended to destroy your soul can be overcome by relying on the supernatural protection of God that will last for eternity.

April 14

Why aren't all rivers straight?

Lead me in the right path, O Lord, or my enemies will
conquer me. Make your way plain for me to follow.
PSALM 5:8

The age of a river makes the difference between one that winds and one that doesn't. Rivers that run along flat land and are ten thousand years old or older are usually crooked. Rivers start uphill and run downhill to the ocean, and the water in them is so powerful that it falls straight down from where it begins. But when water gets to flatter land, it slows down and loses its power, and that is how a river changes directions. There might be bumps or hills or rocks in the way. When the river hits a rock, it moves around it, but the water is still so heavy that it begins to dig out the earth along the banks, or the sides of the river. This causes the river to curve as the dirt of the banks is washed away. Younger rivers are straighter because they haven't had as long to erode or change the land that shapes them.

Although the course that a river will finally take can't be predicted, it can be clear what course we are to follow in life. Ask God to show you clearly how he wants you to live your life. Pray this way: "Lead me in the right path, O Lord, or my enemies will conquer me. Make your way plain for me to follow" (Psalm 5:8). Instead of floating along, wondering where you will end up, take the straight, sure way to Jesus.

April

How were people able to buy extra time?

For everything there is a season, a time for every activity under heaven. A time to be born and a time to die.
ECCLESIASTES 3:1-2

It all started because Carlton Magee was trying to solve a car-parking problem. When people parked to go shopping, their cars often weren't moved for hours, which made it impossible for new shoppers to find a spot to park, causing nearby stores to lose the money from more sales. In Oklahoma City in 1935, Carlton was hired to install his new invention at each parking spot. It was a machine that had a crank like a candy machine, except that when you put money in, no candy came out. Drivers were required to put coins in the machine to reserve that spot for their car. It turned out that when shoppers had to pay to park or risk getting a ticket, they shopped faster. That's how the parking meter began selling time, and shoppers bought some, even though they didn't like paying for something that used to be free.

When you have given your heart to God, you can be sure he will keep track of your minutes for you. He invented time, and he planned out every second of your time on earth for you. The Bible tells us, "For everything there is a season, a time for every activity under heaven. A time to be born and a time to die" (Ecclesiastes 3:1-2). It goes on to list many other ways that God is in control of the minutes, hours, years, and centuries. God doesn't expect you to have a dime in your pocket so you can buy time on a parking meter. He gives you your time on earth for free, without your even having to arrange for it.

April 16

What's so nutty about the nuthatch?

Fear of the LORD is the foundation of true wisdom.
All who obey his commandments will grow in wisdom.
PSALM 111:10

You won't see a nuthatch just fly into its hole like other birds. It lands above its house and then climbs into it upside down. Most birds spread their legs from side to side, giving them good balance, but the nuthatch spreads its legs from front to back, which allows it to walk down a tree trunk headfirst. And all the while, the nuthatch is making a *yank, yank* sound and just won't be quiet. Not only that, but the nuthatch takes a piece of animal fur or smashed insect and rubs it all around the hole of its house, maybe to keep its enemies from being able to find its house by smell. What a full day's entertainment you can have just by watching all the nuthatch's busy little habits!

What seems nutty to humans is nothing more than the birds following the instincts God gave them to help them survive. But God gives us much greater potential and opportunities than he gives birds and other creatures. Instead of just using instinct, we can attain true wisdom. The Bible tells us, "Fear of the LORD is the foundation of true wisdom. All who obey his commandments will grow in wisdom" (Psalm 111:10). Keep your heart open to God, and he will open your mind for wisdom.

April 17

What's wrong with the way we draw raindrops?

God will wipe every tear from their eyes.
REVELATION 7:17

Even though we draw raindrops like teardrops, they are never really shaped that way. Actually, each raindrop has a shape that looks like a bagel or a doughnut. But the place where the hole should be doesn't go all the way through. The surface tension of the water dents the raindrop in the middle, but it doesn't make a complete hole. There's something to think about next time you draw a raindrop!

When you are God's child, you can be sure that he cares about every hurt you feel and every tear you cry. You can tell how much he loves you when you read in the Bible that "God will wipe every tear from their eyes" (Revelation 7:17). That means yours, too. No one will ever want to take away your sadness more than God does.

April

Where did the name *motel* come from?

There is more than enough room in my Father's home.
If this were not so, would I have told you that I am going
to prepare a place for you? When everything is ready, I will
come and get you, so that you will always be with me where
I am. And you know the way to where I am going.

JOHN 14:2-4

The word *motel* is a combination of *motor* and *hotel*, and that's what it was intended to be—rooms for people who were traveling. The idea was that they could drive their cars right up next to their cabins to stay and rest. Arthur Heineman thought of the name and was the first to use it on the motor hotel he built in 1925. Called the Milestone Mo-tel (the hyphen was there so that people would understand the new name), it had small cottages built around a courtyard. Each little house—there were forty of them—had its own kitchen and garage. The best part was an indoor bathroom with a shower! In the middle of the courtyard there was even a swimming pool. There was much more privacy and luxury for people than having to camp outside when traveling by car. All of this luxury cost only two dollars and fifty cents a night. That long ago, cars were driven slowly, so people were hired to stand by the roadside in front of the motel to hand brochures about the motel to the passengers as they rode by.

When you're weary of traveling, it's welcoming to see a motel, especially if you and the people you're traveling with were worried that you wouldn't be able to find one. A motel offers good things for you to enjoy. But there is a place reserved for you that is much better than a motel. The Bible tells us that Jesus said, "There is more than enough room in my Father's home. If this were not so, would I have told you that I am going to prepare a place for you? When everything is ready, I will come and get you, so that you will always be with me where I am. And you know the way to where I am going" (John 14:2-4). What could be better than a place that Jesus himself made sure was ready for you?

April

How long can a sermon be?

Commit yourself to instruction; listen
carefully to words of knowledge.
PROVERBS 23:12

There are two unusual sermons on record, both because they were so lengthy. The first was given by Clinton Locy, of West Richland, Washington, in February 1955. His sermon lasted forty-eight hours and fifteen minutes—that's more than two days!—when he preached on some of the text from every book of the Bible. By the time he finished, there were eight people left sitting in the congregation. The second sermon set a new record. The speaker was Reverend Donald Thomas of Brooklyn, New York. He started speaking on September 18, 1978, and finished his last word on September 22, for a grand total of ninety-three hours.

Sometimes it is hard to be patient and listen to your minister or teacher or parent when you'd rather be outside playing or spending time with your friends. But God has put adults in your life to teach you valuable things that will help you in the future. It is especially important to listen when people teach about the Word of God. The Bible tells us, "Commit yourself to instruction; listen carefully to words of knowledge" (Proverbs 23:12). Do your best to listen in church, and the message that you keep in your heart will be the most valuable one you hear.

April 20

What huts were popular in the 1940s?

You are my strength; I wait for you to rescue
me, for you, O God, are my fortress.
PSALM 59:9

Imagine a long, low building with a curved top that looks like a cylinder sliced in half lengthwise. Many people lived in buildings like this in 1941 when the military sent more than 160,000 of them to places all over the world. These buildings were named Quonset huts because they were made at a naval air base in Quonset Point, Rhode Island. These oddly shaped Quonset huts were very useful because they stayed warm in the winter and cool in the summer, were easy to put up and take down, and were convenient to ship from one place to another. They were also inexpensive to build and to buy. They were made of steel and could be used as houses or churches or hospitals. When World War II was over, people continued to live in Quonset huts because there was a shortage of houses for many of the soldiers returning from war. Finally, when enough regular houses could be built, the need for Quonset huts stopped. Interestingly, the early settlers in the 1600s lived in buildings very much like Quonset huts.

The Quonset hut had lots of good things about it, but nothing could be as good as having God himself as your shelter from trouble. The Bible tells us how to thank God for caring about us so much: "You are my strength; I wait for you to rescue me, for you, O God, are my fortress" (Psalm 59:9).

April
21

What do bats and dolphins have in common?

The LORD hears his people when they call to him for help. He rescues them from all their troubles.

PSALM 34:17

Both bats and dolphins have a high-pitched shriek. When they cry out, they are trying to bounce sound waves off objects. They hear an echo returning, and from that they know how far away their dinner is and where to find it. Both dolphins and bats use this method, called echolocation, to figure out what the response means.

When we cry out to God, we already know what his response will be. Our prayers don't just echo back to us—he hears us and responds, and he will help us with whatever we need. The Bible reminds us, "The LORD hears his people when they call to him for help. He rescues them from all their troubles" (Psalm 34:17). Don't be shy about asking God into your daily life!

April

Why do we feel cold when we're wet?

When I am afraid, I will put my trust in you.
PSALM 56:3

You've just had a shower, and the bathroom is full of warm steam. But you still begin to feel cold. Why? When you are wet, the heat that your body is always giving off turns some of the drops of water into a gas called water vapor. When water changes from a liquid to a gas, it is called evaporation. The reason you start feeling cold is because evaporation uses up the heat that your body has produced. That's similar to what a hair dryer does. The droplets of water in your hair are heated up until evaporation happens.

Sometimes we shiver when we feel cold, and other times we shiver when we feel afraid. You don't need to worry either time. God has designed your body to help take care of the cold, and God has designed your spirit to run for his protection. We can do what David in the Bible did: "When I am afraid, I will put my trust in you" (Psalm 56:3). That's the best way to warm your heart!

April

How was a bird responsible for starting _Guinness World Records_?

Jesus shouted, "Lazarus, come out!"
And the dead man came out.
JOHN 11:43-44

Hugh Beaver was a hunter, and one day he shot at a bird but missed because the bird was flying so fast. Hugh began to wonder how fast that bird could fly and which was the fastest flier of all. He couldn't find the answer anywhere, and he decided that the world needed a book that contained information about things like what was tallest, fastest, or longest. He found the perfect people to write the book: identical twins Ross and Norris McWhirter, who had already been researching and collecting facts and information they loved for years. Amazingly, they could answer just about any question anybody could think of, and they put what they knew into a book. The first _Guinness Book of Records_ was published in 1955, and since then people all over the world have been looking things up in the book that began with a bird.

It's interesting to find out about what records people have set, but their accomplishments don't compare to the miracles described in the Bible. No one in _Guinness World Records_ has ever raised someone from the dead, but Jesus did. After his good friend Lazarus had been dead for four days, Jesus went to his tomb and asked that the stone be rolled away. The Bible says, "Jesus shouted, 'Lazarus, come out!' And the dead man came out" (John 11:43-44). _Guinness World Records_ is fun to read, but what's in the Bible will always be much more amazing.

April

Why did a hearing aid weigh sixteen pounds?

We must listen very carefully to the truth we
have heard, or we may drift away from it.
HEBREWS 2:1

Before many of our modern technological advances, people who had difficulty hearing also had difficulty getting help. Many solutions were tried. In 1819, the biggest hearing aid ever built was actually a throne for King John VI of Portugal. People who came to see the king had to speak into the arms of the throne, which were hollow, and the sound went into tubes that the king wore in his ears. In the early days, men hid their hearing aids in top hats or walking sticks with tubes coming out of them. Women's hearing aids were hidden in bonnets, handbags, or crowns (if they were royalty). The first battery-powered hearing aid was invented in 1923, but all the equipment that needed to go along with it had to be carried in a case that weighed sixteen pounds. Finally, in the 1950s, a newer technology called transistors made it possible for hearing aids to be smaller and lighter so they could be hidden behind the ear, and now they fit in the ear itself.

It's a gift to be able to hear clearly with our earthly bodies, even if we need technology to help us. But we should work even harder to hear what God wants us to hear. The Bible says, "We must listen very carefully to the truth we have heard, or we may drift away from it" (Hebrews 2:1). What could be more important than that?

April

Have you ever wondered why we blink?

Let me reveal to you a wonderful secret. We will not all die, but we will all be transformed! It will happen in a moment, in the blink of an eye, when the last trumpet is blown. For when the trumpet sounds, those who have died will be raised to live forever. And we who are living will also be transformed.

1 CORINTHIANS 15:51-52

Most parts of your body get the oxygen they need from a supply of blood that flows through them. But the cornea (the outer layer) of your eye doesn't have a blood supply, even though it needs oxygen. When you blink, your eye gets moistened, and the cornea can then absorb some oxygen from the water. The other reason you blink is to wipe the surface of your eyes clean from little particles of dust or dirt that land on them. The average person blinks fifteen times in a minute, which means you spend the equivalent of nine full days of every year blinking.

Blinking is fast, and it happens before you even realize it. But do you know what else will happen that fast? The Bible says, "Let me reveal to you a wonderful secret. We will not all die, but we will all be transformed! It will happen in a moment, in the blink of an eye, when the last trumpet is blown. For when the trumpet sounds, those who have died will be raised to live forever. And we who are living will also be transformed" (1 Corinthians 15:51-52). Each time you notice yourself blinking, remember that someday heaven will be yours . . . faster than you can blink your eyes!

April

What's the largest living thing on earth?

It is like a mustard seed planted in the ground.
It is the smallest of all seeds, but it becomes the
largest of all garden plants; it grows long branches,
and birds can make nests in its shade.

MARK 4:31-32

Would you guess an elephant or a whale? You might be surprised to find out what it really is—a mushroom! Stranger still, most of this mushroom, called the honey fungus, grows underground. The mushroom grows rootlike tentacles, called mycelia, that form a connecting mat under the soil. This mushroom is between two thousand and eight thousand years old, and it has grown to the size of 2,200 acres in Malheur National Park in Oregon.

Jesus taught us about things that grow, even things that start out small. In the Bible Jesus says, "It is like a mustard seed planted in the ground. It is the smallest of all seeds, but it becomes the largest of all garden plants; it grows long branches, and birds can make nests in its shade" (Mark 4:31-32). Jesus isn't really talking about plants. He is saying that every time we tell other people about him, it's like we are planting a tiny seed of faith inside their hearts. And we hope that their faith grows to be the biggest thing on earth!

April

Eaten any Twinkle Fingers lately?

If you look for me wholeheartedly, you will find me.
JEREMIAH 29:13

Twinkies, the vanilla-filled yellow cake snacks, were invented by a Hostess baking plant manager named James Dewar. James put two ideas together and came up with a winning product. Times were hard during the Depression in the 1930s, and the bakery needed a product that could be made and sold cheaply. Also, James noticed that the pans where strawberry shortcakes were baked stayed empty except for in strawberry season, which was only six weeks long. He thought, *Why not use those pans* (which made long, finger-shaped cakes) *and add a banana filling* (which was later changed to vanilla when there was a shortage of bananas)? So that is exactly what the Hostess bakery did, and Twinkies became the company's best-selling cake. The name came from a shoe factory sign that said "Home of Twinkle Toe Shoes." The cakes were first called "Little Shortcake Fingers," but James decided against his friend's later suggestion of Twinkle Fingers and settled on Twinkies.

The story of Twinkies was a long process of beginning and beginning again. Jesus wants us to have that kind of patience and desire to keep looking for him, because he promises it will be worth the effort. God says, "If you look for me wholeheartedly, you will find me" (Jeremiah 29:13). Look for Jesus every day, and don't get discouraged if you have to keep trying again and again.

April

What tales does a squirrel's tail tell?

Wild animals and all livestock, small scurrying animals
and birds . . . let them all praise the name of the LORD.
PSALM 148:10, 13

The squirrel's tail is a kind of all-purpose tool. The squirrel uses its tail like a balancing pole to help it stay on wires and branches when it crosses them. If a squirrel falls, it uses its tail as a parachute. Did you know squirrels can fall more than one hundred feet without hurting themselves? The squirrel's tail is also an umbrella to keep it dry when it rains, a blanket to keep it warm on cold nights, and a shade to keep it cool on warm days. The squirrel's tail is also a flag that warns other squirrels of danger and a shield in case it has to fight another animal.

The squirrel is just one of the animals created to praise God, and it has so many things to give praise for. Its tail doesn't do only one job; it does many. God designed the squirrel in a special way, unique from other animals. He has thought of everything. The Bible tells everything to praise God, including "wild animals and all livestock, small scurrying animals and birds. . . . Let them all praise the name of the LORD" (Psalm 148:10, 13). Every animal—and every person—can praise the Lord for the gifts we've been given, far and wide.

April

What sparked the idea for the first fire hose?

He will come with his mighty angels, in flaming fire, bringing judgment on those who don't know God and on those who refuse to obey the Good News of our Lord Jesus.
2 THESSALONIANS 1:7-8

B. F. (Benjamin Franklin) Goodrich knew how to make things out of rubber. He owned and ran a factory that made products out of rubber, like rubber tires. But one day in 1870, he decided to make another product out of rubber. He was in the backyard of his house in Akron, Ohio, when he smelled smoke. He hurried down the street to see that the house of one of his neighbors was on fire. B. F. watched as the horse-drawn fire truck arrived and rolled out the leather hose, connected it to the water pump, and tried to put out the fire. But the hose was brittle and had a leak, and then it burst. All anyone could do was watch as the house burned to the ground. Soon after, B. F. Goodrich began making the world's first fire hoses. They were heavy-duty cotton-covered rubber hoses that became his best-selling product.

B. F. Goodrich was sorry to see what happened to his neighbor, and he wanted to make sure that something like that wouldn't happen again. But as terrible as a fire is here on earth, there is a much worse kind of fire: the fire of judgment: "He will come with his mighty angels, in flaming fire, bringing judgment on those who don't know God and on those who refuse to obey the Good News of our Lord Jesus" (2 Thessalonians 1:7-8). When we follow Jesus, we are saved from the fire of judgment, and we can show other people how they can be saved too.

April

How was a little electricity tamed?

God said, "Let there be light," and there was light.
GENESIS 1:3

In the 1800s, when electricity first became available for homes, the supply came on for only a few hours a day, so no one bothered to unscrew the one lightbulb from its socket on the wall or ceiling. To use anything else electric, you had to figure out how to attach it to the lightbulb socket or attach the wires directly to the wires of the house. Not many people knew how to do either. So there was a real need for Harvey Hubbell of Connecticut and his two electrical inventions. In 1896, he invented a pull-chain socket so that people could turn off the lights by tugging on a chain where the lightbulb was screwed in. And in 1904, he invented a plug plate that would allow people to plug in electrical appliances through the wall. Harvey got his idea for the wall plug when he was helping a janitor who was trying to reattach some wires to the wires in the wall. It was the janitor's job to clean behind a large arcade machine that allowed people to play a boxing game electrically. But the janitor struggled to disconnect and reattach the machine each time he had to move it. Harvey invented a plug-and-socket box for the wall that only had to be wired once and could be used easily after that. Harvey solved the janitor's problem, along with making life easier for everyone else.

"God said, 'Let there be light,' and there was light" (Genesis 1:3). It was one thing when Harvey found a way to fix the plug, and another thing entirely when God first brought light into being. But maybe Harvey felt a little bit like he was following in God's footsteps in some small way. If we each take steps to follow our Lord, the world will be a better place.

May 1

What was the best way to park a covered wagon?

The LORD is my rock, my fortress, and my savior; my God
is my rock, in whom I find protection. He is my shield,
the power that saves me, and my place of safety.
PSALM 18:2

Many pioneers rode covered wagons from the eastern United States out toward the West. Each night, it required some planning to stop and sleep as safely as possible. The idea was to "circle the wagons" in a way that would give the most space inside for a cooking fire and places for sleeping, while still offering protection. The wagons had to be as close together as possible to discourage anything or anyone from getting through from outside the circle to attack the center space. What was the best solution? If there were enough wagons traveling together, covered wagons were parked in groups of ten, forming a chain that made a circular shape. This provided the most space inside, with the best protection created by the outer side of the wagons.

It is wise for us to use the good ideas God gives us to practice safety. But the Bible explains, "The LORD is my rock, my fortress, and my savior; my God is my rock, in whom I find protection. He is my shield, the power that saves me, and my place of safety" (Psalm 18:2). As God's children, we know that in the end it is not a circle of wagons or a lock on the door that protects us but God's plan for our lives. God is greater protection than any kind of human security. We can always run to our Father and ask for his help. He is not afraid of anything.

May

Where could you shop for items from around the world?

Cry out for insight, and ask for understanding. Search for them as you would for silver; seek them like hidden treasures. Then you will understand what it means to fear the LORD, and you will gain knowledge of God.

PROVERBS 2:3-5

Long ago, people got together to do their shopping several times a year in different cities along the busiest and most traveled routes. Merchants, farmers, and craftsmen from certain areas of the world would sell their products. But those meetings changed in 1851, when the English decided to build fairgrounds and invite the whole world to gather there. The Crystal Palace was built to make the spot in London spectacular. The palace was made of three hundred thousand pieces of glass and was the largest and only building of its kind ever built. Many different countries brought their newest and best products to show off and sell in the Crystal Palace. The first World's Fair was a huge success, with over 6 million people visiting during the five months the fair was open. It was a chance for people to keep up with what was being created and developed all over the world. Later, other cities held World's Fairs and Expositions of their own.

People who went to the World's Fair were looking for understanding of the latest ideas and inventions, and searching for treasures from other parts of the world. But there is something much more valuable to spend your time searching for. The Bible tells us, "Cry out for insight, and ask for understanding. Search for them as you would for silver; seek them like hidden treasures. Then you will understand what it means to fear the LORD, and you will gain knowledge of God" (Proverbs 2:3-5). Make searching for God the most important thing you do, and you will find riches of heart and soul that will be much more exciting than what the world has to offer.

May

Who first declared war on germs?

Create in me a clean heart, O God.
Renew a loyal spirit within me.
PSALM 51:10

Dr. Joseph Lister had a suspicion about something in the 1860s. He was put in charge of a new surgical unit in the Glasgow Royal Infirmary, but he didn't like the way so many patients were dying after successful surgery. Some doctors called it "hospital fever," but Joseph suspected another cause. He studied some information from Louis Pasteur, a famous scientist, and then Joseph got an idea. People in the hospital were getting sick because germs were being passed from one patient to the next in the surgical operating rooms by unclean hands and instruments. People thought Joseph was crazy, because nobody believed in germs then—you couldn't see them! But one day in 1865, a boy with a broken shin, which usually led to infection and death, became Joseph's patient. Joseph set the broken bone and then did something new—he treated the wound with bandages dipped in carbolic acid to kill any germs. James Greenlees, the young patient, left the hospital six weeks later, walking and healthy. After that, operating rooms were treated with carbolic acid as the world began paying attention to getting rid of germs. By the way, you may recognize a product named after Dr. Lister: Listerine mouthwash.

Having hands free of germs helps keep our bodies strong. And having clean hearts helps our souls stay strong too. We can pray like this: "Create in me a clean heart, O God. Renew a loyal spirit within me" (Psalm 51:10). God wants us to be encouraged that if we are watchful against things that could harm our spirits, like lying, or stealing, or cheating, we will get stronger in our faith and closer to him every day.

May

Why would you give someone a "white elephant"?

Love your enemies! Do good to them.
LUKE 6:35

The idea came from the king of Siam (which later became Thailand). In ancient times, a white elephant was considered a sacred animal that could never be made to do work. If the king was angry with someone, he gave a "present" that wasn't very appreciated—he gave the person a real live white elephant. A gift from the king was always considered too special to give away, so the new owner had to keep it. Of course, that meant that the new owner had to feed the elephant and care for it, which was expensive and took a lot of time. For his trouble, though, he would never get one bit of help from the white elephant. What appeared to be a gift was actually something that the king didn't want himself, so he gave it to somebody else. That's the kind of gift you should choose to take to a "white elephant" party—something useless or something you don't want to keep.

White elephant gifts can be fun to give, as long as they don't harm anyone else. But doing something mean to someone on purpose—even if it is someone you don't like—is not God's way for us to live. The Bible says, "Love your enemies! Do good to them" (Luke 6:35).

May

What kind of jar could make you jump?

Use your hands for good hard work.
EPHESIANS 4:28

In 1775, people were experimenting with electricity, and two men came up with the idea of the Leyden jar. This jar, covered with metal, could either store electricity or give off a powerful spark that could cause a shock. To show just how strong the shock could be, an experiment was once demonstrated. A thousand monks lined up, all holding hands. When the Leyden jar was attached to the first monk and then to the last one, the shock went through every monk and made each one of them jump.

Because the monks were part of an experiment, their work at that time involved something unpleasant. But fortunately their normal days weren't spent this way. The Bible teaches us to "use your hands for good hard work" (Ephesians 4:28). Sometimes your hands are involved in special projects, but usually your daily work is plenty to keep you busy, hopefully doing tasks that won't include a shock.

May

Why was everyone talking about the temperature?

Jesus Christ is the same yesterday, today, and forever.
HEBREWS 13:8

It's almost certain that the townspeople of Spearfish, South Dakota, were doing exactly that on January 22, 1943. On that one single day, the temperature changed in a big way—not just once, but twice! First, in only two minutes, the temperature rose from -4 degrees Fahrenheit to 45 degrees. In that short amount of time, the air outside got 49 degrees warmer! But that was not the end of the weird weather. On the same morning, a little while later, the temperature fell way back down in twenty-seven minutes. It went from 54 degrees Fahrenheit back down to -4. In other words, the air outside got 58 degrees colder! The reason seemed to be that both cold and warm fronts hit the nearby Black Hills before sweeping across the Great Plains and on to Spearfish.

Weather can change quickly. We can't depend on it to stay the same. But God's people can depend on him. The Bible tells us, "Jesus Christ is the same yesterday, today, and forever" (Hebrews 13:8). You can count on the Lord all the time.

May

What did Wilt the Stilt do to make basketball history?

O LORD God of Heaven's Armies! Where is there anyone as mighty as you, O LORD? You are entirely faithful.

PSALM 89:8

Wilt Chamberlain played basketball, and he played it well. But no one knew just how well until March 2, 1962. That night the New York Knickerbockers and the Philadelphia Warriors were playing a game in Hershey, Pennsylvania. It was a small town at a small National Basketball Association game, but Wilt Chamberlain was not small. And he accomplished something very big—basketball history! Wilt was seven feet one inch tall. "Wilt the Stilt" heaved one hundred points into the basket during that game! He scored 36 field goals in 63 tries and sank 28 out of 32 free throws. His team won 169–147, and basketball won a new record.

God knows all about how to take charge of a team, like Wilt did that night. God runs the whole world, after all. The Bible says, "O LORD God of Heaven's Armies! Where is there anyone as mighty as you, O LORD? You are entirely faithful" (Psalm 89:8). Whenever you need to perform for any reason, like acting in the school play or reading out loud in front of the class, you can count on God to help you be strong. He will be beside you every moment, and he will give you victory over your fears.

May

Do all mosquitoes bite?

I will give you back your health and heal your wounds.
JEREMIAH 30:17

The female mosquito is designed to bite because she needs your blood to help her eggs develop. But the male mosquito never bites. His mouth is not built to be able to pierce your skin or drink your blood. The male mosquito drinks plant juices or water but nothing else, because he has no eggs he needs to provide for.

God cares about what happens to you. Even when you're bothered by a little mosquito bite, that matters to him. God tells us, "I will give you back your health and heal your wounds" (Jeremiah 30:17). Take all of your cares to Jesus, both large and small. He loves his children and wants to help.

May

Could the tortoise really beat the hare?

This hope is a strong and trustworthy anchor for our souls.
HEBREWS 6:19

Most of us remember the story of the tortoise and the hare. The hare is much faster, but it gets distracted and doesn't keep patiently plodding along like the tortoise does. In the end the tortoise wins, and we are advised that "slow and steady wins the race." The interesting thing is that in real life, the fastest speed a giant tortoise can manage to go is about five yards a minute—that's less than two yardsticks placed end to end. A hare, on the other hand, can cover that same distance in less than a half of a second. That must mean there would have to be a big difference in attitude between the two creatures if the tortoise came out ahead!

When we hope for something, it makes us cheerful and happy and willing to keep going. Much more important than winning a race here on earth is the finish line we will cross as we go to heaven. The Bible says, "This hope is a strong and trustworthy anchor for our souls" (Hebrews 6:19).

May 10

How many offspring are springing off?

When I was a child, I spoke and thought and reasoned as
a child. But when I grew up, I put away childish things.
1 CORINTHIANS 13:11

The number of babies in a birth can vary widely. The elephant gives birth to only one very large baby at a time. The opossum can have thirteen babies in one litter. That's nothing compared to the giant toad, which lays thirty-five thousand eggs at one time. But the termite wins the prize—it can lay eight thousand eggs *per day* for years.

Every year you are getting older. You are not a baby or a little kid anymore. The Bible has something to say about that: "When I was a child, I spoke and thought and reasoned as a child. But when I grew up, I put away childish things" (1 Corinthians 13:11). Think of all the things you've already learned—and there will be much more to come. But you already know the most important thing. It is simple, and that truth will never change. No matter how old you are, Jesus wants you to understand that you belong to him.

11
May

How does a sponge hold so much water with all those holes?

My purpose is to give them a rich and satisfying life.
JOHN 10:10

Long before anyone thought to copy them with artificial material to be used in kitchens, sponges were sea creatures, living in the ocean. And it's exactly because the sponge has so many holes near its surface that all the extra water can get into it. Without the holes, sponges wouldn't be able to hold much water, and no one could squeeze much water out.

Jesus wants us to have a life full of love and laughter and faith and forgiveness, a little like a sponge that is soaked with water. He says, "My purpose is to give them a rich and satisfying life" (John 10:10). Some people think of God as selfish or stingy, as if he only wanted us to have a life like a worn-out rag that nothing could be squeezed out of. But God isn't like that! He is a generous God, and he wants us to have a full, satisfying life.

May

What tricky words can you use to stump your friends?

Do you love me?
JOHN 21:16

There are so many games you can play with the letters of the alphabet, including where they appear in words and in what order. A good question to stump your friends requires only that you memorize how to say two words, how to spell them, and what they mean. Then you can shock people you know (including many grown-ups) by asking this question: What two words in the English language have the vowels *a, e, i, o,* and *u* in them—in that order? The two words are *abstemious* (ab-STEE-mee-us), which means disciplined about what you eat and drink, and *facetious* (fuh-SEE-shus), which means sarcastic. How's that for sounding smart?

It is sometimes fun to know questions that make people think and that make them view you as very intelligent. But all the knowledge in the world isn't as valuable as a simple question from Jesus and your simple answer. The Bible tells us the question that Jesus really wants us to answer: "Do you love me?" (John 21:16). Your one-word answer—*yes*—is the only one that will affect your life for eternity.

May 13

Can lightning strike twice?

He causes the clouds to rise over the whole earth. He sends the lightning with the rain.
PSALM 135:7

Yes, and it may even strike as many as ten times in one spot! There's an old legend that says, "Lightning never strikes twice in the same place," but science and photography have proved otherwise. For example, engineers of the General Electric Company have taken successful photographs of lightning flashes in repeat locations in the Berkshire Mountains of Massachusetts. Pictures have been taken in many other places that show the same thing. As for the power in a lightning strike, think about this. An ordinary household electric socket wired at 115 volts can give you quite a shock if you come in contact with its electricity. A single flash of lightning has been estimated to carry a charge of one hundred million volts.

No matter how much we learn about lightning, the main thing we really need to know is that, along with everything else, it comes to us from the power of the Lord. The Bible tells us, "He causes the clouds to rise over the whole earth. He sends the lightning with the rain" (Psalm 135:7). God is the only one who thought of and created lightning. No human being could make it happen the way God did.

May 14

Why did people bounce up and down in the 1920s?

God, the source of hope, will fill you completely
with joy and peace because you trust in him.
ROMANS 15:13

It was because of an invention made by George Hansburg in 1919 in Germany. You've probably even tried out this toy—it's the pogo stick. No one knows for sure what made George think of it, but people loved his idea. He sent a shipment of pogo sticks to America, where a large department store sold them. Along the way, George changed the wood pole to a metal one for durability, and other improvements have been made by other people over the years. But nothing could top this amazing story from the 1920s: one couple actually got married while bouncing on pogo sticks!

Have you ever been so excited that you couldn't stay still? Maybe you even jumped up and down without a pogo stick because you couldn't contain all the joy inside of you. God's love for you can make you feel like that. The Bible says, "God, the source of hope, will fill you completely with joy and peace because you trust in him" (Romans 15:13). The happiness that God adds to your life will last much longer than a ride on a pogo stick!

May

15

What got grown-ups practicing their painting?

We are God's masterpiece. He has created us anew in Christ Jesus, so we can do the good things he planned for us long ago.
EPHESIANS 2:10

In the 1950s, a new type of painting swept the country. Called "paint by number," it was patterned after the way Leonardo da Vinci, a great painter in the 1500s, did some of his work. Leonardo had apprentices who would fill in the easy parts of his paintings for him. He did this by leaving spaces with numbers in them, which the apprentices matched by numbers on the paint palettes and filled in. In the 1950s, an artist named Dan Robbins borrowed the idea, and America went crazy over it. Dan made patterns without colors in them, similar to coloring book pictures. He added a number to each empty space and included paints with those same numbers in the kits. Suddenly grown-ups were carefully painting to fill in all the spaces, and the more colors they added, the closer they got to seeing what they were painting a picture of!

In a way, Jesus has already drawn lines for our lives, and we are encouraged to fill them in with our personalities. He knows the perfect picture our lives should make in the end, which is why we need to follow his direction. The Bible says, "We are God's masterpiece. He has created us anew in Christ Jesus, so we can do the good things he planned for us long ago" (Ephesians 2:10). Watch for the Lord's direction, and you will make a beautiful work of art from your life that will be pleasing to him.

May 16

Which bird prefers to live underground?

The eternal God is your refuge.
DEUTERONOMY 33:27

A small owl called the burrowing owl looks for holes in the ground that were dug by squirrels or prairie dogs. Those creatures lived in the holes at one time, but now the holes are vacant. The burrowing owl makes a nest in a hole, and if it senses danger, it makes a noise. The noise doesn't sound like the screech or hoot that most owls make. Instead, it sounds like a rattlesnake!

Just as the burrowing owl looks for a safe home, sometimes we look for a safe place to escape to. The Lord is waiting with open arms to welcome you—and that's the safest place you can be. The Bible tells us, "The eternal God is your refuge" (Deuteronomy 33:27). He will be with you at all times, and he will supply you with a protected place to rest.

17
May

How fast was the Pony Express?

You have been taught the holy Scriptures from childhood,
and they have given you the wisdom to receive the
salvation that comes by trusting in Christ Jesus.
2 TIMOTHY 3:15

It all started when the mail was so slow. In 1849, it took almost a month to receive a letter sent from the East Coast of the United States to the West Coast. The choices back then were to send it around the edges of America by boat or across the land in a slow-moving stagecoach. William Russell believed that mail could be carried on horseback much faster than that. People didn't believe it when he said a letter could get from one side of the country to the other in ten days. So he proved it. William and some other businessmen started the Central Overland California and Pikes Peak Express Company, nicknamed the Pony Express. They set up resting stations along the route the Pony Express riders would take, and they picked eighty men and four hundred horses to do the job. The Pony Express rider's task was to ride for six hours and travel sixty miles by riding six different horses. The rider would stop at a rest station, grab the saddlebag full of mail, jump off the tired horse and onto a fresh one, and take off again, all in less than two minutes. Sure enough, the mail arrived in ten days. The Pony Express riders faced heavy snowstorms, high and narrow mountain trails, and possible attacks from Native Americans as their land was crossed. And yet the mail continued to get to its destination for more than a year and a half. The end of the Pony Express came because the telegraph was invented, and people could then send messages to each other without sending letters.

These days there are many ways for people to get messages to each other. But the way God gets his message to you has never changed. He doesn't need a pony, a mailbox, a telephone, or a computer to communicate with you. His words are in the Bible. His words tell you how to contact him. The Bible says, "You have been taught the holy Scriptures from childhood, and they have given you the wisdom to receive the salvation that comes by trusting in Christ Jesus" (2 Timothy 3:15).

18

May

What was so sweet about Milton Hershey?

I hope all is well with you and that you are as healthy in body as you are strong in spirit.
3 JOHN 1:2

Milton Hershey's favorite place to go as a child was the candy store, where he spent lots of time trying to decide how to spend his pennies. When Milton was fourteen, he worked in a candy store, learning how to make different candies. At eighteen, Milton opened his own store. He opened and closed several stores before he settled on making caramels as his special candy. He was very successful at it. But Milton learned two things. He found out that his biggest customer in Europe was ordering the caramels but then covering them with chocolate before selling them to wealthy people for a treat. Then one day at a party in England, Milton saw children take some chocolate-covered candies from the table and run to the side of the house. Milton was curious and followed them. He saw the children lick the chocolate off the candies and throw away the centers, even if the centers were peppermint or caramel. Milton had always wanted to make candy for children, and he now saw the kind of candy children liked best. That's when Milton Hershey decided to switch from making caramel candy to making chocolate candy. *Chocolate* and *Hershey* are two words that have gone together ever since.

Milton Hershey wanted to make people's lives better, and he kept trying until he found just the right thing they liked. If you want to help someone but you don't know how, the Bible gives you a way. It tells you how you can pray for other people: "I hope all is well with you and that you are as healthy in body as you are strong in spirit" (3 John 1:2). Let someone know that you care and are praying for them. It will make their day as sweet as chocolate candy!

19 May

What's the sweetest place on earth?

They share freely and give generously to those in need.
Their good deeds will be remembered forever.
PSALM 112:9

Milton Hershey decided he needed a huge factory to make his chocolate candy quickly, so he picked out a cornfield. He dreamed big dreams. He thought he would need about six hundred people to work for him, and he wanted to make a whole town for them where the factory would be built. It would have houses and schools and churches, and the streets would have chocolate names. Even the streetlights would be shaped like Hershey's Kisses. (No one knows for sure how Kisses got their name, but it is believed that the factory machine makes a kissing sound when it drops the chocolate onto the conveyor belt to make a Hershey's Kiss.) In 1906 Milton chose a town called Derry Church in Pennsylvania to build his factory, and the name of the town was changed to Hershey. The next thing Milton and his wife, Kitty, wanted to give the town was an orphanage for boys, since they had never had children of their own. Milton wanted the boys to go to school and learn skills for a job, so the Hershey Industrial School was started, with a six-year-old boy and his eight-year-old brother being the first students. All the boys loved living at Hershey. When the Great Depression came to America in the 1930s and a third of all Americans were out of work, Milton wanted to make sure his townspeople didn't lose their jobs. So he hired them to build a gym, a library, a high school, a theater, and an office building for Hershey, Pennsylvania—the town that became a tourist attraction people love to visit.

Milton Hershey wanted to create a town where people felt loved and respected, and people visited from all over the world to see such a marvelous place. Milton didn't keep all the gifts God blessed him with to himself. He shared them. The Bible says, "They share freely and give generously to those in need. Their good deeds will be remembered forever" (Psalm 112:9). When your heart is in the right place, it's a wonderful place to be.

May

What's so great about these two states?

They agreed that they were foreigners and nomads here on earth.
Obviously people who say such things are looking forward to a
country they can call their own. . . . They were looking for a better
place, a heavenly homeland. That is why God is not ashamed
to be called their God, for he has prepared a city for them.
HEBREWS 11:13-14, 16

Along the East Coast of America, the northernmost state and the southernmost state are special for two different reasons. In the north, Maine is unique because it touches only one other state in all of America. New Hampshire is the state that connects Maine to the rest of the United States. When you look at a map, you will see that all the other states touch the sides of at least two states. The state that's farthest south along the East Coast is special because the oldest city in the United States is located there. Florida is where you will find St. Augustine, the city that was first settled by the Spanish in 1565, making it the first official American city ever to be lived in.

It is a good thing to love the country you live in and to be proud of it and to want to know more about it. But the Bible says there's an even more important place we should consider our home country. It tells us, "They agreed that they were foreigners and nomads here on earth. Obviously people who say such things are looking forward to a country they can call their own. . . . They were looking for a better place, a heavenly homeland. That is why God is not ashamed to be called their God, for he has prepared a city for them" (Hebrews 11:13-14, 16). We will be so full of joy when we live in our heavenly homeland at last!

21 May

What was the big breakthrough for whipped cream?

I will take away their stony, stubborn heart and
give them a tender, responsive heart.
EZEKIEL 11:19

For a long time, not many people served whipped cream with dessert, because the cream had to be whipped by hand, which required time and effort. Then along came Charles Goetz, a senior chemistry major at the University of Illinois. In high school, he had worked part-time at an ice cream shop, where his job was often to whip the cream. When he was in college in 1931, his part-time job was in the dairy bacteriology department, where there was work going on to improve milk sterilization. Charles put all his experiences and knowledge together and came up with an idea. He thought milk should be stored under high gas pressure to keep bacteria from forming. When he experimented, he found that milk under high pressure came out as foam. Then he tried using cream, but the gases he used gave it an odd flavor. Finally he talked to a dentist and began using the same tasteless gas that was used in a dental office as an anesthetic. The official name was nitrous oxide, but it was commonly known as laughing gas. Not only did Charles invent whipping cream that could be sprayed from a can, but the method also worked for shaving cream, and his discovery began an era when many other products could be produced in a spray can.

Just like cream can be made into soft and fluffy whipped cream, God can even more easily make our hearts soft toward him, ourselves, and one another. When you are feeling angry or bitter or upset, ask him to make your heart soft again, just like whipped cream. Then you can truly experience the love God wants to give you every day. In the Bible, God says, "I will take away their stony, stubborn heart and give them a tender, responsive heart" (Ezekiel 11:19).

22
May

Which brand of coffee was named after a hotel?

When you open your hand, you satisfy the hunger and thirst of every living thing.
PSALM 145:16

J oel Cheek, a traveling salesman, couldn't get the perfect cup of coffee off his mind—perhaps because he had sampled so many cups of coffee in his travels. He finally created a blend in 1882 that he thought was just right, so he decided to make and sell the coffee. A famous hotel in Nashville, Tennessee, was the first customer to buy and serve it, which is why Joel used the name. This hotel was so popular and elegant that even presidents of the United States stayed there. One of the presidents, Theodore Roosevelt, declared that the coffee was "good to the last drop," which Joel used as the advertising slogan for his drink. The hotel and the coffee were called Maxwell House.

Coffee is an important drink to many people, but nothing can be more important than the drink Jesus supplies. The Bible says, "When you open your hand, you satisfy the hunger and thirst of every living thing" (Psalm 145:16). Jesus talks about thirst because he knows it's something every human being understands. When we accept Jesus into our lives, we will never again feel thirsty for the goodness only God can provide.

23

May

What's unusual about "home sweet home" for these animals?

Christ will make his home in your hearts as you trust in him.
EPHESIANS 3:17

Some creatures never build homes for themselves because they carry their houses with them or borrow another animal's. A green turtle's "house" is always available because it carries its house on its back. This turtle has a shell that grows bigger as it does, with plates of hard bone joined in a jigsaw style and stuck together and coated with keratin, which is what our fingernails are made of. The shell is permanently attached to the green turtle's back and protects it like a suit of armor. Although lots of crabs carry their shells the way a turtle does, the hermit crab is different. It has a spiral-shaped body and strong back legs that can grab the inside of an empty shell. As the hermit crab grows, it looks for bigger and bigger empty shells. It never kills an animal to get its shell but searches only for ones that are already vacant. The hermit crab keeps its old shell close until it is sure it wants to switch to a new one. If the new one is still too small or is too heavy, the hermit crab returns to the old shell and keeps looking.

Hermit crabs are constantly looking for homes, but we already have one waiting for us in heaven. And Christ has made his home in us! The Bible says it all: "Christ will make his home in your hearts as you trust in him" (Ephesians 3:17).

May 24

Does each tree grow only one kind of leaf?

There are different kinds of spiritual gifts, but the same Spirit is the source of them all.

1 CORINTHIANS 12:4

No, certain trees grow several different leaf shapes at the same time. The sassafras tree has three uniquely shaped leaves growing from the same tree, and in fact, all three shapes grow on the same branch! If you look closely, you can find one that's a mitten shape, one with a "thumb" on each side and three lobes in between, and a third shape that's a plain oval.

God made so much variety in his creation; he even designed the sassafras tree to have several different kinds of leaves. The Bible tells us, "There are different kinds of spiritual gifts, but the same Spirit is the source of them all" (1 Corinthians 12:4). Look for your different talents. Maybe you are good at singing or helping people or understanding the Bible. Whatever your gifts are, let them grow bigger, just like the leaves on a tree.

25

May

What's going on when you yawn?

He himself gives life and breath to everything.
ACTS 17:25

To stay alive, people and animals need to breathe air. The most important gas for us in the air is oxygen, and lots of oxygen is breathed in by living creatures every day. Why don't we ever run out of it? God has created a wonderful plan. When we breathe out, we push carbon dioxide, another gas, out of our bodies. Carbon dioxide goes back into the air and is taken in by plants, which need carbon dioxide to live. The plants use the carbon dioxide and in return put new oxygen back into the air, which we then breathe in again. Sometimes, when you are tired and your body is working more slowly, you keep more carbon dioxide inside than usual. To get rid of the extra carbon dioxide in a hurry, you open your mouth wide and gulp in a big blast of oxygen. Then you breathe out all the extra carbon dioxide gas. That's what is happening when you yawn!

It is amazing to realize that our God thought of every single detail when he made all living things on earth. For our minds, that would be a *lot* to keep organized! But God is all-knowing and all-powerful, and the Bible tells us, "He himself gives life and breath to everything" (Acts 17:25). We can trust that he can come up with the greatest plans of all!

26

May

Are the Pennsylvania Dutch really Dutch?

You will be given a new name by the LORD's own mouth.
ISAIAH 62:2

The Pennsylvania Dutch were a group of people who came to America in the late seventeenth and early eighteenth centuries, in search of a land that was peaceful and would allow them to work hard and worship God. But these people aren't, and never have been, Dutch at all. They were at first called the Pennsylvania Deutsch (pronounced DOICH), because they came from Germany, and the German word for Germany is *Deutschland*. But after moving to America, the word *Deutsch* sounded to the American ear like *Dutch*, and this group of people has been called the Pennsylvania Dutch ever since.

The Pennsylvania Dutch did not get to keep their original name, but they had what was important—the freedom to worship God. The Bible tells us what God does for all of us: "You will be given a new name by the LORD's own mouth" (Isaiah 62:2). God provides what is most necessary when we need to have it, and you can trust him to judge correctly what he should supply.

27 May

What question started the Quadro Jump?

A cheerful look brings joy to the heart;
good news makes for good health.
PROVERBS 15:30

Fifth grader Wendy Johnecheck had an idea to improve jump roping in 1984. Her school held a contest, so she entered her project. But putting it together took some effort at first. Wendy wanted to create a way to jump rope that didn't take two friends to turn the rope just so one person could jump. What if you only had one friend to play with? Wendy lived on a farm, so she looked around for something that would help her build her idea, and she decided that the handle of a shovel would work well as a pole. Then Wendy wanted to attach something that swiveled on the top of the pole. Her mother took her to the hardware store, and her grandfather showed her how to use the tools to assemble the swivel. Her brothers and sisters helped her braid a long rope, which Wendy attached to the swivel on the pole. Now just two could play! But Wendy thought some more and attached three other ropes. Now lots of kids could jump rope with only four turners. Her classmates loved using her invention at recess. Wendy's teacher taught her how to write letters advertising the idea, so Wendy sent them out and found a company that sold her new Quadro Jump.

It's good to take time to have fun. When you find something that you really enjoy doing, treat yourself to "recess" once in a while and give yourself a chance to play. After all, God is a God of joy, and he wants us to enjoy life too. The Bible tells us, "A cheerful look brings joy to the heart; good news makes for good health" (Proverbs 15:30).

May

How does a newspaper machine know what day it is?

We are pressed on every side by troubles,
but we are not crushed.
2 CORINTHIANS 4:8

Have you ever seen the machines that hold newspapers? They're kind of like vending machines, and people put money in them to get their newspapers. There is a mechanism inside the machine that has different slots for coins, and people have to put in the right amount of coins so they can take their copy of the paper out. But newspapers are more expensive on Sundays. So how does the machine know which price to charge for which day? Actually, the machine is reset, by hand or electronically by pushing a button, for the following day by the people who bring the new newspapers. Some electronic machines can even provide the newspaper people with information such as what coins are usually used or what day and what time the newspapers are bought. This information helps the sellers decide how to best sell the papers.

Almost everywhere you look—in newspapers, on television, or on the computer—it seems as if the news is all bad, all the time. News can sometimes make us feel that the whole world is not a very nice place to be. But don't forget that we have God on our side, and he turns what's bad into good. The Bible tells us, "We are pressed on every side by troubles, but we are not crushed" (2 Corinthians 4:8). We can take hope in the promise from Jesus Christ that better things are coming.

May 29

How do some books travel the world?

The LORD sees every heart and knows every plan and thought.
1 CHRONICLES 28:9

Some libraries float on rivers, like the seven floating libraries in Indonesia. At one time, the boats had to wait until people finished reading their books before the boats could go anywhere! Later, containers of books were left so the boats could move on to the next town. In the Indonesian city of Surabaya, bicycles with big boxes built onto them served as a way to deliver library books through the narrow, winding streets. In Kenya, librarians use camels to transport books through the desert sand that even a car can't get through. Two library camels are needed: one carries five hundred books weighing four hundred pounds total, while the other camel carries the tent that will be set up as a temporary library building. Some library books in Thailand travel by elephants that deliver books for about twenty days to remote villages. The capital city of Bangkok uses old railroad cars that don't run anymore as libraries. The police make them look new again, and homeless children who have nowhere to go are welcome there.

Reading books is a great way to find out about our world. God gave you a mind to think and honor him. Even when information is new to you, remember that there is someone who knows more than any book. "The LORD sees every heart and knows every plan and thought" (1 Chronicles 28:9). Search for special knowledge of God first!

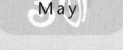

May

How was the first sports drink connected to alligators?

Anyone who is thirsty may come to me!
JOHN 7:37

Dr. Robert Cade wanted to find a drink that would replace the liquids and salt that the human body loses through sweating when the body exercises. Incredibly, it took Dr. Cade only three minutes to analyze the body liquids and decide on a formula for his drink. The doctor chose the football team from the University of Florida to test how well his new drink worked. The results were excellent, and that is how the drink got its unusual name. The football team was called the Florida Gators, and the drink was Gatorade.

When you give your heart and soul to Jesus, you receive a gift much better for you than a sports drink. Through his Son, God has planned a way to refresh your soul forever. Jesus tells us, "Anyone who is thirsty may come to me!" (John 7:37). You can look to Jesus for all your needs, and he will give you what is good for you.

May

When could doing your homework get you into trouble?

Fix your thoughts on what is true, and honorable,
and right, and pure, and lovely, and admirable.
Think about things that are excellent and worthy of praise.
PHILIPPIANS 4:8

A teacher in England had an unusual idea. Why not make the next ordinary writing assignment more exciting for his class and stretch their imaginations? He gave his students maps of a fake town and instructed them to describe the perfect way to rob the town's imaginary bank. The whole class was encouraged to let their plans go wild! That's when the crazy part really began. The teacher's phone rang just a few days later. The caller was the local police chief, who had earlier received a call from a worried parent. The parent anonymously described how there might be a crime wave soon in their town, and the police chief wanted the teacher to explain what in the world was going on. Fortunately the project didn't lead to any arrests of pretend bank-robbing students, and everything ended well when the police chief was asked to be the judge of the perfect bank robbery projects.

Even though these students didn't really intend to rob a bank, they almost got into big trouble for spending their time thinking about it. God wants us to keep our minds free from bad thoughts and concentrate on healthy, helpful things instead. He might be asking you to pitch in and weed your neighbor's garden or to make sure your dog always has fresh water or to offer to carry a bag of groceries for the lady behind you in line. The Bible says, "Fix your thoughts on what is true, and honorable, and right, and pure, and lovely, and admirable. Think about things that are excellent and worthy of praise" (Philippians 4:8). God promises that the more you think this way, the further you will stay away from trouble.

June 1

What was so wonderful about the wheelbarrow?

My yoke is easy to bear, and the burden I give you is light.
MATTHEW 11:30

Before the invention of the wheelbarrow, if you wanted to take something from one place to another, you carried it. Sometime between the years AD 50 and AD 200, there lived a man named Chuko Liang in China. He had a better idea than doing the backbreaking work of lugging everything around by hand. He took a tub-shaped container that could be pushed with handles and attached a wheel to the front and two wheels in the back. His invention has been used ever since to roll heavy loads—letting wheels do the hard work.

Life without and with a wheelbarrow is like life without and with Christ. When you don't have something like a wheelbarrow to help you, the work seems hard and long and tiring. But when the wheelbarrow shows up, things get much easier. You make a lot more progress, and you don't get so worn out. Jesus invites you to team up with him. In the Bible Jesus says, "My yoke is easy to bear, and the burden I give you is light" (Matthew 11:30). It doesn't seem like too hard a choice to let Jesus help you with everything you need to do.

June
2

How did Canada get its name?

How wonderful and pleasant it is when
brothers live together in harmony!
PSALM 133:1

The explorer was Jacques Cartier, the continent was North America, and the time was the sixteenth century. Jacques didn't know where he was, but he was anxious to find out what to call the land he had discovered. Jacques came upon an Iroquoian village, so he asked the chief what the name of this country was. The only way Jacques could think of to help the chief know what he was asking was to move his hands far and wide, pointing to the village and meaning to include all the surrounding areas too. But the chief only noticed that Jacques was looking at the village, so he answered Jacques with the word for "a cluster of huts, a village"—and that name was *kanata*. Later, when Jacques wrote about his travels, he described the country he had seen and mentioned it by a form of the name the chief had given him: Canada.

Jacques Cartier noticed all the homes together in that foreign land, and the chief was proud to tell him it was a group of friends and family—people in the cluster of huts that made up the village. It is good to live at peace with others. But the Bible tells us it is especially wonderful to live with other believers who get along. It says, "How wonderful and pleasant it is when brothers live together in harmony!" (Psalm 133:1). God wants us to have unity with others and treat them kindly. Then when people ask us why we do that, we can answer, "Because Jesus did." That is how to be a good witness for our faith.

June

Where could you catch dinner without leaving the kitchen?

Come, follow me, and I will show you how to fish for people!
MATTHEW 4:19

Once there was a Cistercian monastery in Alcobaça, Portugal. Whenever the cooks there wanted to make some fish, they didn't even have to leave the kitchen to get them! In the middle of the floor was an area where they could just dip their nets into the water of a branch of the Alcoa River, which just happened to flow right underneath the middle of their big kitchen.

Fish and fishermen are mentioned many times in the Bible. But God isn't just talking about wanting us to be good at catching dinner. The Bible tells us what Jesus is really concerned about when he says: "Come, follow me, and I will show you how to fish for people!" (Matthew 4:19). In the same way some people try hard to hook a fish and reel it in, Jesus wants us to try to bring people to his love. The rewards will be so much greater than a simple meal.

June
4

What happened to the caboose?

Riches don't last forever.
PROVERBS 27:24

In the 1990s, for the first time since the invention of the train, cabooses began disappearing from the ends of trains. Why were they being left off? Technology was replacing the work that the crew in the caboose used to do. Originally, an engineer and a brakeman sat in the engine at the front of the train, and another brakeman and the conductor sat in the caboose at the end. The caboose had a little lookout tower on top so the conductor and brakeman could watch what the train was doing. Before the radio was invented, the men in the back used lanterns and hand signals to tell the engineer if the train had smoke coming from somewhere or if it was dragging something that shouldn't be there. But three new devices were added to the engine of the train and changed the way things used to be done. Flashing Rear End Devices (called FREDs) allow the engineer to tell when brakes should be applied in the rear of the train. That means the brakeman didn't need to apply the brakes anymore—the engineer could do it when the light told him to. The Hot Box Detector (HBD) tells the engineer if the wheels are overheating, so a crew in the caboose isn't necessary to watch for smoke or fire. The End of Train Device (ETD) tells the engineer when the back of the train is moving, so there is no reason for the conductor to be watching for whether the train cars have slack spaces between them. Once in a while a caboose is still needed if the train has to back up a very long way. Otherwise, there are just flashing lights at the end of the train where the caboose used to be.

As time passes, things change. Children grow up, new toys get worn out, and cabooses disappear from view. The Bible says, "Riches don't last forever" (Proverbs 27:24). There is only one thing that is forever, and that's heaven. Enjoy things while you have them, but don't worry about them when they're gone. As God's child, you can hold on to his promise for your future forever, and that will never change.

June

Why would people eat oysters only during the months spelled with an *r*?

If you need wisdom, ask our generous God, and he will give it to you. He will not rebuke you for asking. But when you ask him, be sure that your faith is in God alone.
JAMES 1:5-6

These are the months with the letter *r* in their spellings: January, February, March, April, September, October, November, and December. Notice what's missing? The summer months—and that's when people wouldn't eat oysters. Back before refrigeration, it was hard to keep food cool when it was being shipped from one place to another. Oysters spoil easily in warm temperatures and then become poisonous. So if people didn't want to eat a bad oyster, they wouldn't eat any until the weather was cool enough for the oysters to stay fresh.

People learn some things through experience, like when it's the best time to eat oysters. But if you want to be wise about something you haven't experienced before, the Bible tells you what to do. "If you need wisdom, ask our generous God, and he will give it to you. He will not rebuke you for asking. But when you ask him, be sure that your faith is in God alone" (James 1:5-6). The Lord will be your teacher and your guide. You can trust him to help you.

June

What does D-day mean?

Everything that is covered up will be revealed,
and all that is secret will be made known to all.
LUKE 12:2

You will see this in your history books, and you might have heard about it from your relatives or in movies. D-day happened during World War II on June 6, 1944, in Normandy, France. It was a significant and memorable battle that allowed American forces to gain control of certain areas of Europe. Many people think that D-day is the name for that confrontation alone. But what most people don't know is that there have been many D-days, with the *D* standing for "the day." It was a term used by the military because the time and location of any battle could be kept secret that way. The day before the invasion is called "D minus one," and the day after is "D plus one." During World War II, the American, Canadian, and British soldiers practiced for months, but they didn't know when D-day was going to be until the night before. Likewise, the enemy found out that a big attack was coming, but they didn't know when or even where. Actually, D-day was supposed to be on June 5, but the weather was so bad that everything was stopped and delayed for twenty-four hours.

People went to a lot of trouble to keep D-day a secret. Sometimes people can keep secrets from each other, but the Bible reminds us of the power of God. It says, "Everything that is covered up will be revealed, and all that is secret will be made known to all" (Luke 12:2). God is all-knowing, all the time.

June 7

What color are goldfish?

Praise God for the privilege of being called by his name!
1 PETER 4:16

The answer to that question is not as simple as it seems. The Chinese are responsible for the color of the pet goldfish in the bowl in your bedroom. Several hundred years ago, fish like yours were green, swimming in streams in China. But these green fish were patiently bred with other fish over many generations, after careful consideration over the colors. Finally, many different colors of goldfish existed—there are now gold, silver, gray, black, blue, and multicolored goldfish to choose from. The average goldfish lives only a few years, but the Chinese have been taking care of some special Oriental goldfish that can live up to seventy years. Imagine having a pet goldfish that lived about as long as you!

It is strange to think about fish that are called goldfish even though they aren't always gold. But when we call ourselves Christians, we are taking on Christ's name. That means we need to make sure our lives reflect his character. The Bible puts it like this: "Praise God for the privilege of being called by his name!" (1 Peter 4:16).

June

How do you speak to an alligator egg?

My sheep listen to my voice;
I know them, and they follow me.
JOHN 10:27

For many years, people tried to raise alligators in captivity. The problem was that the alligator mothers would lay their eggs, bury them, and then appear to forget about them. None of those eggs hatched. Then someone in Florida had an idea. That person approached a nest of alligator eggs and began to make the same grunting noises that mother alligators make. When the baby alligators in the eggs heard the noise, they answered. The eggs were uncovered, and the safe, healthy baby alligators came tumbling out. Finally the mystery had been solved, and alligators could be raised in captivity at last!

There is something wonderful about hearing the familiar voice of someone whom you trust. It makes you feel happy and relieved inside. In the Bible Jesus says, "My sheep listen to my voice; I know them, and they follow me" (John 10:27). Do you recognize Jesus' voice when he's speaking to you through prayer and through his Word?

June

What was on the menu for the king?

God blesses those who hunger and thirst
for justice, for they will be satisfied.
MATTHEW 5:6

King Louis XIV of France was known for his large appetite. At a typical meal he would start with four bowls of different soups, then a whole pheasant *and* a whole duck or chicken or partridge—stuffed with mushrooms, of course. Then came a gigantic salad, some lamb, and two slices of ham, and then it was time for dessert. He ate preserves and raw fruit and a dish of pastry. When he died, his body was examined, and it was found that the interior of his stomach was huge, and his intestines (the tubing attached to his stomach) were twice the length of a normal person's.

God knows we need food to use as fuel for our bodies, but he also knows that food alone will not make a person feel complete. The Bible says, "God blesses those who hunger and thirst for justice, for they will be satisfied" (Matthew 5:6). Only when you have a huge appetite for God's Word will you be able to fill up until your heart is content.

June

Why did two sea creatures become buddies?

He calls his own sheep by name and leads them out.
JOHN 10:3

Two kinds of sea creatures have gotten together underwater in an unusual way. The sea anemone fastens itself to shells or a rock most of the time because it moves extremely slowly. It can only move about three or four inches an hour, and that is too slow to catch much food. It has long, deadly stinging tentacles for protection. The other creature is called a clown fish. It moves slowly too. It is a bright orange color, which makes it easy for other fish to see, chase, and catch. The sea anemone and the clown fish become partners underwater. Here's how it works. The clown fish is amazingly immune to the stinging poison in the tentacles of the sea anemone, so the clown fish can dart in and out between the sea anemone's tentacles. Other sea creatures see the bright clown fish wriggling under the sea anemone and come over to investigate. That is when the sea anemone stings the new creature with its tentacles and kills it. Then the sea anemone and the clown fish share dinner together. The clown fish attracts creatures that the sea anemone couldn't attract on its own, and the sea anemone kills food that the clown fish wouldn't be able to. As a team, the two sea creatures live and work together well.

Having a friend or a teammate can be good for you when you need help. But the best thing of all is having a friend named Jesus, who calls you to be his. The Bible says, "He calls his own sheep by name and leads them out" (John 10:3). Jesus knows all about you, and he chooses you to be right by his side every day of your life.

June

What are some inventions that never became popular?

Plans go wrong for lack of advice;
many advisers bring success.
PROVERBS 15:22

Sometimes an idea that seems wonderful to one person doesn't appeal to anyone else. Consider John Boax—he thought he had a better way to give a haircut than just using scissors. His solution was to invent a helmet for the long-haired person to put on. The helmet had small holes in it that sucked the hair through them. Then electric coils burned the hair to make it shorter. No wonder this method wasn't popular! Another inventor, Elmer Walter, came up with an idea that was gentler but not much more appealing. He created a knife with a mirror on the handle. The idea was that a person sitting at the dinner table could check his or her teeth in the mirror to see if there was food stuck between them. Not very appetizing for the others who were eating at the table!

Just because an idea seems like a good one to you, it's wise to run it by the Bible's checklist for success first. It says, "Plans go wrong for lack of advice; many advisers bring success" (Proverbs 15:22). If you follow this formula, it will help you avoid some of the blunders that the people in this story encountered.

June

How do mother animals and their babies keep track of each other?

Can a mother forget her nursing child?
Can she feel no love for the child she has borne?
But even if that were possible, I would not forget you!
ISAIAH 49:15

Lambs, kittens, fawns, puppies, and all kinds of other baby animals are usually found right beside their mothers because these babies each have their own unique smell. Their mothers sniff them the moment they are born. From then on, their moms can pick them out just by smelling them, even if the babies are surrounded by dozens of other babies that look just like them. But the babies don't always do such a good job of finding their moms. Little ducklings or chicks, for example, think that the first thing they see when they open their eyes is their mother. Usually that turns out to be right. But sometimes, if the duckling sees a dog or a person first, that is who the duckling thinks is its mother. So if you happen to see a duckling following a dog around, you'll know why these animals are not quite matched up correctly!

We enjoy watching animals and learning about their ways. God tells us that his love for us is even greater than the kind of love a mother has for her child. He says, "Can a mother forget her nursing child? Can she feel no love for the child she has borne? But even if that were possible, I would not forget you!" (Isaiah 49:15). How special we are to our God!

June 13

How does the automatic store door know you want to come in?

I am the gate. Those who come in through me will be saved.
JOHN 10:9

It doesn't know by itself. You tell it to open by moving toward it. The doors that open for you have an electronic "eye" that sends out an invisible beam. Look above the door the next time you are about to go in—the electronic eye is probably up at the top of the door in some sort of round case. It sends down a beam that spreads in front of the door, and your body will break through the beam when you cross it. Then a motor begins working that opens the door.

The doors at the supermarket certainly aren't the most important doors you will enter in your life. The Bible tells us which one is: Jesus. He said, "I am the gate. Those who come in through me will be saved" (John 10:9).

June 14

Why do fruits and flowers have such bright colors?

Look at the lilies and how they grow. They don't work or make their clothing, yet Solomon in all his glory was not dressed as beautifully as they are.
LUKE 12:27

The colors of flowers and fruits are signals that tell insects and animals how to act. A red flower, which birds can clearly see, tells them to stop and eat some nectar. Bees are attracted to yellow flowers. And flowers with stripes look like a runway to a bee, showing the way to the nectar. The brighter the colors, the more they appeal to certain insects and animals, sending an invitation to spread the seeds or bring pollen from other flowers so that seeds can get started. Fruits and flowers are colored to compete for the attention of animals and insects.

It is amazing to look around our world and see all the variety God has given us. He thought up the colors, smells, and shapes of every fruit and flower there is. The Bible says, "Look at the lilies and how they grow. They don't work or make their clothing, yet Solomon in all his glory was not dressed as beautifully as they are" (Luke 12:27). Maybe when you have some imagining time, you can try to think of a new tree or plant you would design and what would grow on it. That would make God smile.

June

15

What made air-conditioning cool?

The wind blows wherever it wants. Just as you can hear the wind but can't tell where it comes from or where it is going, so you can't explain how people are born of the Spirit.

JOHN 3:8

The first air conditioner was invented to help ink dry. A printing plant was having trouble getting the ink to dry evenly, so Willis H. Carrier came up with a solution in 1902. He made a machine that cooled air until the water in it condensed and could be drained away. Willis then applied the same idea to cooling air in other buildings—for the benefit of people, not just ink and paper. Willis discovered that when air is hot and also has high humidity, sweat cannot evaporate and our bodies cannot get cool. So he found a perfect balance of air temperature and airflow. When the water was removed, the temperature cooled faster, and rooms were made more comfortable. By 1919, movie theaters and department stores had begun installing "air-cooling," although individual houses didn't have it for many years. Many people went to those public places just to cool off. Offices with air-conditioning claimed that employees worked more efficiently, which paid for having the air-conditioning installed. They arrived at work early and stayed later instead of going home, just to keep cool.

When God made the world, he provided his own air-conditioning. It's called wind. The Spirit of God is compared to the wind, but he does something much more valuable than cooling people down on a hot day. The Bible says, "The wind blows wherever it wants. Just as you can hear the wind but can't tell where it comes from or where it is going, so you can't explain how people are born of the Spirit" (John 3:8). God gives us the Holy Spirit to guide us, and we can listen to his guidance, even if we don't understand everything about him.

June 16

Is it true that fish can't drown?

You are truly my disciples if you remain faithful
to my teachings. And you will know the
truth, and the truth will set you free.
JOHN 8:31-32

That belief is what is called a fallacy—a statement that is not true. Humans breathe with lungs, but fish don't have lungs. They get their oxygen from the gills on their sides, which bring oxygen through their bodies by taking it out of the water around them. If the water is not supplying enough oxygen for the fish, it needs to find a place with more oxygen or it will drown from the lack of it.

You never need to worry if what you read in the Bible is a fallacy. Jesus said, "You are truly my disciples if you remain faithful to my teachings. And you will know the truth, and the truth will set you free" (John 8:31-32). You can be free to believe every word of the Bible and have no doubt that it is true.

June

Why are marbles so marvelous?

You will show me the way of life, granting me the joy of
your presence and the pleasures of living with you forever.
PSALM 16:11

Children and adults have been playing with marbles for thousands of years. The first marbles were simply baked clay balls or shiny round stones. Later marbles were made of decorated glass. All you need for playing is a smooth, flat piece of ground, a circle marked on the ground, and a few small balls. Players take turns trying to knock other players' marbles out of the circle with their own marble. There are marble collectors around the world, and there have been many marble players throughout history. When John Tyler found out that he was elected president of the United States in 1841, he was busy playing marbles. And when Neil Armstrong, the first man on the moon, saw the earth from space, he said it looked like a big blue marble. Each marble has a unique name to describe what it is made of or how it looks. Some of the names are onionskin, steelie, turtle, toothpaste, and cat's-eye.

Lots of people have enjoyed playing marbles. Christians know that all good things come from God and that he wants us to enjoy his gifts. The Bible says, "You will show me the way of life, granting me the joy of your presence and the pleasures of living with you forever" (Psalm 16:11). The joys that God gives us bring us much more pleasure than just a game of marbles!

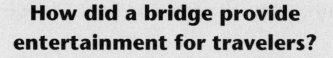

June

How did a bridge provide entertainment for travelers?

Those who trust in the LORD will find new strength.
They will soar high on wings like eagles. They will run
and not grow weary. They will walk and not faint.
ISAIAH 40:31

When builders were constructing the suspension bridge across a body of water called the Puget Sound in the state of Washington in 1940, they noticed how much the bridge swung in the wind. It was moving because the roadway part of the bridge was hanging from high, strong steel cables, sort of like a very stiff hammock. After the bridge was completely built, everyone talked about the way it pitched from side to side. More cars than usual began driving on the bridge, just so passengers could feel their cars swinging with the road. They nicknamed the bridge Galloping Gertie and thought of it as a fun ride. One day, when the bridge was only four months old, the winds across Washington were blowing very fast at forty-two miles an hour. The bridge was acting like a roller coaster, and it was giving the best rides ever. Fortunately, everyone drove off the bridge before the trouble started. The roadway began to break apart and fall into the sea, leaving the wires dangling, holding nothing. What went wrong? The straight, solid roadway part of the bridge was so much like an airplane wing that it began to rise and lower in the wind. Bridge builders learned to test small models of new bridges in a machine called a wind tunnel to make sure no other bridge would buck like Galloping Gertie.

The wind under the bridge was dangerous because it lifted the road. People didn't know how to make the bridge correctly then. But when God lifts you up, he is giving you a gift that will never harm you. Since he created everything, he already knows how it will work. The Bible tells us, "Those who trust in the LORD will find new strength. They will soar high on wings like eagles. They will run and not grow weary. They will walk and not faint" (Isaiah 40:31). The wind makes birds rise easily, and God will make sure you will feel lifted up safely also.

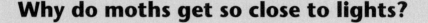

June 19

Why do moths get so close to lights?

I could ask the darkness to hide me and the
light around me to become night—but even
in darkness I cannot hide from you.
PSALM 139:11-12

Moths use the light of the moon or the sun to travel by. When you see a moth being drawn to any other kind of light, that's because the moth thinks the light is the moon or the sun, and it's trying to get its sense of direction back. Before there were artificial lights, moths used the angles of the sun and the moon in their eyes to fly straight. But with the addition of electric lights, moths get confused. When moths circle the light and come closer, they are really trying to get into position so that the artificial lights are at the same angle that the moon's or sun's light would be. That can never happen since the moths are so close to the electric lights, so they feel the need to keep circling them. By the way, moths can't see the colors yellow and red, so if you'd like to watch moths without disturbing them as they feed at night, use a red light and they'll never know you're there.

Like moths, we need lights to be able to see where we're going, but God doesn't need any light to be able to see where we are. God already knows what happened and what's on your mind, so you can go to him and talk about it. He'll give you a chance to start over again. One of the writers of the Bible says, "I could ask the darkness to hide me and the light around me to become night—but even in darkness I cannot hide from you" (Psalm 139:11-12).

June

What's the biggest flower in the world?

Even the wilderness and desert will be glad in those days.
The wasteland will rejoice and blossom with spring crocuses.
ISAIAH 35:1

On the island of Sumatra in the rain forests lives the biggest flower on earth. Called the rafflesia, it is just one flower measuring three feet across, with no stem or leaves. It can hold twelve pints of nectar and weighs fifteen pounds. It lives by growing on the vines of other plants or on the exposed roots of trees and sucking nutrients from them to survive. The seeds of the rafflesia are spread by the feet of elephants! When a rafflesia dies, it crumples into a big gooey, sticky blob with seeds in it. An elephant walking along steps on this gigantic mess, and the seeds stick to its feet. Since the elephant doesn't enjoy having sticky feet, it rubs its feet back and forth across the roots of trees to get the mess off. And that is exactly where the rafflesia seed needs to be dropped so it can feed on the exposed root and grow into another flower.

The rafflesia, as the biggest flower, must bring extra joy to the creatures that eat its nectar. There is something about flowers that makes us happy too. The Bible says, "Even the wilderness and desert will be glad in those days. The wasteland will rejoice and blossom with spring crocuses" (Isaiah 35:1). Try to take the chance today to give joy to someone the way flowers do. Be encouraging to someone; say something kind. The person will think about your words all day, and you will make them feel like they got a whole bouquet of flowers.

June

Which is the oldest vegetable on earth?

The Sovereign LORD will show his justice to the nations of the world. Everyone will praise him! His righteousness will be like a garden in early spring, with plants springing up everywhere.

ISAIAH 61:11

Botanists, who study plants of all kinds, agree it's possible that cabbage is the most ancient vegetable still grown today. Cabbage is the fourth-leading vegetable eaten in the United States. Can you guess the other three before reading on? The most popular vegetable is potatoes, with lettuce in second place and tomatoes coming in third.

Gardens bring us good food to eat, and God is the one who makes it possible for vegetables to grow. He also makes it possible for the world to know all about him. The Bible says, "The Sovereign LORD will show his justice to the nations of the world. Everyone will praise him! His righteousness will be like a garden in early spring, with plants springing up everywhere" (Isaiah 61:11). The more you tell people about your heavenly Father, the more people will get to understand who he is.

June

How does a kaleidoscope work?

God has made everything beautiful for its own time.
ECCLESIASTES 3:11

It seems a little unusual that a physicist would invent a toy, but that's what happened in 1816. David Brewster from Scotland devised what looked like a telescope, but you couldn't see faraway things through it. Instead, there were two mirrors at the end, with little colored pieces that moved between them. When the kaleidoscope was turned, the pieces would fall into different patterns as you saw them in the mirrors. Kaleidoscopes are entertaining because you will likely never see the same thing twice when you look into them. The name is Greek and means "to see beautiful shapes."

When you look into a kaleidoscope, it is a reflection of the world in pieces. Even those small particles hold beauty. Even without the little scope, the whole world is astounding. It is true, as the Bible says, that "God has made everything beautiful for its own time" (Ecclesiastes 3:11).

June

What can you do in case of fire?

When you walk through the fire of oppression, you will
not be burned up; the flames will not consume you.
ISAIAH 43:2

Kindergartner Emily Giles was listening when the fireman came to speak at her school in Buffalo, New York, in the 1980s. The fireman said that it is always very important to get out of a burning room. But Emily was worried about what would happen if there were a fire in the middle of the night when it was too dark to see anything. How could she find her way out? She thought of an answer, entered it in her school's invention program, and won. Her project was called the Kids' Fire Escape, and it also won the award in the state competition. How did Emily solve the problem of escaping a fire in the dark? She put glow-in-the-dark teddy bear footprints on the floor. They were easy to see and easy to follow, and led from her bed to the door of her bedroom and to safety.

Sometimes God gives us good ideas to protect us from bad things that could happen. Thinking ahead about how to get away in case of a fire is a way to use the wisdom God has given you. The Bible says, "When you walk through the fire of oppression, you will not be burned up; the flames will not consume you" (Isaiah 43:2). God wants you to be safe, and he wants to help you make plans just in case.

June 24

What's a Cracker Jack?

How sweet your words taste to me;
they are sweeter than honey.
PSALM 119:103

The taste of Cracker Jack wasn't new. As far back as AD 800, North American tribes added heated maple syrup to popcorn to preserve it longer. But it was F. W. Rueckheim who began boxing the mixture of popcorn, peanuts, and a candied coating. It was first shown to the world at the 1893 Columbian Exposition even before it had a name. The name came from a salesman in 1896 who tasted the treat and said, "That's crackerjack!" At the time, that was a term that meant "super," or "the best thing ever." The little sailor boy and dog on the box was a picture of F. W.'s grandson and his dog, Bingo. Inside every box or bag of Cracker Jack is a small prize. The small toys are picked by a committee, cost the company less than half a penny, and are scanned in their containers by three electric eyes at the factory to make sure they are never missing.

It's fun to have a sweet treat every once in a while, especially one that comes with a little present, too! But it's even more exciting to think of God's goodness to us and the gifts he wants to give us. The Bible says, "How sweet your words taste to me; they are sweeter than honey" (Psalm 119:103).

June

How do owls hunt at night?

God alone understands the way to wisdom; he knows where it can be found, for he looks throughout the whole earth and sees everything under the heavens.
JOB 28:23-24

The owl has many tools that make it easy for the owl to hunt in the dark. Many owls have one ear higher than the other to help them pinpoint the exact location of the smallest rustling of a mouse or a vole on the ground. Owls can't turn their heads completely around to 360 degrees, but they can turn 270 degrees because of their extra neck vertebrae and specialized muscles. Owls cannot move their eyes, so they need to move their heads to change the scenery. The owl's nonmoving eyes are actually an extra tool for hunting. Because its eyes face forward, the owl's binocular (or three-dimensional) vision is greatly increased, which makes night vision easier. The eyes of the owl are also more round than human eyes, which makes them one hundred times as sensitive to light. Owls can see well enough to hunt by the light of a single candle placed five hundred yards away. And the owl's eyes are really large so they can let in the most light possible. If our eyes were to the same scale on our faces, we'd have eyes the size of grapefruits!

As amazing as the owl's eyesight is, God can see even more. He sees everything in creation, and he sees you every moment! The Bible says, "God alone understands the way to wisdom; he knows where it can be found, for he looks throughout the whole earth and sees everything under the heavens" (Job 28:23-24).

June

What country helped inspire Lincoln Logs?

Unless the LORD builds a house, the
work of the builders is wasted.
PSALM 127:1

Lincoln Logs are round pieces of wood with grooves in them that allow you to make a small, sturdy version of an American pioneer's log cabin. They were named after President Abraham Lincoln. Even though the inventor gave Lincoln Logs an American name, the design of the logs didn't come completely from America. It also came from ancient Japan. The inventor's name was John Lloyd Wright, and he was the grown son of a very famous American architect, Frank Lloyd Wright. John went with his father to Tokyo in 1916 when his father built a fancy hotel there. The same kind of construction was used for the hotel that the Japanese had used to build a bridge many years before. The logs fit together so snugly on the bridge that no nails or steel parts were needed to make it safer. When John came back to America after that trip, he designed and sold the first Lincoln Logs. Some of the children who played with Lincoln Logs later grew up to be architects themselves.

People can build buildings that are greatly admired. But the Bible says, "Unless the LORD builds a house, the work of the builders is wasted" (Psalm 127:1). God is in charge of our lives, and if we try to live without his safety and structure around us, no house can keep us safe by itself. Invite Jesus to live with you wherever you are, and he will watch over you.

27 June

Do humans copy animals' homes?

Lord, through all the generations you have been our home!
PSALM 90:1

Early humans probably lived first in caves, just as the animals did. Later, we can assume people built their homes from what they found in their surroundings: the same wood, mud, and dried grass that birds use to build their nests. When towns became more permanent, people looked for sturdier materials to build with, like mud bricks and eventually concrete, similar to the way termites make natural cement out of sand and saliva and other ingredients. Termites' homes can be as tall as twenty-five feet, and only dynamite can destroy them. Skyscrapers are like our human version of the same thing. Humans have also built large buildings where different people are living in each apartment, just as a beehive has many compartments for the bees to live in.

No matter what kind of home you live in, as God's child, your home is really with him. Your heart and soul are safe in his keeping. You can rest in his presence without fear, and he will watch over you always. The Bible says, "Lord, through all the generations you have been our home!" (Psalm 90:1).

June 28

What was a Pig Stand, and what could you do there?

The manna came down on the camp
with the dew during the night.
NUMBERS 11:9

Texan Jesse Kirby had an opinion that gave him an idea. He said, "People with cars are so crazy they don't want to get out of them to eat." Jesse decided to make it easy for the drivers to get their food. In Dallas in 1921, his restaurant opened. Called the Pig Stand, it provided a totally different way to receive a meal. When a car drove up, workers would run out of the building, take the order, race back inside to grab the bags of food, and then bring them back to the car. That was a lot of activity! Ten years later, Kirby thought of an even more efficient way to run his restaurant. Because of his new idea, all the workers could stay inside the restaurant and stop their running, which made getting the food even faster. Drivers were able to pull their cars right up to a window on the side of the restaurant and have their food simply handed to them. The drive-through restaurant had arrived at last!

God had an even more amazing way of delivering food to his people. When the people of Israel were wandering in the desert, they were hungry. God arranged for their food, called manna, to fall from the sky! The Bible tells us, "The manna came down on the camp with the dew during the night" (Numbers 11:9). All the people had to do was bend over, pick up their meal, and eat it. Only God could make a way for food to be delivered that easily.

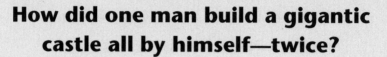

June 29

How did one man build a gigantic castle all by himself—twice?

You are coming to Christ, who is the living
cornerstone of God's temple.
1 PETER 2:4

Nobody knows. But a man named Edward Leedskalnin, who was just five feet tall and weighed only one hundred pounds, somehow managed to do it. Edward moved to Florida from the country of Latvia and started to build his castle in 1920. He chose a part of Florida where not many people lived, because he wanted to be alone. He was a mysterious person, and he worked secretly at night, carving coral boulders out of the land using handmade hammers, chisels, saws, chains, hoists, and recycled auto parts as tools. He made a nine-ton gate that was balanced so perfectly that a five-year-old could touch it with one finger and it would open. Edward also made half-ton rocking chairs that could be rocked with just a light push. After twenty years, the castle was finished. But when people wanted to live nearby, Edward decided to relocate his castle ten miles farther away near a town called Homestead. Piece by piece, boulder by boulder (some weighing thirty tons each), he took the castle down. He hired a man to drive the trailer loaded with boulders to the new location. But not even the driver got to see how the boulders were lifted on and off that trailer. Edward asked him to leave and then come back after the trailer was loaded. Years later, when Edward died, his secret for building the Coral Castle still had not been told.

Each stone in the castle had to be carefully placed so that the building would be strong. The Bible tells us, "You are coming to Christ, who is the living cornerstone of God's temple" (1 Peter 2:4). The surest way to be strong in your faith is to believe that Jesus Christ is your Savior. When you build your life on him by following what he says, you can count on Jesus to stand firm for you and not let you tumble down.

June

What bird uses a spear to catch its dinner?

Give all your worries and cares to God, for he cares about you.
1 PETER 5:7

Birds have lots of tools for finding and eating their food. They use their beaks, their claws, and their wings to get themselves to food and to get the food into their stomachs. But one bird, at first glance, seems to have been left out. The Galapagos woodpecker finch tries to behave like a regular woodpecker. Like the woodpecker, it uses its beak to chop up plants, which allows it to get closer to its food: the grubs inside. The real woodpecker then unrolls its long tongue to scoop up the grubs. But the little woodpecker finch doesn't have a long tongue. How does it get the grubs? Amazingly, the woodpecker finch has a solution. It picks a spine off a cactus and holds it in its beak to use as a spear. This little bird then pokes the spear into the plant and pulls grubs out where they are easy to reach and eat.

The Creator provided a surprising way for the woodpecker finch to eat. The finch doesn't have to worry about how to feed itself. It just uses the way God made it, even if it isn't the same way the other birds are made. We, too, can trust in the Lord to provide a way for us to have what we need. Worrying about it will not make it turn out right. Only giving our concerns to God will make things right, because God always works things out for good. The Bible says, "Give all your worries and cares to God, for he cares about you" (1 Peter 5:7). How wonderful to know that God has a solution for every one of our problems. We just need to trust in him and look around for the tools he has already given us.

July

What does it mean to be
there "with bells on"?

We are here to bring you this Good News. The promise was made to our ancestors, and God has now fulfilled it for us, their descendants, by raising Jesus.
ACTS 13:32-33

You may have heard someone say this in a cheerful voice, as if you should be pleased. What are they trying to tell you? It all goes back to the days of the covered wagon. A team of six horses pulled each wagon, and each horse weighed at least 1,800 pounds (as much as a whole class full of fourth graders!). These were special horses, and they each wore a special arch attached to their collars. On each arch there were bells— five bells each on the two front horses' collars, four bells on each arch of the two middle horses, and three bells on the two horses closest to the wagon. The bells jingled when the wagon was moving to announce that this big vehicle was coming, warning people and animals to move to the side to let the horses and wagon through. So when people say they'll be there "with bells on," they mean that they will make a grand and special entrance and attract lots of attention. Nothing could stop them from arriving to join you.

If bells on horses trotting by could get people's attention, imagine how the apostles felt when they had such good news to share about the gospel! They surely were looking forward to being there "with bells on" to tell people about Jesus. "We are here to bring you this Good News. The promise was made to our ancestors, and God has now fulfilled it for us, their descendants, by raising Jesus" (Acts 13:32-33). Now that's something worth ringing bells about all over the earth!

July

Why does a baseball field have a raised pitcher's mound?

O LORD, you are righteous, and your regulations are fair.
PSALM 119:137

The first time a rule was made about the pitcher's mound was 1903. The rule was that the pitcher's mound could not be more than fifteen inches higher than the rest of the field. Why was that rule necessary? It began when pitchers started pitching overhand instead of underhand. Batters needed more time to decide how to hit the ball, so the pitcher was moved farther and farther away from the batter. In the 1870s, the pitcher used to stand forty-five feet away from the batter, and now the pitcher is located exactly sixty feet, six inches away. Before 1903, though, different ball fields made the pitcher's mound any height they wanted to, which made it hard for outfielders to know if they would trip over an outrageously high mound while they were trying to catch a ball overhead and they weren't watching the ground. After the ruling in 1903, every mound was the same size. Pitcher's mounds are helpful for several reasons. In rainy weather, the mound allows rainwater to run off the slope and away from the middle of the field. Another reason pitchers like the mound is that being up higher provides extra gravity, which gathers more energy for the ball and makes it go a little faster. There is more challenge when the ball comes from a higher angle, because it is harder for the batter to connect with it. And lastly, the pitcher moves in a downward motion as he heads into his pitch, which makes it easier to throw the ball than if he were standing downhill from the batter or even on flat ground.

Rules can be good when it comes to playing games, because they keep things fair for everyone. In the Bible we read, "O LORD, you are righteous, and your regulations are fair" (Psalm 119:137). In this case, that seems to be what happened for baseball. Everyone knew what to expect, and everyone enjoyed the game more.

July

How could a loud band help with a bad tooth?

He grants the desires of those who fear him;
he hears their cries for help and rescues them.
PSALM 145:19

In the 1800s, doctors didn't know many of the things they know today. Just about any idea was tried to see if it worked or not. There was one dentist who was determined to practice dentistry really quickly. One day, in less than an hour, he pulled out seventy-four teeth from various patients! In the office there was a loud brass band that played on and on so the patients couldn't hear each other in pain. Fortunately, dentists have come a long way since then!

Whenever you are hurting, you don't have to worry that God will just drown out your cries for help. He always hears you, he always listens, and he always cares. The Bible tells us, "He grants the desires of those who fear him; he hears their cries for help and rescues them" (Psalm 145:19).

July 4

What are some little-known secrets of the Statue of Liberty?

I was a stranger, and you invited me into your home.
MATTHEW 25:35

The Statue of Liberty on Liberty Island in New York Harbor is a familiar sight to most Americans. But not everyone knows some of the astonishing details about the statue. The tablet the woman is holding in one hand has Roman numerals carved on it that say July 4, 1776, the day our country declared its independence. Her fingernails are each as large as a sheet of notebook paper. Her nose is four and a half feet long. The Statue of Liberty was completely built in France first. Then in 1884, it was taken apart and put into 214 packing cases to be sent as a gift to the United States, where it was put back together again, piece by piece. And although the statue is green, it has never been painted; it is made of copper, which has turned green with time.

America is proud of the Statue of Liberty because many people who traveled far to live here viewed the statue as one of their first sights of the United States. The statue seemed to say, "Welcome!" Jesus tells us how important it is to be kind to others, no matter who they are or where they are from. He says, "I was a stranger, and you invited me into your home" (Matthew 25:35). This is something we can do, whether it means welcoming someone into our country, our home, or our conversation.

5

July

Can your cat talk?

How wonderful to be wise, to analyze and interpret things.
ECCLESIASTES 8:1

There are several clues a cat can give you about what it is thinking. First of all, a cat can make more than one hundred different sounds, depending on if its voice is high or low or quiet or loud. But a cat can also tell you how it feels with its ears and its tail, without making any sound at all. Watch your cat's ears carefully. When its ears are pointing forward, your cat is alert and watching or just happy. When the ears are flat, something has scared your cat. But be careful of a cat whose ears are lying back on its head—that means it's angry. That's heads—now let's look at tails! The best position for a cat's tail is when it is standing straight up, because that means your cat is happy to see you. If its tail is waving slowly, your cat is content. If your cat's tail is twitching quickly, your pet is annoyed or excited. Your cat will hold its tail low, with the fur fluffed out, if it is afraid, and a tail between the legs means your cat is worried. Even though your cat doesn't use words, there are many ways it still can talk to you!

The Bible tells us, "How wonderful to be wise, to analyze and interpret things" (Ecclesiastes 8:1). The more observant you are about things around you, the more wisdom you will obtain as you get older. Plus, your cat will probably enjoy all the attention it gets as you practice on it, trying to figure out what it is thinking.

6

July

How did Abraham Lincoln make fun of how he looked?

The LORD doesn't see things the way you see
them. People judge by outward appearance,
but the LORD looks at the heart.
1 SAMUEL 16:7

It happened during a political debate with Senator Stephen Douglas, who accused Abraham Lincoln of being two-faced on one of his policies. To be two-faced means that you say one thing and do another. But Lincoln turned that criticism into something funny that amused the listening crowd. He answered Senator Douglas by saying, "I leave it to my audience. If I had two faces, would I be wearing this one?" Lincoln knew that he had never been considered handsome, and he was joking that if he had a choice of two faces, he would have picked the other one instead.

It didn't bother Abraham Lincoln that he wasn't handsome. He was wise enough to realize that there are many more important things in life, like how much you care for others and how serious you are about doing the right thing. The Bible reminds us of this when it says, "The LORD doesn't see things the way you see them. People judge by outward appearance, but the LORD looks at the heart" (1 Samuel 16:7). You can make sure your heart is beautiful every single day of your life by loving the Lord and following what he teaches you.

July

How did an accident that caused broken glass end up protecting people?

We put our hope in the LORD. He is our help and our shield.
PSALM 33:20

In 1903 French chemist Edouard Benedictus was on a ladder reaching for something on a shelf and accidentally knocked over a glass container. When it crashed to the floor, Edouard noticed the broken pieces of glass stuck to each other instead of shattering everywhere. The container had been full of liquid plastic, which evaporated and left a clear film that held the glass pieces together. He spent the next twenty-four hours straight experimenting with coating glass and breaking it, and finally he was sure that safety glass had been invented. Edouard tried to convince carmakers that this new glass would be perfect for windshields to protect people from getting cut in a crash. But they were not interested until ten years later. In the meantime, the U.S. Army began using the glass for lenses in soldiers' goggles, and safety glass has been used in many products since.

The windshield was designed to protect a car's passengers from wind and debris that could fly into the vehicle while it is traveling. Safety glass made the windshield even more effective, since it protects against injury from broken glass. But nothing can compare to the power of God as he protects you. We are told: "We put our hope in the LORD. He is our help and our shield" (Psalm 33:20). God is the best windshield you could possibly ask for as you travel through life.

July

Which insect flies faster than all the rest?

At the right time, I, the LORD, will make it happen.
ISAIAH 60:22

The winner of the speeding contest is the dragonfly. But the dragonfly is not the insect that beats its wings the fastest. Strangely enough, the dragonfly flaps its wings only about twenty to forty times a second, and yet it can fly thirty miles an hour. This is because of its body shape, which is well adapted for flight, and because of its two sets of powerful wings. On the other hand, a tinier insect like the mosquito, although it beats its wings about six hundred times a second, can only travel one mile an hour.

Whether things go quickly or take a long time, God is in charge of what happens and when. We may try to hurry God by being impatient and getting angry if we feel we have to wait too long for a new bike, summer vacation, or a camping trip. But God pays attention to the details, and he doesn't make mistakes. He can't—he's perfect. He tells us in the Bible, "At the right time, I, the LORD, will make it happen" (Isaiah 60:22). Trust the Lord, not the calendar or the clock.

July

When was a typewriter used for something else?

O LORD, what a variety of things you have made!
In wisdom you have made them all.
PSALM 104:24

Thomas Edison tried his hand at inventing almost anything and everything in the late nineteenth century. One of his inventions was intended to be a typewriter. In fact, his was the first electric typewriter that printed letters on a moving roll of paper. The problem was that his typewriter was never used for typing words. Instead, because of the long roll of paper, it became the first ticker tape machine used in the financial workplace to report on the way stocks were trading and other news during each day. Of course, computers gradually replaced ticker tape machines and typewriters, and both these machines are now just a part of history.

When we humans have ideas or try to create things, they don't always work out the way we'd planned. But that's not how it is with God. Everything has a purpose and a time and a plan, and God doesn't make mistakes. The Bible reminds us, "O LORD, what a variety of things you have made! In wisdom you have made them all" (Psalm 104:24).

July
10

When did it become a good idea to jump?

Without wise leadership, a nation falls; there
is safety in having many advisers.
PROVERBS 11:14

Leonardo da Vinci sketched a parachute in 1495, but a real one wasn't tried until Louis Lenormand invented it in 1783 as a solution to escaping from a burning building. He first tested it by jumping from trees. Then in 1797 André-Jacques Garnerin jumped from a hydrogen-filled balloon when it burst at three thousand feet high. The parachute held Jacques underneath in a bucket that swung so violently that it made him sick, but it took him safely to the ground. The first jump from a plane with a parachute was in 1912 in St. Louis. The parachute was opened by pulling a line attached to the plane, but later that year the first rip cord parachute was used, giving the jumper a second chance to open the chute if the first pull failed. People were fascinated to know for the first time that a plane could still remain stable even after some of the weight was removed while in flight. In 1919 the self-releasing parachute with a rip cord, called the Stevens Life Pack, enabled the passenger to open the parachute by himself. It became the kind of parachute that the military used.

Trying to make decisions without consulting people for advice would be as foolish as getting in a parachute without understanding how to operate it. The Lord sends us people who can talk to us about him when we are not sure we understand what we need to know. The Bible says, "Without wise leadership, a nation falls; there is safety in having many advisers" (Proverbs 11:14). Seek out the wise people you know and ask them to help you make decisions. God will be guiding them—and you.

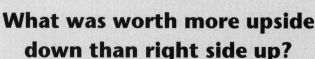

July

What was worth more upside down than right side up?

Give me an eagerness for your laws
rather than a love for money!
PSALM 119:36

People who collect stamps look for ones that are rare and hard to find. Stamps that have printing errors on them are especially valuable. One day in 1918, William Robey went to his Washington DC post office to buy a sheet of twenty-four-cent airmail stamps to attach to an ordinary letter. When he later examined his sheet of one hundred stamps, he noticed something very odd—there were one hundred planes, all printed upside down. William sold the sheet to a collector for $15,000—the same sheet that William had just bought for $24. The sheet was sold again. That time the price was $20,000. Then in the 1940s, just four of the one hundred stamps were sold for $23,000 total. Not too much later, each of the hundred stamps appeared in a catalog that listed each one for $5,000.

William sold his stamps for a quite a bit of money, but later they were sold for even more. Hopefully he was not too upset! God wants us to keep money in its proper place—it is not the most important thing. Wealth is nice to have, of course, but it does not guarantee that you will be loved or safe or saved. God wants us to realize this by believing what Jesus said: "Give me an eagerness for your laws rather than a love for money!" (Psalm 119:36).

July 12

How did a simple cloth become known as a handkerchief?

I am the LORD, and I do not change.
MALACHI 3:6

The Romans started it long ago. They kept a small cloth hanging from their belts. Later the English began to copy the idea, after making a few changes. The English called the cloth a kerchief, the French word for "cloth." And the English hung their kerchiefs from their sleeves. That's when the cloth became known as a "hang-kerchief." Years later, since it was used to wipe the mouth, forehead, or nose, people held the hang-kerchief in their hands. So the spelling was changed, and it became the handkerchief.

With time, changes happen here on earth. The name for the hand-kerchief changed over the years as it was used differently by different people. But you never have to worry that Jesus or the Bible will change. In the Bible God says, "I am the LORD, and I do not change" (Malachi 3:6). You can always believe that what Jesus said and did is true and that what is recorded in the Bible will never turn out to be false.

July 13

Why was a toilet also made into an aquarium?

Those who love money will never have enough.
How meaningless to think that wealth brings true happiness!
ECCLESIASTES 5:10

Before toilets were invented, each bed had a small container underneath it that needed to be emptied the next morning if it was pulled out from under the bed to use during the night. The first real flush toilet was invented by Sir John Harrington in 1596. It needed to be spectacular, because only very wealthy people could afford to have indoor plumbing in their houses, and they wanted to show off the toilet to their friends. So this kind of toilet had a fancy carved base—flowers, animals, shells, or fruit were the favorite carvings of the time—and there were live fish swimming in the tank behind the back of the seat!

In later days, it became more polite not to show off toilets or even mention them. But some people always seem to find possessions to show off—houses or cars or clothes. It is not a good idea to live for other peoples' admiration, especially over your money or your stuff. The Bible says, "Those who love money will never have enough. How meaningless to think that wealth brings true happiness!" (Ecclesiastes 5:10). What you buy will never bring you the happiness or peace of mind that God will give to you for free.

July 14

Why do snakes have forked, or split, tongues?

The tongue of the wise makes knowledge appealing.
PROVERBS 15:2

Snakes have no taste buds on their tongues. Instead, they use their tongues to smell. Actually, they use the two sides of their tongues to give them stereo smell so they can smell things in two directions. Here's how it works. Say a snake is trying to decide whether to turn left or right for food. It sticks out its tongue. The tongue collects information about which animal went left by using the left side of its tongue and which animal went right by using the right side of its tongue. The chemical signal strength on one tip of the tongue is analyzed by the snake's brain and then is compared to the chemical signal strength of the sample on the other tongue tip. The snake does this to be able to locate and follow invisible trails of scents left by passing animals.

Studying the snake's tongue, and all the things a snake can do with it, is a good reminder for us to try to make our tongues useful too. The Bible tells us how when it says, "The tongue of the wise makes knowledge appealing" (Proverbs 15:2). Try to think of what God would like you to say before you open your mouth. He will give you the words if you ask him to tell you the right things to say.

July

Why do baby teeth fall out?

What counts is whether we have been
transformed into a new creation.
GALATIANS 6:15

As you grow up, your jaw gets larger and your baby teeth don't fill it up enough anymore to help you chew, so you need bigger teeth. All teeth have roots that keep them attached to your mouth. Your permanent teeth are lined up underneath your baby teeth to push them out, but the baby teeth have roots that are still too strong to let go. So your permanent teeth shoot out a chemical under your gums that makes the little roots get weak and dissolve. That makes the baby teeth get looser faster and causes them to fall out, making room for your permanent teeth to appear.

When your first teeth leave, there is room for new, better, more useful teeth. But did you know you can also become a new *person*? Once you have asked Jesus into your heart, he makes you kinder and more thoughtful and stronger and so many other things as you become more like Jesus. The Bible tells us, "What counts is whether we have been transformed into a new creation" (Galatians 6:15).

July

16

Where on earth can you see the Atlantic Ocean and the Pacific Ocean at the same time?

The sea belongs to him, for he made it.
His hands formed the dry land, too.
PSALM 95:5

It's not in the United States—the Atlantic and the Pacific have 2,500 miles between them almost everywhere in North America. Central America has better options. In Panama, the narrowest part of Central America, the two oceans are only fifty miles apart. The problem is that there are no mountains in Panama that show a view of both the Atlantic and the Pacific at the same time. However, it is still possible to see both. The country just to the northwest, Costa Rica, has the 11,325-foot-high peak called Mount Izaru, and it is there—the only place in the whole world—that you can get a view of both the Atlantic Ocean and the Pacific Ocean at the same time.

Imagine being at the only place on earth where you can see both of these oceans that God created! It must be inspiring to see so much of God's majesty at once. The Bible tells us, "The sea belongs to him, for he made it. His hands formed the dry land, too" (Psalm 95:5). God pays attention to all the little details, but he also gives us glimpses of his great might and total power. The big and the small all bow down to our God.

July

17

What invention was more than skin deep?

Think of it—the LORD is ready to heal me! I will sing
his praises with instruments every day of my life.
ISAIAH 38:20

Lydia O'Leary knew what it was like to be embarrassed and rejected.
She was born with a dark purplish splotch that covered half her face. She
felt so bad about her looks that she sometimes hid from classmates in the
restroom at school. But when her parents took her to doctors, they said
there was nothing that could be done. She tried getting a tattoo to match
her face color, but even that didn't work. Lydia finished high school and
college and applied for a job. She was not hired because the interviewers
didn't think she should be seen by the public. While painting one day,
Lydia made a mistake, but then she covered the paper with several coats
of paint, and the unwanted mark disappeared. She had an idea—why not
use makeup to do the same thing on her face? She tried, but there was no
makeup strong enough. So she made one herself. She decided to go back
to the same company that had refused to hire her earlier. This time, with
her makeup on, she was hired, and she was the top salesperson in three
weeks. She called her makeup Covermark, and it is the only makeup with
a U.S. patent. When she first applied for the patent, she was told no. But
when she was in court in front of the patent judges, she left the room and
came back wearing her makeup. The panel was so shocked at the difference
and how much it could help others that they granted her the patent as an
exception.

God is in the healing business, for both our bodies and our spirits.
Often, we long to be like everybody else when we have something that
seems to make us different. God knows that this is hard, and he wants us
to trust him to work things out for good. The Bible says, "Think of it—the
LORD is ready to heal me! I will sing his praises with instruments every day
of my life" (Isaiah 38:20). Trust that God sees you, he feels your pain with
you, and he is working to help you while holding your hand.

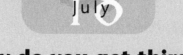

July 18

Why do you get thirsty?

O God, you are my God; I earnestly search for you.
My soul thirsts for you; my whole body longs for you.
PSALM 63:1

Your body lets you know that you don't have enough water in your bloodstream by giving you the feeling that you need to drink. One reason you might be thirsty is if you've eaten something salty, since salt absorbs water. When people who are thirsty are allowed to drink all they want to, they usually drink exactly the amount their body needs. This has caused scientists to guess that our bodies have a "water meter" that measures the moisture we need to be balanced, and it signals us how much to drink. But so far no one has been able to find where in the body a water measurer might be.

The Bible mentions the thirst of the body and what will satisfy it. But it also tells us about our souls and how they can be filled: "O God, you are my God; I earnestly search for you. My soul thirsts for you; my whole body longs for you" (Psalm 63:1). Come to the Lord as quickly as you would run to the drinking fountain when you're thirsty.

July

19

Why did clothes dryers need windows in the front?

Those who accept my commandments and obey them are the ones who love me. . . . And I will love them and reveal myself to each of them.
JOHN 14:21

When the clothes dryer was first invented, there was a problem with it. It worked just fine, but people didn't know what it was for. At that time clothes were dried outside and hung from a clothesline. The Hamilton Company wondered how it could sell its new clothes dryer. That's where Brooks Stevens came in. When he was a young boy, Brooks had polio, a sickness that forced him to spend much of his time in bed. During Brooks's illness, his father urged him to spend his time drawing. And that's what Brooks did for the rest of his life—he grew up to be a designer, and he thought up ideas and drew them. It was Brooks who came up with the idea of putting a window in the clothes dryer. He thought people needed to see clothes tumbling dry so they would know why they should buy the machine. Following Brooks's advice, salesmen would run the dryers in the store, where people could watch the clothes going around and around, getting dry. Once everyone knew what a dryer could do, the window wasn't necessary anymore. Brooks also designed many other products besides the clothes dryer. He designed the Harley-Davidson motorcycle and the Wienermobile, a car shaped like a hot dog that was driven around to advertise Oscar Mayer franks.

God gave Brooks the talent to see things in a unique way that other people hadn't thought of yet. When you read God's Word, he will show you new things about himself that you haven't noticed before. Jesus teaches that "those who accept my commandments and obey them are the ones who love me. . . . And I will love them and reveal myself to each of them" (John 14:21). Be alert for new ideas—God may be giving you a special gift!

July

What do a snail and an engine have in common?

You are a God who does what is right, and you smooth out the path ahead of them.
ISAIAH 26:7

When a snail moves along the ground, it goes forward because its base, or foot, contracts and expands like a muscle. Because the foot is the soft part of the snail under the shell, it could easily get dried up or worn away or snagged on rough ground as it moves. But none of those things happen, because the snail secretes a mucus from its foot that makes a smooth jelly for it to glide on. You might see a silver trail of dried mucus on the sidewalk in the morning that will tell you a snail crawled by in the night. In the human world, engines are machines with lots of moving parts that would rub and wear away if they didn't have the protection of some kind of oil or jelly to keep the parts turning smoothly. An engine moves fast and a snail moves slowly, but both move easily because they have a lubricant making their movements slick.

Sometimes as we go through life we have a tendency to get stuck in tough places. But God knows exactly what is going to be difficult for us, and he doesn't leave us on our own. He promises to go in front of us and smooth out the way for us to go. The Bible says this about God: "You are a God who does what is right, and you smooth out the path ahead of them" (Isaiah 26:7).

21 July

When was it very inconvenient to listen to a stereo system?

Faith comes from hearing, that is, hearing
the Good News about Christ.
ROMANS 10:17

Hearing something "in stereo" means you can hear it from two places at the same time, either from two different speakers in the room or from both earphones of a headset. When the stereo was first invented in 1881, many people went to a lot of trouble to hear it. They paid to have a device resembling a telephone installed in their house. At a prearranged time, the telephone wires would carry a broadcast of live music. To hear it, listeners had to watch the clock for when the music would begin. Then they had to hold two telephone receivers through the entire performance—one against each ear—for the stereo sound to come through to both ears at the same time. Finally, in 1925, stereo music was broadcast over radio speakers instead of through phone lines, and that was the first time people could stop holding phone receivers up to their ears. They could just relax and enjoy the entertainment.

More than a hundred years ago, people had to try very hard just to hear music in stereo. As God's children, we have something much more important we need to listen for. We want to hear, over and over again, every word that Jesus says to his people. The Bible tells us why this is important: "Faith comes from hearing, that is, hearing the Good News about Christ" (Romans 10:17). When you pay attention to what Jesus says, you can keep a joyful song in your heart all the time, and you won't need phone receivers, speakers, or headphones to hear it.

July

Why was a tree named after a president of the United States?

Here on earth you will have many trials and sorrows.
But take heart, because I have overcome the world.
JOHN 16:33

It all started with the game of golf. President Dwight Eisenhower loved to play the game so much that he had a putting green created on the White House lawn and practiced swinging his golf club as he walked through the White House. He played golf on as many as 150 days of the year, but he wasn't all that good at it. For example, at the Augusta, Georgia, golf course, where he often played, there was a tree he kept hitting with his ball. He finally requested that the pine tree be cut down. The tree stayed standing, but it was known after that as the "Eisenhower tree."

President Eisenhower couldn't seem to avoid the tree, so he wanted it removed. All of us have things in our lives that we wish were different. Some of us wish our parents were not divorced. Some of us wish we had more money. Some of us wish the bullies would leave us alone at school. God doesn't promise us that only good things will happen. Jesus says, "Here on earth you will have many trials and sorrows. But take heart, because I have overcome the world" (John 16:33). Jesus wants us to have courage and patience and to understand that things on earth won't be perfect, but things in heaven will be.

July

How did a shoe polish gimmick turn into a tangled-up game?

Decide instead to live in such a way that you will
not cause another believer to stumble and fall.
ROMANS 14:13

Reyn Guyer and his father were in the advertising business, and they had a good idea when a shoe polish company asked them for a unique gimmick to sell their shoe polish in 1965. Reyn and his dad decided to put a coupon for a gift in magazines, comic books, or newspapers for kids to cut out and send in with a dollar. Then the kids would get a gift back in the mail. The gift, Reyn decided, would be colored patches for kids to put on their shoes, and then he added the idea of putting a plastic board with colors on the floor. The kids would have to match their patches to the board by stepping on the board and reaching for the right color. To test the idea, Reyn asked his office workers to play the game, and soon everyone was tangled up and laughing. Reyn realized he had just invented a game that kids and grown-ups would like. He gave the patches to the shoe polish company and sold the game (called Pretzel) to Milton Bradley, a toy company. The game's name was changed to Twister, but there wasn't much interest from the public until one night when a famous TV talk show host played Twister on the air for everyone to watch. The next day, everyone wanted to play. Twister has been a favorite party game for many years.

When people go tumbling down in Twister, it's fun because it's only a game. But the Bible cautions us to be more careful in real life, because you can cause people problems if you put a stumbling block in their way. For example, if you do someone else's homework, not only are you cheating, but that person may flunk the test on the material later in the semester. It would be better not to let your friend take the easy way out, because even if it seems like a good idea, it will cause him or her to stumble in the future. The Bible says, "Decide instead to live in such a way that you will not cause another believer to stumble and fall" (Romans 14:13).

July 24

How did a stoplight experiment end up catching speeders?

The fastest runner doesn't always win the race.
ECCLESIASTES 9:11

John Barker was working on a project in 1947. He was trying to use radar to prompt stoplights to change automatically. It just wasn't working. Every time a car came by, the radar measured the car's speed instead of the stoplight's. Eureka! Without knowing it, John had just discovered the beginnings of the radar gun. He made some improvements, such as attaching the radar antenna near the edge of the road. This way it could send out a beam of radio waves. When a car got within five hundred feet of the beam, the radar gun began recording how fast the car was going. The speed always registered slightly lower than the car was actually going, and radar became the accepted way, even in court, to prove that a car was speeding.

A driver who is stopped for speeding has to sit on the side of the road as the police officer writes a ticket, while the slower drivers, who used to be behind, drive past and go on their way. Not only will these people get where they are going, but they won't have to pay extra money for a ticket. The Bible tells us, "The fastest runner doesn't always win the race" (Ecclesiastes 9:11). That means it's more important to work hard than to be the first to raise your hand in class. It's more important to treat others respectfully than to be at the front of the lunch line. Try to see the benefits of being polite and obeying the law. Doing what's right will make you a winner in the end.

July

Which word never existed?

Faith is the confidence that what we hope for will actually happen; it gives us assurance about things we cannot see.
HEBREWS 11:1

The word was *dord*, and it appeared in the 1934 dictionary as a joke. It all began when a linguist who was working on writing the dictionary put an abbreviation for the word for *density* on a slip of paper and added it to the stack for the letter *d*. The next worker who received the papers thought the abbreviation was written incorrectly, so he put all the letters together, and they spelled *dord*. When the dictionary's editors caught the mistake, they made a decision. They wanted to see if anyone reading the dictionary would find the fake word, so they allowed it to be printed in the dictionary. It stayed there through several more printings and was finally taken out when new editors started working on a revised version of the dictionary.

There is only one book on earth that you can absolutely believe every word of—it's the Bible. Anything else is created by only humans and cannot be perfectly reliable. The Bible is God's Word to us and contains his message, and it represents our Christian faith. The Bible tells us, "Faith is the confidence that what we hope for will actually happen; it gives us assurance about things we cannot see" (Hebrews 11:1). Don't just rely on what you see, like a word that doesn't really mean anything. Put your trust in the Word, which means everything.

26

July

Why did people want to sit on top of a flagpole?

The LORD is high above the nations; his
glory is higher than the heavens.
PSALM 113:4

It all began with one man, Alvin Kelly, when he sat on a flagpole as a stunt for a movie. Then he got an invitation to repeat his display outside a Los Angeles theater to draw people to the movie. After that, there were more requests from advertisers for his flagpole-sitting, and the press reported on his accomplishments. People started copying him as they read about him, and soon flagpole-sitting was a national fad. Alvin Kelly's best record was staying up on a flagpole for forty-nine days in Atlantic City, where more than twenty thousand people saw him. One person who didn't have a flagpole available—fifteen-year-old Alvin Foreman—still participated by climbing his backyard tree, which inspired other people to climb trees as well.

Going up and down a flagpole can be risky and slightly dangerous, although no one seemed to get hurt. Whether we are involved in harmless fun or are in more serious danger, the Bible tells us there is one thing we can count on: "The LORD is high above the nations; his glory is higher than the heavens" (Psalm 113:4). That is the kind of great God we have!

27 July

Are those birds really humming?

We must quickly carry out the tasks assigned us by the one who sent us. The night is coming, and then no one can work.
JOHN 9:4

Hummingbirds are named after the sound their wings make when they fly. Hummingbirds can fly left, right, forward, backward, down, up, and even upside down. They flap their wings in figure-eight patterns at seventy times a second. They are considered nature's helicopters. They have slim bills to nose into deep flowers for the nectar and a long tongue that can flick out and lick the nectar at thirteen times a second. Unlike other birds that sit on a perch, the hummingbird hovers near the flower where it's taking nectar and then backs out to remove its beak. The hummingbird goes backward by doing something no other bird can do—it turns its wings over.

Even a bird like the hummingbird has its work to carry out, and it does that each day. The little bird is a good example to us. The Bible says, "We must quickly carry out the tasks assigned us by the one who sent us. The night is coming, and then no one can work" (John 9:4). Try to keep busy during the day so that when it's time for bed, you will have completed what God planned for you.

July

What does a skateboard have to do with the ocean?

Here is the ocean, vast and wide, teeming with life of every kind, both large and small.
PSALM 104:25

Skateboarding started in the early 1960s along the California coastline. Surfboarders used skateboards to practice on land when the weather was too bad to get in the ocean. Skateboards were originally made just like their name, with roller skate wheels attached to a flat board. The wheels were made of steel, clay, and rubber, which didn't stay usable very long, often snagged on obstacles, and didn't work for performing tricks. But at least kids all over the country could ride them like surfboards without having to be near an ocean. In 1973 Frank Nasworthy moved from Virginia to California to surf, and he brought some wheels with him that were difficult for a roller skate company to sell. They were too slow for roller skates, but they turned out to be just right for skateboards. Frank started a company that sold ten thousand sets of his Cadillac Wheels in one year. The wheels allowed skateboarders more ability to maneuver their boards and gave them more traction. More improvements followed on every part of the skateboard, and it soon became a common way for kids to travel. Skateboarders could do all kinds of stunts on sidewalks or special ramps. In 1976 the first paved park built especially for skateboards was created in Port Orange, Florida.

People who loved the ocean were the first to try skateboards. God loves the ocean too—he's the one who made it! The Bible says, "Here is the ocean, vast and wide, teeming with life of every kind, both large and small" (Psalm 104:25). Whenever you see something God made—the ocean or animals or human beings—you can thank him for it. And you can remember that he is the one who gives us life!

July 29

How did a young person name a former planet?

The heavens proclaim the glory of God.
The skies display his craftsmanship.
PSALM 19:1

It was an eleven-year-old girl from England who named what was once considered the ninth planet in our solar system. Until then, the planet that was discovered in 1930 by Clyde Tombaugh was called Planet X. Astronomers had suspected Planet X was there, but Clyde saw it through a telescope he had made himself. He patiently took many photographs of the night sky, and finally Planet X was visible in them. Many people wanted to name the planet, but Venetia Burney's choice for a name was selected out of hundreds of entries sent in. Her suggestion? Pluto. In 2006 a group of scientists decided that Pluto doesn't actually fit the requirements for a planet, so it has now been reclassified as a dwarf planet or a minor planet.

When you see the stars and the moon and the planets and the sun, it takes your breath away because the show is so spectacular. It is amazing to think that God created things we never even would have imagined if we were in charge of thinking them up. The Bible says, "The heavens proclaim the glory of God. The skies display his craftsmanship" (Psalm 19:1).

July

When were oysters used in court?

The LORD demands accurate scales and balances;
he sets the standards for fairness.
PROVERBS 16:11

The ancient Greeks ate a lot of oysters, and they used the empty shells for a number of different purposes. In an election, the Greeks would write the names of their candidates on the oyster shells and then give them to the vote counters. And in court, jury members would write their verdicts on oyster shells. If there were more shells with "guilty" written on them than shells with "not guilty," the person on trial would face punishment—perhaps being sent far away and never allowed to return. The Greek word for oyster was *ostreon*. So if someone was sent away and excluded from the rest of the people, then that person was "ostracized" by a vote of oyster shells.

When you are trying to decide what is fair, you don't need an oyster shell. You need a talk with God. He will tell you what his wisdom is. The Bible says, "The LORD demands accurate scales and balances; he sets the standards for fairness" (Proverbs 16:11).

July 31

What would be a good reason to turn down an invitation to the White House?

The King will say to those on his right, "Come, you who are blessed by my Father, inherit the Kingdom prepared for you from the creation of the world."
MATTHEW 25:34

When famous author James Michener was invited to a celebrity dinner at the White House by President Eisenhower, there was a problem. James had already promised three days earlier to speak that same night at a dinner in honor of the high school teacher he credited with teaching him how to write. He wrote a note to the president to decline his White House invitation and told him why. President Eisenhower sent back a note in his own handwriting that said, "In his lifetime a man lives under fifteen or sixteen presidents, but a really fine teacher comes into his life but rarely. Go and speak at your teacher's dinner."

As a child of God, you have an invitation every day that is much more special than a request to eat dinner with the president of the United States. You have an invitation from God to come and live with him in heaven for eternity. The Bible gives you these words of welcome from Jesus Christ himself: "The King will say to those on his right, 'Come, you who are blessed by my Father, inherit the Kingdom prepared for you from the creation of the world'" (Matthew 25:34). Now that's an invitation you never want to turn down!

August 1

Seaweed is just a weed, right?

Rejoice because your names are registered in heaven.
LUKE 10:20

Actually, when your feet get tangled in seaweed, you are putting knots in somebody else's dinner! Hawaiians use more than seventy-five different kinds of seaweed in their cooking. Many types of seaweed are delicious as sauces and soups. Did you know that seaweed is full of vitamins and minerals? Seaweed is also used in some parts of the world as medicine. Weeds have never been so helpful . . . or delicious!

This plant doesn't deserve a name with the word *weed* in it, because that makes it sound like it is useless and should be thrown away. Seaweed has medicinal benefits, and it is delicious. Maybe someone has called you a name you don't deserve. You don't have to believe or accept that it is truly who you are. As God's child, you can remember how special you are. The Bible tells us what God thinks of you and what he has done with your name because he loves you. "Rejoice because your names are registered in heaven" (Luke 10:20). That's the highest compliment you could receive.

August

Was there really such a thing as a "bat bomb"?

This foolish plan of God is wiser than
the wisest of human plans.
1 CORINTHIANS 1:25

In 1943, the United States Army came up with a plan involving bats. The idea was to attach explosives to the bodies of 30 million bats and then turn them loose in enemy territory with their delayed fuses running. It was hoped that the bats would get into people's attics or under roofs, and then the bats would be exploded, causing widespread damage behind enemy lines. In 1945 the whole operation was ready, at a cost of over $2 million, but the bat bombs were never used. However, a general's car and an aircraft hangar were destroyed when some of the bats accidentally got loose.

Many times the plans of people don't work out, because we don't have the understanding that God does. Sometimes we think we are being smart, when really we are far from it. Invite God to help you when you are solving a problem, and he will give you the wisdom to overcome it. The Bible says, "This foolish plan of God is wiser than the wisest of human plans" (1 Corinthians 1:25).

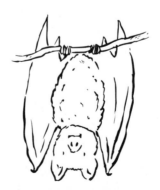

August

Are canaries supposed to bark?

To everyone who is victorious I will give . . . a white stone, and on the stone will be engraved a new name that no one understands except the one who receives it.

REVELATION 2:17

When you hear about the Canary Islands, you might guess they got their name from all the beautiful little yellow finch birds that live there. But you would be wrong. When the Romans first came to the islands, what they saw were large packs of roaming wild dogs. So they called the islands Insula Canaria, which means "island of the dogs." It was much later when the yellow birds got the name *canary* to match.

The meaning of the Canary Islands' name is surprising until you know the reason behind it. We have names given to us by our parents, but we also have a surprise name that God will keep a secret until we are in heaven with him. He has chosen this name especially for us, and it will describe us perfectly. The Bible says, "To everyone who is victorious I will give . . . a white stone, and on the stone will be engraved a new name that no one understands except the one who receives it" (Revelation 2:17).

August 4

What did a little girl discover in the cave?

Good news from far away is like cold water to the thirsty.
PROVERBS 25:25

When Maria Sanz de Sautuola was eight years old, she discovered something that no one except her father would believe she found. Maria and her father often went exploring together in a cave on their property in northern Spain. Maria's father found out about the cave because a man who was hunting with his dog suddenly couldn't see his pet but still heard it barking. He rescued his dog from the crack it had fallen into, which turned out to be the opening to the cave. When Maria's father explored the cave further, he took Maria with him. She would hold the candle while he dug in the ground, or sometimes she dug a little herself. They found pieces of tools, pottery, shells, and bone—all near the entrance. But Maria wanted to see farther into the cave, and one day in 1879 her father allowed her to take the candle and go in a little deeper than they had gone before. When he heard her yell, "Toros! Toros!" he couldn't imagine why she was screaming about bulls in the cave, but he ran in to rescue her. She pointed, and there they were on the wall. Cave drawings! They were thousands of years old but had been beautifully preserved because the cave was sealed up for so long. Maria's father knew that other cave drawings had been found in France, and he wrote letters inviting French professors to come and see the drawings. But the French did not believe the drawings in Spain could be real. They accused Maria's father of hiring someone to paint them and would not even come to see. Finally, many years later, the French professors came, and that is when the discovery became famous and the professors apologized for not believing before.

Maria's family wrote many letters to tell the story of the cave. But the most important letter you could ever write would be to tell someone the story of Jesus. Why not try it? The Bible says, "Good news from far away is like cold water to the thirsty" (Proverbs 25:25). Send a little of God's love to someone soon!

Au**g**ust

Where does the world's smallest fish live?

Whoever is the least among you is the greatest.
LUKE 9:48

In Hawaii there is an ocean fish that native Hawaiian people simply call O. Since it has such a short name, you might think it's small, but that's not the case. Then there is a much smaller Hawaiian fish with a much longer name: homomomonukunukuaguk. But the smallest fish of all lives in the creeks of the Philippines. Called pandaka pygmea, it measures only 6/16 of an inch and is almost transparent. The only parts of the fish you can really see are its eyes, which are large for its body. Never mind trying to catch this fish with a fishing pole, though—it is only about the size of an ant!

God has a different way of looking at things than the world does. People like to be the biggest, the best, and the strongest. But God looks at the heart, and he searches for those who are willing to be humble and serve others, not people who expect to be served. Just as the little fish has the big name and the big fish has the shortest name, God will make sure that we get our reward for volunteering to be the least instead of the most. "Whoever is the least among you is the greatest" (Luke 9:48).

August

What did a raisin start out as?

Other seed fell among rocks. It began to grow,
but the plant soon wilted and died for lack of moisture.
LUKE 8:6

Before a raisin turns brown and before it gets wrinkled and before it shrinks, what is it? Raisins start out as grapes that are juicy and plump and full of liquid. Then the grapes are dried. As the water leaves the grapes, they turn from red or green to a dark brown, and the skin of the grapes starts to shrink. The skin gets wrinkles because there is no water left inside to keep it stretched smooth. You would be telling the truth if you said your box of raisins is really a box of old, shriveled grapes. And what does the word *raisin* mean? It's the French word for "grape."

Without water, a grape becomes a raisin. But if plants don't have water, they're in big trouble. The Bible explains it this way: "Other seed fell among rocks. It began to grow, but the plant soon wilted and died for lack of moisture" (Luke 8:6). Humans need water too—not just for our bodies but also for our spiritual thirst. If we don't have God and his Word to help us grow, we'll get dry and shriveled up . . . much worse than a raisin!

August

Why did people wear those wacky glasses?

A glad heart makes a happy face;
a broken heart crushes the spirit.
PROVERBS 15:13

In the earliest black-and-white movies, actors had to wear green makeup while being filmed, because the film in those days was only sensitive to red light, which changed the way objects and people appeared on-screen. But it was the audience that looked odd in the 1950s, when cardboard 3-D glasses, with one red-tinted lens and one green-tinted lens, were worn by everyone watching the movie. Starting in 1952, some movies were made in 3-D (meaning three-dimensional), which made objects appear to be jumping right off the screen when people watched through the special glasses. The movies were fun to watch at first, but the fad that was supposed to be a huge success never really caught on with the public. The movies were poorly made, blurry, and gave people headaches. Technology has advanced since then, and now they can make 3-D movies that don't require funny glasses.

"A glad heart makes a happy face; a broken heart crushes the spirit" (Proverbs 15:13). The Bible encourages us to laugh and have fun and enjoy the funny things we see around us. Being cheerful will make your day brighter.

August

Why did a father encourage his children to play with food at the table?

I am the living bread that came down from heaven.
Anyone who eats this bread will live forever.
JOHN 6:51

George Lerner had an idea after his kids had been playing with their food at mealtimes and nothing seemed to stop them—not punishing or scolding or even begging. George sat down with some supplies and began to entertain his children. He stuck thumbtacks into a potato to make a smile. Bottle caps became the eyes, and the nose was a strawberry on a toothpick. Although the original name for his creation was Funny Faces for Food, you have probably guessed that George had just created the first Mr. Potato Head. Plastic eyes, ears, mouths, noses, and other parts were made, and later on, a plastic potato was added so people wouldn't be wasting food. Mr. Potato Head was the first toy ever to be advertised on television, and George Lerner may have been the first dad ever to be happy his kids were playing with food instead of eating it.

Maybe there have been times you were so hungry you could barely wait for the next meal or snack. God does care that you have enough food to eat, but did you know there's something you need even more? The Bible tells us what Jesus said about himself: "I am the living bread that came down from heaven. Anyone who eats this bread will live forever" (John 6:51). Jesus gives you all you need to live forever. He's the one your soul is hungry for.

August

What kind of hats did the first baseball players wear?

May he equip you with all you need for doing his will.
HEBREWS 13:21

When organized baseball began in the 1850s, the players wore straw hats—the kind with a brim that went all the way around the hat. When America became involved in the Civil War, the soldiers wore a hat that had a visor in front. After the war was over, baseball players began copying the uniforms the soldiers had worn, and that's how the easily recognized baseball cap with a visor came to be the standard headgear for the sport.

The equipment that baseball players use for their sport includes caps and bats. Christians need equipment to follow God too. The Bible says that Jesus will "equip you with all you need for doing his will" (Hebrews 13:21). When you use the tools that God provides for you, you will certainly be a winner in the Lord's eyes.

August

What do a deer and a dollar bill have in common?

Choose a good reputation over great riches.
PROVERBS 22:1

The clue to this riddle is in the nickname people gave a dollar bill—a "buck." That name came from what you could buy for a dollar in the 1700s in America. The hide or pelt of a male deer was priced at a dollar, and the name for a male deer is a buck, so people used the same word for both the deer and the dollar bill.

Money can be useful, and many people wish they had a lot of it. But money is not the most important thing for you to want. Being someone people trust and consider a friend is a better thing to ask God for. The Bible says, "Choose a good reputation over great riches" (Proverbs 22:1). Having money will not make you a good person, but giving your soul to God will make your life great.

August

11

What were the rules of the road?

God's law is written in their hearts, for their
own conscience and thoughts either accuse
them or tell them they are doing right.
ROMANS 2:15

In 1909 in America, there were few traffic laws of any kind. People could pretty much drive however they wanted to, and it was still legal. In fact, at that time, only twelve states even required that drivers have drivers' licenses at all. In England, driving tests were not given to license would-be drivers until 1935, after people had been driving for almost twenty-four years.

Just as many drivers drove responsibly for all those years without a license, it pleases God when you choose to do the right thing in your own life, even when no one is forcing you to. God knows you and knows your good heart, and he rejoices that you are a trustworthy person. The Bible says, "God's law is written in their hearts, for their own conscience and thoughts either accuse them or tell them they are doing right" (Romans 2:15). You are giving praise to the Lord when you choose well.

August

How do you know how "hot" spicy food really is?

Who else has held the oceans in his hand?
Who has measured off the heavens with his fingers?
Who else knows the weight of the earth or has
weighed the mountains and hills on a scale?
ISAIAH 40:12

There is a way to measure how hot a food is—it is called the Scoville scale, after Wilbur Scoville, who invented the test for hotness and the scale to measure it. It all starts with an ingredient called capsaicin, which is what makes peppers taste hot. Wilbur decided to gather a group of people and ask them to swish part of a pepper combined with sugar water around in their mouths. Then they would try a different pepper and decide which one was hotter—the first or the second. The hotter the taste, the higher the number on the Scoville scale. Sweet peppers measure 0, jalapeño peppers get 1,000 to 5,000 Scoville units, and the world's hottest pepper, the Scotch bonnet, earns 300,000 Scoville units.

It took a lot of work to figure out how to measure the hotness of peppers. Can you imagine what it would take to measure the whole world? The Bible draws our attention to this question: "Who else has held the oceans in his hand? Who has measured off the heavens with his fingers? Who else knows the weight of the earth or has weighed the mountains and hills on a scale?" (Isaiah 40:12). Creating the universe was not hard at all for God—he knew long before he created it exactly what the measurements would be.

August

Do sharks have metal detectors?

Anyone who obeys God's laws and teaches them
will be called great in the Kingdom of Heaven.
MATTHEW 5:19

They don't have detectors for metal, but they do have detectors for food that work in a similar way. People can use metal detectors to find metal objects buried under the ground. The detector creates electrical fields that penetrate the soil. When something metal, such as a coin, is covered up nearby, it interacts with the electrical field, and a signal is sent to the earphones that are worn while a person uses the metal detector. Then the coin can be located, dug up, and looked at. A shark's nose operates in much the same way as a metal detector. Sharks' noses have special organs in them called ampullae of Lorenzini. These organs can detect the tiny electrical signals a fish produces when it twitches its muscles. Even though the fish may be buried in sand and completely out of sight, the shark's nose can still tell where the fish is. It blows away the sand and snatches the fish.

The shark follows the laws of nature that God created. How much more important it is for us to learn and listen to God's plans for us! The Bible says, "Anyone who obeys God's laws and teaches them will be called great in the Kingdom of Heaven" (Matthew 5:19). God has worked out all the details for how we can have the best possible life, with an even better life to follow in heaven. We just need to study what he wants us to follow to get there.

August

Where do the butterflies go?

The earth will yield its harvests, and God,
our God, will richly bless us.
PSALM 67:6

Throughout the summer, all across America, you can see beautiful black and orange monarch butterflies flitting and flying peacefully. But starting in August, they all begin a five-thousand-mile journey to the exact same place on earth—where they came from last spring: the High Sierra mountains of Mexico, to a spot more than ten thousand feet high. On average, it takes the monarch butterflies forty days to arrive. They travel in flocks, sometimes moving along at thirty-five miles an hour on a breeze. Their cool and quiet secret spot wasn't discovered until 1975. When the 300 million butterflies are there through the American winter, it is said that the trees appear to be covered from the ground to the tips with orange flowers. In March, the butterflies rise up from the mountains of Mexico and begin the journey back to America. They lay their eggs in Texas and Louisiana, and when the caterpillars hatch, these monarchs will continue the rest of the journey across the United States until winter comes once again.

It is incredible to think that an insect can take as long a journey as the monarch butterfly does and still care for itself along the way. But God created this world with a delicate balance to make sure the animals are provided for. That means he arranged for the rains and the growing flowers long before the butterflies even knew they'd need them. The Bible reminds us, "The earth will yield its harvests, and God, our God, will richly bless us" (Psalm 67:6). He does this just in the correct times and places—the way God always does things!

August

What was so good about a cut?

The LORD will guide you continually, giving you water
when you are dry and restoring your strength.
ISAIAH 58:11

Conrad Geiser invented an antistatic sheet for the dryer, because he saw that his wife kept wondering when to go down the three flights of their apartment building to pour the fabric softener into the washing machine they used there. He sold his idea to a company that then hired him to work on improving it. Employees at the company brought their laundry to work so tests could be done on it. One of the ladies in charge of doing the laundry was Agnes Mcqueary. She noticed that when there was only a small load of clothes in the dryer, the antistatic tissue would get pulled to the air outlet of the dryer, where it blocked the flow of air. This caused the dryer to shut itself off, and the clothes didn't get dry. Agnes thought about this problem and what could be done to fix it. She took some of the tissues home and made an improvement on them, just using her kitchen table and a knife. She cut some slits in the antistatic sheet. That one small change made a big difference, and the dryer didn't get clogged anymore.

It is very rewarding to think of a solution to a problem that's been bothering you. God gives us that gift of problem solving. Ask him for help when you need it. The Bible tells us, "The LORD will guide you continually, giving you water when you are dry and restoring your strength" (Isaiah 58:11).

August

What does God know about you that you don't even know about yourself?

The very hairs on your head are all numbered.
MATTHEW 10:30

Consider your hair. Each individual hair grows out of its own hair follicle—you have between 100,000 and 150,000 hair follicles on your scalp. Each hair follicle can grow twenty hairs, one at a time, during the course of your lifetime. Yet God knows exactly how many hairs are on your head at any given time. Maybe you think multiplication will get you close to knowing what God knows. But there's another fact about your hair: since it doesn't grow all at the same time, you have new hairs coming in and old ones falling out all the time. So how many hairs do you have on your head today?

The Bible tells us, "The very hairs on your head are all numbered" (Matthew 10:30). Not only does God know how many hairs are on your head right at this very minute, but he knows when one falls out or another one grows in. He also knows how many hairs are on the head of each student in your class and on the heads of all the people in your school, in your town, in every town, and in every part of the world! To us, that's an impossible number of hairs to keep track of. But to God, who made each person, it is just a small thing compared to everything else he knows about us.

August

How did a man who was blind make it safer for people to drive a car?

Do not neglect the spiritual gift you received.
1 TIMOTHY 4:14

Not many young people build gasoline-powered cars, but at the age of twelve, Robert Teeter did, even though he had been blinded in an accident when he was five. But Robert wasn't finished working on cars. When he was older, he was riding in a car when he began noticing the sounds of other cars' engines around him. He could tell that the cars were going faster and then slower and then faster again. He thought he could help drivers stay at the same speed all the time, which might save gas and avoid accidents. Robert made a device called the Speedostat. The driver could select a number, like 55, and push a button. The car would not go over 55 miles an hour, even when the gas pedal was tapped. But the Speedostat only worked halfway, because the cars still slowed down. Robert wasn't satisfied; he wanted a device that controlled the car at the same steady pace. The problem was finally solved in 1956 when Robert made an adjustment to his invention and created a true cruise control, which drivers can use to keep the car at just one speed. Because drivers weren't going faster and slowing down so much, they could pay more attention to problems that might come along, like other drivers who weren't being careful or animals running across the highway. Amazingly, it was a man who couldn't see who made watching the road easier for everyone else.

Listening to the sounds of cars helped Robert invent something new. He couldn't see, so he paid special attention to what he heard. Each of us has some talent we can do especially well. Try to discover which things you are good at, and God will be pleased that you found the gifts he gave you. The Bible says, "Do not neglect the spiritual gift you received" (1 Timothy 4:14). God has a plan for you, and he has equipped you with all the talents you will need.

August 18

Which animal was chosen to be the first animal-shaped balloon?

May you have the power to understand, as all God's people should, how wide, how long, how high, and how deep his love is. May you experience the love of Christ, though it is too great to understand fully. Then you will be made complete with all the fullness of life and power that comes from God.

EPHESIANS 3:18-19

The very first time you could have made a toy balloon on your own was in 1865, but you needed a kit to make it happen. You had to squirt rubber and glue out of a syringe like the ones used for shots. The balloon that formed at the end of the syringe then had to be hung to dry for about four minutes before you could pull it off and tie a knot. But in 1931, an exciting thing happened at the annual Patriots' Day parade in Massachusetts—the first animal-shaped toy balloon was created. Neil Tillotson, who worked for a rubber company, had been experimenting. He drew an animal face with ears, cut it out of cardboard, and dipped the cardboard into a new kind of rubber, called latex, to see what would happen. When the face dried and was blown up with air after being pulled off the cardboard—surprise! There was a cat's face, complete with painted whiskers! Two thousand of the cat balloons were sold that day at the parade. After that Mr. Tillotson took a bus trip around the United States to show off the balloons, and he sold enough orders to start making the new toy balloons every day.

You are so much more important to God than a toy balloon. What do you think he fills you—his best invention—full of? The Bible tells us, "May you have the power to understand, as all God's people should, how wide, how long, how high, and how deep his love is. May you experience the love of Christ, though it is too great to understand fully. Then you will be made complete with all the fullness of life and power that comes from God" (Ephesians 3:18-19). God cares about you all the time and wants to fill you up with his love!

August

How did a fifth grader invent a way to help people in wheelchairs?

Fill in the valleys, and level the mountains and hills.
Straighten the curves, and smooth out the rough places.
ISAIAH 40:4

Alison's teacher asked for an invention project, due in two weeks—which started Alison thinking fast. Since Alison used a wheelchair herself, she knew what problems wheelchair users face. Her invention was the "Rampanion," a portable, lightweight ramp that could be folded into a bag and attached to a wheelchair. The person using it could put it on the ground to get up and down over curbs. Alison made a model out of Popsicle sticks, and her dad helped her build the real Rampanion after they improved the design several times. The work was worth it: her project won the fifth grade grand prize at an inventor's convention, and it had a great deal of potential to really help people at the same time.

Alison had a special understanding of how important it is for people in wheelchairs to have easier ways to get around. She found a way to do exactly what the Bible talks about: "Fill in the valleys, and level the mountains and hills. Straighten the curves, and smooth out the rough places" (Isaiah 40:4). And it's not just land or sidewalks God is talking about. He will help us clear the way so his glory can be seen in our lives.

August

Can you top this toy?

A gentle answer deflects anger.
PROVERBS 15:1

The top is a toy that comes from ancient times and existed all over the world. Its name comes from a Dutch word meaning "to whirl." Stone Age people learned about spinning from watching seedpods fall to the ground, and they copied the movements. People in ancient Japan made tops with painted designs that looked amazing when they spun. They also put holes in the tops to make them whistle and added miniature lanterns in them that could be lit at night. Europeans in the Middle Ages made tops as big as people. When it was cold, the villagers would gather and slap the top until it started spinning—this movement of their bodies warmed them up. Some tops were spun with whips, and playing with them became a contest. A skilled top-whipper could make the top jump fifteen feet in the air and land on a target. There were also obstacle races, in which tops would be lifted over piles of snow with a spoon and then be made to jump from ice patch to ice patch. The winner was the person who kept the top spinning the longest. Some American toy manufacturers created tops that gave off sparks, launched a "flying saucer," or could balance on a clothesline.

The most fascinating thing about a top is the way it spins and turns. When you see a top turning around and around, maybe it will remind you of what the Bible says about the best way to turn a bad situation around. It advises, "A gentle answer deflects anger" (Proverbs 15:1). If someone is speaking angry words to you, don't speak angry words back. That person who is upset won't have anyone to fight with if you don't enter into the argument.

August

What's the secret to scissors?

Look at the ravens. They don't plant or harvest or store food in barns, for God feeds them. And you are far more valuable to him than any birds!

LUKE 12:24

Scissors may have been inspired by the jaws of animals and the beaks of birds. The crossbill bird, for example, has an overlap at the tips of its beak so that it can split the scales of a pinecone and then pick out the tiny seeds inside. Human fingers would have a hard time doing the same thing, but with a pair of scissors, we can copy the crossbill. All animal jaws have a hinge that allows the two parts to open and close together again. Scissors have a screw that allows them to open and close the same way. Even a human jaw works like a pair of scissors with teeth stuck to the blades.

God likes it when you notice the way he takes care of every living thing on earth. The Bible tells us, "Look at the ravens. They don't plant or harvest or store food in barns, for God feeds them. And you are far more valuable to him than any birds!" (Luke 12:24). God hopes that you will be amazed when you discover all the different ways he has planned to provide for so many creatures, large and small. Then you will realize how much he loves you and how he uses his power to take care of the needs, large and small, of each one of his children. You are so special to God!

August

What mistake did President Truman find in the White House?

Do all that you can to live in peace with everyone.
ROMANS 12:18

The president of the United States is very busy running the country. That's why it was so unusual for President Harry Truman to be standing in what is called the Green Room at the White House, just staring at the rug. That's when he realized what was bothering him about what he saw. On the rug was printed the presidential seal, which includes an eagle, some arrows, and an olive branch. But the president noticed that the eagle's head was turned in the wrong direction; it was facing the arrows instead of the olive branch. Right away, he requested that the rug be redesigned to correct the mistake.

The meaning in the rug's picture was changed when the eagle's head was facing the arrows. Arrows are used for fighting. The olive branch is a symbol of peace and friendship. It is much more inspirational to think of peace instead of war, so it is good for each president to have a reminder in the room. The Bible tells us, "Do all that you can to live in peace with everyone" (Romans 12:18). That advice is meaningful for presidents, as well as for each one of us.

August

Which invention was called a "slide fastener"?

Take control of what I say, O LORD, and guard my lips.
PSALM 141:3

It was created to replace shoelaces on boots. This invention was taken to the 1893 World's Fair, where twenty thousand people were in attendance, but only twenty of the items (which eventually broke) were sold to the U.S. Postal Service for their mailbags. Fortunately for everyone, even though several improvements needed to be made to their product, the creators didn't give up, and in 1913 the military wanted to use this invention, ordering many of them. Ten years later, the creation finally was used on boots, which was the original goal, but soon it became common on all kinds of clothing. The name it ended up with came from the sound it makes as it slides up and down. You call it the zipper.

You may have heard someone say, "Zip your lips!" when they wanted you to be quiet. Sometimes it is better not to say anything. For example, when you want to yell something mean that will hurt another person's feelings, choose silence instead. It is not always easy, but it is much kinder. The Bible gives you a prayer that will bring you the strength to do the right thing. We are taught to ask, "Take control of what I say, O LORD, and guard my lips" (Psalm 141:3). When you close your mouth like a zipper, you will have more time to think of something nice to say.

August

What dessert was once called the "I-Scream Bar"?

No eye has seen, no ear has heard, and no mind has imagined what God has prepared for those who love him.
1 CORINTHIANS 2:9

Christian K. Nelson was a schoolteacher, and he also owned an ice cream store. One day he noticed that a little boy in his store couldn't decide whether to buy a chocolate bar or some ice cream, because he didn't have enough money for both. Christian wondered if he could make a sweet treat that would blend candy and ice cream together so people could have both at the same time. He began to experiment with how to get a coating of chocolate to stick to some vanilla ice cream. Finally he was successful, and the people in Iowa, where Christian lived, were the first in the world to see the new dessert, called the I-Scream Bar. You may have eaten one of these treats yourself, but you call it another name. After Christian changed the name, this dessert became known as the Eskimo Pie.

Most people save dessert as a treat to eat at the end of a meal. Heaven is better than the most wonderful dessert you can imagine. If you believe in Jesus Christ, heaven is waiting for you to enjoy when your life on earth has come to an end. Just like you wait to eat an after-dinner treat, you can look forward to saving the best reward for last. The Bible says, "No eye has seen, no ear has heard, and no mind has imagined what God has prepared for those who love him" (1 Corinthians 2:9).

August

Which trip would most people take only once?

Do not throw away this confident trust in the Lord.
Remember the great reward it brings you!
HEBREWS 10:35

Imagine you are taking a hot-air balloon trip with Count Zambeccari and two of his assistants back in 1804. You take off from the ground one afternoon in Bologna, Italy, and your balloon starts to rise. At first it seems like fun. But your control of the balloon is not good, and you rise so high that you almost freeze to death. Then the balloon starts going down. By then it is too dark to read the instrument that tells you how high you are. The next thing you know, you are hearing the roar of waves below you, and your balloon with its basket is splashing into the Adriatic Sea. Now you have to lighten the balloon to get it back up in the air, so you throw many things overboard from the basket you're riding in. Up your balloon goes, so fast and high that your sopping-wet clothes freeze solid and it's almost impossible for you to breathe. Once again the balloon starts floating down, and you end up back in the sea, where you are not rescued until after dawn. Count Zambeccari goes ballooning again another day, but you do not! No, thank you!

Many useful items had to be thrown off the balloon to make the trip safer. When you travel with God at your side, he wants you to hold on to what is valuable—your belief in him—and bring it with you. The Bible says, "Do not throw away this confident trust in the Lord. Remember the great reward it brings you!" (Hebrews 10:35). God promises to deliver you safely to heaven. He is the best pilot you could ever hope to find.

August

What made groups of soldiers turn blue?

The one who is the true light, who gives light
to everyone, was coming into the world.
JOHN 1:9

It all started in 1916 with Dr. Edmund Newton Harvey, a scientist who was interested in studying bioluminescence, or what makes sea creatures glow. It was hard to see the creatures underwater, and the creatures didn't live very long when they were removed from their habitats. But Edmund found a solution in Japan, where he discovered the very small shrimplike ostracods, with their see-through shells. Ostracods are amazing because they can project clouds of blue light from their bodies to scare away other creatures that might want to attack. Edmund found that the ostracod shells could be turned into powder and still show a blue glow up to twenty years later when mixed with water. Edmund went back to America and had ostracods shipped to him there, where he studied them and made many important scientific contributions in the area of bioluminescence. Meanwhile, back in Japan, Japanese soldiers in World War II had also noticed the blue light of the ostracod. They added the shell powder to water and rubbed the blue mixture on their skin. The soldiers then glowed blue, which helped them find each other in the dark.

The Bible makes this prediction about Jesus coming to be born in Bethlehem: "The one who is the true light, who gives light to everyone, was coming into the world" (John 1:9). When we give our hearts to Jesus, we do not need to find a special glowing paint so we can see in the dark. He makes his plan for our lives clear to us when we follow him step after step. Keep your eyes on Jesus, and he will make sure that you can always see where he is. Then you can always stay right beside him.

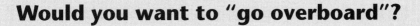

August 27

Would you want to "go overboard"?

He calmed the storm to a whisper and stilled the waves.
PSALM 107:29

To go overboard means you are so enthusiastic and excited about something—sports, for example—that you are likely to get very involved in it and let it take your attention away from your daily life. Where did the phrase *go overboard* come from? It is tied to ships and sailors from long ago. Sailors called the sides of the ship the "board." It was the captain's duty to decide when something on the ship was too old or damaged to be useful, and if it was, he would order the sailors to throw it "over board" into the sea. So when someone says you are going overboard, they mean you are so involved with something, it's as if you went right off the side of the boat and into the ocean where the waves could carry you away.

If you find yourself getting carried away in something like being too involved with sports or video games or talking too long on the phone or just being too noisy or rowdy at home, ask Jesus to calm you down and get things back in balance for you. You can trust him to help you. The Bible says, "He calmed the storm to a whisper and stilled the waves" (Psalm 107:29). Surely he can do the same for you, too.

August

How does a rattlesnake protect itself?

My eyes are always on the LORD, for he rescues
me from the traps of my enemies.
PSALM 25:15

The answer is in its name, of course. The rattlesnake has colors on its body that blend in with where it lives, which is a good way to hide. But the snake could be stepped on by mistake by large animals, so it shakes the rattle in its tail. The noise is loud, and animals run away. The rattlesnake doesn't want to strike and inject its venom unless it is absolutely necessary. If the animal is too big for the rattlesnake to eat, the snake would be wasting its poison. And if the rattlesnake bites and fights, it could be injured along with its enemy.

There are all kinds of dangers in the world; a rattlesnake is just one of them. But as God's children, we do not need to be afraid. No matter what problem you are facing, you have a protector. At all times and in all circumstances, you can say, "My eyes are always on the LORD, for he rescues me from the traps of my enemies" (Psalm 25:15).

August

How could there be a "folding bathtub"?

Wash me clean from my guilt. Purify me from my sin.
PSALM 51:2

In the late 1800s, the only running water in a house came from a pump in the kitchen. It didn't make a difference which room the bathtub was in, because it didn't need to be attached to plumbing pipes in the wall. No matter where it was, the tub still had to be filled with bucketfuls of water that people carried themselves. Since a tub might appear anywhere in the house, some people made bathtubs fancier by building them inside big, decorated wooden cabinets or wardrobes. Each of these showy wooden pieces of furniture, with a bathtub inside, could be opened to pull the bathtub down or fold it out of the cabinet. They could be placed in any room where people wanted to show off their fancy furniture when no one was taking a bath. Inside the cabinet there was also a heater to get the water warm once the tub was full, but when the bath was finished, a faucet at the bottom had to opened so the water could be drained back into buckets and carried outside. Folding the bathtub down was definitely the easiest part of getting a bath ready back then!

It is much easier to take a bath and get clean today than it was several hundred years ago. But there is still only one way to be clean on the inside, and that's by asking God to forgive you and wash away your sins. You can pray like this: "Wash me clean from my guilt. Purify me from my sin" (Psalm 51:2).

August

How did a basketball player get the name "Chicken Man"?

It is better to say nothing than to make
a promise and not keep it.
ECCLESIASTES 5:5

As an incentive, the Ron Krispy Fried Chicken restaurant promised a free fast-food chicken dinner to everyone who bought a ticket to any game that the Houston Rockets played if the team scored 135 points or more. The Rockets had only reached that goal once in eight years, which made it seem like a pretty easy promise never to have to honor. In the 1978 season opener, the Rockets were beating the New York Knicks by forty points in the fourth quarter. But no fans left the game. The announcer had just reminded them of the Krispy promise, and the fans began to yell, "We want chicken! We want chicken!" That's when the Rockets really began to move! When there were fifty-one seconds left in the game and the score was favoring the Rockets 133–83, Mike Dunleavy scored with a layup, and the crowds went wild. The next day, four thousand ticket holders ate a total of $6,000 of free chicken, and Mike Dunleavy had a new nickname—his teammates began calling him "Chicken Man."

Ron Krispy Fried Chicken did the honorable thing by giving all the ticket holders the chicken dinner reward they had been promised. You should always try to keep your word, because as a follower of Christ you want people to believe you when you talk about all the good things he has done for you. The Bible advises, "It is better to say nothing than to make a promise and not keep it" (Ecclesiastes 5:5).

August

How did pilots' uniforms help with the invention of the electric blanket?

He guards the paths of the just and protects
those who are faithful to him.

PROVERBS 2:8

The pilots' uniforms entered the story much later, but it began in 1912, when American inventor S. I. Russell invented an electric heating pad that could be put on the chests of tuberculosis patients to help them breathe better. Even though the heating pad had some flaws—it was small, and the wires were not dependable and could possibly start a fire—many people thought that a full-size electric blanket would be a good idea. But no one could figure out how to make one. Finally, almost thirty years later, during World War II, the problem was solved. The answer came from the Air Force, when electrically heated flying suits were invented to keep pilots warm. A few changes were made, and the suits for flying became blankets for sleeping instead.

We use blankets to protect us from the cold. But God is a much greater protector for us. The Bible says, "He guards the paths of the just and protects those who are faithful to him" (Proverbs 2:8). When you are God's child, you can believe that he will cover your soul like the warmest, softest blanket and keep you wrapped up safely and permanently in his love.

September

Is that real gold on top?

How much better to get wisdom than gold,
and good judgment than silver!
PROVERBS 16:16

Have you ever looked at an important building with a dome on the roof, like a courthouse, and wondered if its round gold top is really gold? Chances are good that it is. Even though it may seem to be a very expensive way to decorate, many buildings do have tops that are decorated with real gold. Gold is a soft metal, and it can be carefully tapped on and spread thinly into what looks like a large amount. This process is called gold leafing, and you would be surprised at how much the leafing can cover. It only takes a lump of gold that weighs about as much as two packs of chewing gum to spread over something as big as a football field! A little gold can go a long way.

Precious metals like gold and silver look valuable and impressive. But the Bible tells us what is really valuable: "How much better to get wisdom than gold, and good judgment than silver!" (Proverbs 16:16). Imagine! You might be on your way to riches of wisdom and good judgment right this minute!

September 2

How has the Bible been important to presidents of the United States?

Grow in the grace and knowledge of our
Lord and Savior Jesus Christ.
2 PETER 3:18

Some of the presidents, including George Washington and John Adams, have given strong clues that the Bible was meaningful to them. It was George Washington who established the custom of kissing the Bible after taking the oath to become president. And John Adams read the entire Bible every year.

Knowing that the leader of a country is seeking the Lord brings joy to the hearts of Christians. Anytime someone wants to "grow in the grace and knowledge of our Lord and Savior Jesus Christ" (2 Peter 3:18), whether that person is a president or not, it is a time for thankfulness and encouragement.

September

What made a chair fit for a king?

God reigns above the nations, sitting on his holy throne.
PSALM 47:8

Several hundred years ago, there were not many chairs with high backs on them. Those few were reserved for very important people, like kings, to sit on. Everybody else used stools or benches. In the fifteenth and sixteenth centuries, there was so little furniture of any kind that even kings owned palaces that were empty unless they brought their chairs with them from another one of their palaces. Eventually, everyone was allowed to sit in those special chairs with high backs, and soon chairs with backs began to appear everywhere. Another kind of chair, the rocking chair, was invented many years later in America. At first skates were attached to the bottom of a chair so it would have movement. Then two curved pieces of wood were added to a chair to make it rock. Since the curved wooden slats wore down and ruined carpets, rocking chairs were also called "carpet cutters."

Special seats were reserved for kings to show how important and respected they were. Did you know that the King of kings has an even more special place to sit? He has a throne reserved only for him, because no one else could ever rule with the kind of power and love he has. The Bible tells us, "God reigns above the nations, sitting on his holy throne" (Psalm 47:8).

September 4

What are those crab shells doing on the sand?

The LORD . . . blesses the home of the upright.
PROVERBS 3:33

Many people think that all the crab shells they find on the sand are the remains of crabs that have died. Sometimes that's true. Most often, though, they are just abandoned shells. Just as snakes shed their skins, crabs grow bigger and need to get out of their small shells to grow bigger houses for themselves. They leave their old shells behind, and these shells sometimes wash up on the shore.

Sometimes, just like the crab, we think the house we live in isn't right for us. Maybe we believe it is too small or not fancy enough or not filled with all the newest toys and technology. But God cares much more about one thing that's inside your house—he cares about you. The Bible tells us what God thinks about where we live: "The LORD . . . blesses the home of the upright" (Proverbs 3:33). That's the best kind of home to live in!

September

Who stuck to making gum?

*My people will live as long as trees, and my chosen
ones will have time to enjoy their hard-won gains.*
ISAIAH 65:22

When William Wrigley Jr. was eleven, he kept getting suspended from
school about once every three weeks. He was smart but bored in school,
and he finally ran away to be a newspaper boy in New York City. Then
he became a sailor. But finally he returned home to work in his father's
soap factory. At the age of twelve, he spent six days a week, ten hours a
day doing the hardest job—stirring the soap with a paddle. He eventually got promoted to salesman, and he loved that job of traveling around
talking to people. He even became the top salesman. Later he started
his own soap company. To get companies to buy and sell his soap, he
offered them prizes. He tried umbrellas, purses, razors, scales, and baking powder, which was his customers' favorite. In 1915, William started
selling baking powder instead of soap, and he gave gum as a reward with
each purchase. William then noticed that his customers liked the gum
best of all, and he finally decided to make a chewing gum business. He
advertised in interesting ways. He sent free samples of gum in the mail
to 8.5 million people in the American phone book. He sent two-year-
old children two free pieces of gum on their birthdays. And he was the
first person to invent a singing commercial for the radio—all to make
Wrigley's a household name for gum.

What a long road it was for William Wrigley! And yet he was faithful
to his talent, and he saw his reward. The Bible says, "My people will live
as long as trees, and my chosen ones will have time to enjoy their hard-
won gains" (Isaiah 65:22). Stick with something long enough, and your
hard work will eventually pay off.

September

Does everything with the word *scotch* in its name come from Scotland?

In the beginning the Word already existed.
JOHN 1:1

Actually, long ago the word *scotch* had a meaning all its own. To scotch something meant to cut or mark it or make lines on it. Take the candy butterscotch. When it is being made, the candy is cut, or scotched, into small pieces. But what about the game hopscotch? To play that game, the sidewalk must be marked with chalk to divide it into squares that you jump onto. You have just scotched the sidewalk with your chalk. So even if you eat butterscotch candy while playing hopscotch, it won't mean you are anywhere near Scotland!

There are all kinds of words and all kinds of explanations of where they came from. But there is one Word that stands apart from the rest. The Word with a capital *W* means God's Word, or the Bible, and it also means Jesus. The Bible tells us, "In the beginning the Word already existed" (John 1:1). One Word, one Jesus. That is the most important Word you can ever learn about.

September 7

What delightful drink was invented because someone ran out of ingredients?

History merely repeats itself. It has all been done before. Nothing under the sun is truly new.
ECCLESIASTES 1:9

The idea for ice cream was brought to America by Thomas Jefferson, who first tasted it in France when he was an ambassador and brought the recipe back to Philadelphia. In the 1800s, Philadelphia was considered the ice cream capital of the world. It was there, at a fair in 1874, that ice cream soda was invented by mistake. Robert Green was selling a drink made of carbonated water, cream, and syrup at a soda fountain when he realized that so many people at the fair had bought his drink that he had run out of cream. Quickly he decided to add ice cream instead of cream to his drink, and the ice cream soda was instantly created. It proved so popular that instead of earning his usual six dollars a day from the sale of his old drink, Robert brought in six hundred dollars a day with the new ice cream soda.

It must have been fun for Robert to come up with a new combination of tastes for people to enjoy. But when it comes down to it, the most important thing to discover is the truths of God's Word. His Word is new every time you hear it, because it is always helping you to discover something even more loving about God's heart. As the Bible puts it, "History merely repeats itself. It has all been done before. Nothing under the sun is truly new" (Ecclesiastes 1:9). Stick with God to find out what's truly worth learning about for eternity.

September 8

What's the connection between tall buildings and boats?

Your unfailing love is higher than the heavens.
Your faithfulness reaches to the clouds.
PSALM 108:4

They're connected by a name—skyscraper. The name first started with boats. Skyscrapers were the tallest sails on huge boats that had many sails and traveled by wind power. When you looked at those sails reaching way up into the air, they seemed to be touching the sky. When buildings began to be built taller in the late 1800s, people were amazed to see how high they could be. Early buildings were just built with bricks, which wouldn't stay up if they were stacked too high. But when steel was added to the construction for strength, buildings could be made much taller. Because the new higher buildings reminded people of the high sails they saw on the sea, they borrowed the name.

As humans, we are impressed when people build something much taller than we are. But nothing a human builds will ever be high enough to reach where God can go. The Bible says, "Your unfailing love is higher than the heavens. Your faithfulness reaches to the clouds" (Psalm 108:4). When you are impressed with the mightiness of God, you are focusing your admiration in the right place.

September

Why won't you find a cashew in its shell?

The seeds that fell on the good soil represent honest, good-hearted people who hear God's word, cling to it, and patiently produce a huge harvest.

LUKE 8:15

The first reason is that a cashew isn't even a nut, although many people think it is. A cashew is actually a seed of a fruit called the cashew apple. This sour, pear-shaped fruit is about the size of a regular apple and grows on the cashew tree. Below each cashew apple, you can see nutlike pods of seeds shaped like commas hanging down. Each seedpod has two leathery layers covering it. In between the two layers is a blackish oil called cardol, which is so poisonous and irritating that it is used to make insecticide. The outer nut pod is difficult to remove and has to be taken off without making contact with the cardol. Only machines are able to do this. Then the cashew inside is roasted so no dangerous cardol remains. So when you see cashews in the grocery store, you never see the pods they came out of.

The cashew is considered a valuable and tasty treat. As God's children, we can introduce people to something they want very much—the message of salvation. By being kind and welcoming, we can encourage people to listen to us. The Bible tells us, "The seeds that fell on the good soil represent honest, good-hearted people who hear God's word, cling to it, and patiently produce a huge harvest" (Luke 8:15). God can use us to plant seeds that grow in people's hearts as they learn to love Jesus.

September 10

How do you teach a parrot to talk?

Remember the words of the Lord Jesus.
ACTS 20:35

Parrots can be taught to talk. The number of words each bird can learn depends on how patient its owner is, how talented the individual bird is at copying and repeating and remembering, and how young the parrot was when it first began to receive training. Well-trained parrots are capable of knowing a few hundred words, and some have been known to speak entire passages from memory with practice. There have been some reliable reports, although this has not been confirmed, that one parrot was even taught to recite the entire Lord's Prayer. The United States Biological Survey says that there is no physical or biological reason to doubt that a parrot could indeed recite the prayer.

Teaching a parrot to speak new words is a fun hobby. But for people, the Bible tells us that the most important thing is to "remember the words of the Lord Jesus" (Acts 20:35). The best words to keep in your memory are his. In the words of Jesus you will find every important thing you need to know about life.

September

Which spelling mistake created an embarrassing story in the newspaper?

The word of the LORD holds true,
and we can trust everything he does.
PSALM 33:4

It happened after President Teddy Roosevelt was inaugurated. A type-setter, who in those days had to choose each letter that would be used in printing an article, replaced one very important letter with another by mistake. The result surprised everyone, including the poor reporter, when the article was printed in the newspaper about the ceremony of Teddy Roosevelt's presidential oath of office. The words that appeared in the paper were: "For sheer democratic dignity, nothing could exceed the moment when, surrounded by the Cabinet and a few distinguished citizens, Mr. Roosevelt took his simple bath, as President of the United States." Can you imagine what readers thought when they read that Teddy Roosevelt took a bath, instead of an oath, in front of all those people on that important day?

Jesus tells us, "The word of the LORD holds true, and we can trust everything he does" (Psalm 33:4). You will never have to wonder if what you read in the Bible is some kind of mistake like what you might read in the newspaper. God has carefully given us every word of the Bible to show us how to live, and none of the words are wrong or misleading. The wrong spelling can change a word's meaning a lot, but God's Word never changes.

September

Who is Big Ben?

The LORD is king! He is robed in majesty. . . .
Your throne, O LORD, has stood from time immemorial.
PSALM 93:1-2

In London, England, there is a group of buildings called the Houses of Parliament. There you will find a tower with a clock in it and a bell that rings out the time each hour. Most people will tell you that the name of the clock or the clock tower is Big Ben. But now you will know something most other people don't! The clock itself does not have a name at all, and neither does the clock tower—it is the *bell* in the tower that is named Big Ben. The bell weighs thirteen tons, and the hammer that makes it ring weighs four hundred pounds. At the time the bell was installed in 1859, Sir Benjamin Hall was the commissioner of the project, and that is why the bell is called Big Ben.

Whenever you see a watch or a clock or check the schedule for your next sports practice or notice that it's time to get to class, take a moment to think about who God is. The Bible describes him this way: "The LORD is king! He is robed in majesty. . . . Your throne, O LORD, has stood from time immemorial" (Psalm 93:1-2). Throughout all time, God never changes.

September 13

What old idea made a new kind of pen?

The Sovereign LORD has given me his words of
wisdom, so that I know how to comfort the weary.
ISAIAH 50:4

The first place you could buy a felt-tip pen was in Japan. It was created in 1962 by Yukio Horie and Masao Miura, who wanted to provide people with a way to write more gracefully. They were inspired by thinking about the way the symbols of Japanese writing were so beautifully written with a paintbrush in days gone by.

The felt-tip pen made it easier to write smoothly. Having the right tools to do a job well makes a big difference. As God's children, we have the job of sharing the Good News about God's grace with people who are sad. If you think the task is too hard and you don't know how to do it, remember that God will give you the right words when you need them. The Bible says, "The Sovereign LORD has given me his words of wisdom, so that I know how to comfort the weary" (Isaiah 50:4). You can help people have more joy in their lives, using the tools that the Lord will provide.

September 14

Which came first: the chicken or the egg?

God created great sea creatures and every living thing that scurries and swarms in the water, and every sort of bird—each producing offspring of the same kind. And God saw that it was good. Then God blessed them.
GENESIS 1:21-22

For almost three thousand years, no one was interested in eating chickens—everyone kept chickens so they could eat the eggs. Only chickens that were too old to lay eggs anymore were eaten for their meat. Mass production of chickens and eggs began in the 1800s, which meant that not every household had to raise and keep their own animals. But in 1963, it was still a luxury to have chicken meat that wasn't from old chickens. It wasn't until the 1970s that chicken meat became a favorite with families. If chickens are given hormones and have been selectively bred to mature faster, they grow old enough to be eaten in forty days. If left to nature, a chicken isn't considered grown until it's at least eighty days old.

God made each of his creatures special, with a certain purpose for every one. The Bible tells us, "God created great sea creatures and every living thing that scurries and swarms in the water, and every sort of bird—each producing offspring of the same kind. And God saw that it was good. Then God blessed them" (Genesis 1:21-22). Knowing that God likes his creatures makes us appreciate them also!

September

Can squirrels fly?

Not a single sparrow can fall to the ground
without your Father knowing it.
MATTHEW 10:29

You may never have seen it happen, because flying squirrels are nocturnal and do their gymnastics at night. In America, there are northern flying squirrels in northern states and southern flying squirrels in eastern and southern states. The flying squirrel doesn't flap wings to fly like birds do—it basically glides across long spaces. There is a membrane that attaches the squirrel's front legs to its back legs. The squirrel climbs a tree, moves its head back and forth to check where it's going, then stretches its legs out to activate the membrane. The membrane acts like a sail, and the squirrel takes off into the air. It can go around objects in its way by using its tail as a rudder to steer. It can glide fifty feet or more, even though it is only about the length of your forearm. It can even travel the length of a football field if it starts up around one hundred feet on its tree perch to get going. It lands feet first on a tree trunk and then quickly moves to the other side of the tree in case a predator is following and it needs to make a speedy getaway. Look for flying squirrels on fall nights, because that is when they are most busy gathering nuts for winter.

God equipped the flying squirrel with everything it would need to take care of itself. And God has equipped you with every talent and gift you will need to fulfill his purposes for you. The Bible says, "Not a single sparrow can fall to the ground without your Father knowing it" (Matthew 10:29). God watches over everything you do and everything that happens to you so that he can be by your side whenever you call for him.

September

Why were skates made of bones?

Whoever claims to live in him must walk as Jesus did.
1 JOHN 2:6, NIV

The earliest ice skates that ever existed were cow, horse, or reindeer bones tied to the feet with leather straps. Scandinavia, with all its ice, seems like the place where ice skates would have been needed most, so it is believed they were invented there around 1000 BC. Because metal was scarce, bones were used instead. The oldest ice skates that still exist today came from Sweden. Skates with metal blades didn't appear until about the 1400s, but people in England and Holland were enjoying skating on ice from the twelfth century onward.

God wants you to follow him. He doesn't care if you come to him by boat, by car, or by skates. He just wants to direct the way you live so that you will be eternally happy. The Bible tells us, "Whoever claims to live in him must walk as Jesus did" (1 John 2:6, NIV). That doesn't mean we need to be barefoot or wear shoes like his. The following that Jesus wants us to do takes place in our hearts first, and the rest of our bodies will be right behind.

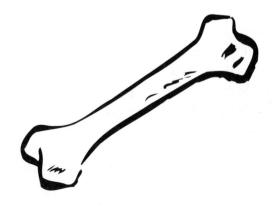

September

17

When can you see a rainbow?

When I see the rainbow in the clouds, I will remember the eternal covenant between God and every living creature on earth.

GENESIS 9:16

Sometimes when it's raining and the sun is still shining, you look up in the sky and see a beautiful rainbow. But if the shower occurs during the noon hour around lunchtime, you won't find a rainbow glittering overhead. A rainbow can be seen through a sunshower only during the morning hours, in the late afternoon, or in the early evening. That's because for you to be able to see a rainbow at all, the sun must be at a certain distance above the horizon.

Whenever you see a rainbow or even just think of one, remember that it is a sign of God's promise of hope for you. The Bible explains what we are promised when it says, "When I see the rainbow in the clouds, I will remember the eternal covenant between God and every living creature on earth" (Genesis 9:16). You are his much-loved child, and he wants you to think about how he keeps you close to him.

September 10

When was a watch first watched?

The Father alone has the authority to set those dates
and times, and they are not for you to know.
ACTS 1:7

The first completely portable clock was invented by a German lock-smith named Peter Henlein around 1500, but it was very awkward. It was the size of a hamburger, had no minute hand, and had a metal cover that had to be lifted to see the time. It had a spring instead of weights to make it work. The wristwatch was invented in Switzerland in 1790, but back then it was called a bracelet watch, and at the time it was considered to be jewelry just for women. In 1810 the sister of Napoleon Bonaparte, a queen herself, requested that a jeweler make her a watch as a bracelet. She received one two years later that even had a thermometer on it. Men's wristwatches were made in 1890 but were still considered too feminine for most men, who preferred to carry pocket watches. In 1904 an inventor from Brazil named Alberto Santos-Dumont needed an easily seen clock to be worn while flying the plane he was building, and Louis Cartier made him a "manly" watch, as Alberto had asked. But it was not until around 1920, when soldiers realized how useful wristwatches were, that people began to think men could wear them. In the 1950s, tuning forks were added inside watches. The battery sent a vibration at a very specific rate to the tuning fork, which has since been replaced by miniature pieces of quartz crystal. These make sure a wristwatch runs accurately to within one minute a year.

Watches and clocks can give us the feeling that we control time, even though we really just watch it pass and try to keep track of it. The Bible reminds us that although we may be able to count hours and minutes and seconds, that doesn't mean we are in charge of them. The Bible says, "The Father alone has the authority to set those dates and times, and they are not for you to know" (Acts 1:7). God knows everything, and we do not.

September

What was one of the first video games?

Be on your guard, not asleep like the others.
Stay alert and be clearheaded.
1 THESSALONIANS 5:6

Pong was the first well-known video game that could be played on a television at home. It consisted of a glowing dot that went back and forth across a line, and players used electronic "paddles," which were tabletop knobs that maneuvered small computer prompters on the screen. The longer you played, the faster the dot moved, so the game would be challenging enough to keep you playing longer. Pong was devised to feel familiar to the players, who recognized it as the electronic version of Ping-Pong. Nolan Bushnell, the founder of the video game company Atari, and employee Al Acorn invented the liquid crystal screen game in 1972. Pong earned 11 million dollars by 1973 because of its popularity.

Video games have changed so much over the years since Pong. Many computerized technologies have appeared, and people often play them so frequently and intensely that they aren't aware of the rest of God's world around them. Be watchful of all you might be missing! The Bible says, "Be on your guard, not asleep like the others. Stay alert and be clearheaded" (1 Thessalonians 5:6). Put down the game, and pay attention to the world around you instead!

September

Why doesn't a jellyfish match its name?

The LORD our God has secrets known to no one.
DEUTERONOMY 29:29

This sea creature is not made of jelly, and it isn't even a fish! The outside of a jellyfish is a gel-like sac that holds almost all pure seawater—more seawater than any other creature—on the inside. If the jellyfish comes out of the water, its body begins to disappear as it dries up. Another odd thing about a jellyfish is that it can shrink or grow larger, depending on how much food is available. Normally it's about twelve inches in size, but if there isn't much for the jellyfish to eat, it can shrink its body down to about the size of a quarter and still be perfectly healthy.

Sometimes we can get very mixed up about what's true—and not just when it comes to jellyfish, either! But we don't have all the knowledge God has. The Bible says, "The LORD our God has secrets known to no one" (Deuteronomy 29:29). We often go by what we see, but our eyes don't always tell the whole story. We are blessed, though, because our Father never makes mistakes like that about us. We are his children, and he knows us perfectly, inside and out.

September 21

Which toy has also been a whistling weapon, a weather watcher, and even a fish catcher?

I stretched out the sky like a canopy and
laid the foundations of the earth.
ISAIAH 51:16

The toy with this interesting history is the kite. Chinese soldiers scared their enemies by hanging stiff paper or pieces of bamboo off a kite. When the wind blew, the sailing kites made whistling sounds and frightened enemy soldiers so they ran away. In the United States, people attached instruments to kites and sent them up to gather weather information before weather balloons and planes and satellites took over this job. And in Asian countries, fishermen sent kites over the water with hooks and lines attached. When a fish bit, the kite was jerked up high into the air, and the fish, hanging from the kite with a hook in its mouth, "flew" back to the fisherman.

Humans have always been interested in the sky. When you fly a kite or watch a thunderstorm or stare at the twinkling stars at night, remember who made all those wonders of the sky for you to see. In the Bible God says, "I stretched out the sky like a canopy and laid the foundations of the earth" (Isaiah 51:16).

September

What's so fascinating about feathers?

He will cover you with his feathers.
He will shelter you with his wings.
PSALM 91:4

Have you ever noticed how many birds you see each day? Every one of them has been equipped by God with a coat of feathers that serve them in all the ways they need. Feathers protect the birds' skin from the weather. Even if they live in the hot desert or the frosty snow country, birds are kept cool or warm by their covering of feathers. Birds stay dry because their feathers are designed so well and laid so thickly over their bodies that no water can get through them. If you hold a feather under a faucet, you will see that the water just runs off. But even though God keeps feathers dry, he doesn't let them get so dry that they break off or crunch up. Instead, birds have oil glands that keep the feathers bendable and usable. Best of all, God designed birds' feathers to make it possible for them to fly.

When you think of how many details God included in the feathers of birds big and small, it is easy to see how much he cares about them. But you are so much more important to God than a bird! You have a soul and a personality, and he loves you very much. If you ever begin to wonder if God really cares about you, think of the birds. The Bible says, "He will cover you with his feathers. He will shelter you with his wings" (Psalm 91:4). All the attention to detail, the protection, and the care God shows for the birds' needs are nothing compared to what he wants to do for you.

September 23

Where did Abraham Lincoln find the nine words he never forgot?

Your word is a lamp to guide my feet and a light for my path.
PSALM 119:105

The book was the story of President George Washington's life; the reader was twelve-year-old Abraham Lincoln. Night after night, Abraham read, until one evening a heavy storm leaked rainwater into his log cabin. Abraham found that the book had been completely soaked, except for the last page. Because the book had been borrowed from a neighbor, Abraham worked to pay for it by clearing off logs from an acre of the farmer's land. Even though the book was gone, Abraham saved in his memory nine words written on that final page. He remembered them for forty years and put them in a speech he wrote when he was president. Maybe you recognize or have even memorized those same nine words yourself. The words—"that these dead shall not have died in vain"—became part of history in one of the most famous speeches ever written, the Gettysburg Address.

There are words that are even more important to remember than the ones Abraham Lincoln memorized. Every word of the Bible is something God wants you to learn from. The Bible says, "Your word is a lamp to guide my feet and a light for my path" (Psalm 119:105). What you learn from the Bible will give you advice on how to live your life well. Choose a verse in the Bible to remember, and you will find more value there than in the words of any other book.

September

What's the story behind the glow-in-the-dark rock?

I say to you that you are Peter (which means "rock"),
and upon this rock I will build my church.
MATTHEW 16:18

Shoemaker Vincenzo Casciarolo found the unusual rock in 1602 when he was busy with his hobby in his hometown of Bologna, Italy. Vincenzo was looking for a special rock that would help make gold. Since then, it has been discovered that there is no such rock, but in Vincenzo's day, many people looked for the special rock they thought would create gold. One day Vincenzo found his special rock. He took it home, turned part of the rock into powder, and heated it up. Of course, it didn't turn anything into gold. But it did do something equally strange and surprising. Vincenzo's rock would store up light when it was left in the sun and then release the light by glowing in the dark. Sometimes Vincenzo mixed the powder with egg whites or water and shaped it into animals. He created the first glow-in-the-dark toys! This unusual rock was called the Bologna Stone or Vincenzo's sun rock, and when Vincenzo showed it to scientists, it helped them learn a lot more about the science of light.

When most of us look at rocks, we don't see the potential in them. They are just ordinary to us. But God has a purpose for the rocks he created. And did you know he has a purpose for ordinary people like us too? Jesus said these words to one of his disciples: "I say to you that you are Peter (which means 'rock'), and upon this rock I will build my church" (Matthew 16:18). Our faith in the Lord can be as unchanging as a rock, and that belief will light up our lives with the brightness of a future spent with God.

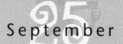

September

Where do you hide a traffic policeman?

Don't hide from your servant; answer me
quickly, for I am in deep trouble!
PSALM 69:17

The first speed trap was for cars racing above the eight-miles-an-hour speed limit in Massachusetts in 1905. Constable Peabody set up his new idea. There were two lookout posts—dead tree stumps placed exactly a mile apart along the road. Behind each one was a policeman with a stopwatch and a telephone. When a car approached, the first policeman clicked his stopwatch and called the next policeman in line, who then clicked his stopwatch at the same time. Then he looked at a speed chart. If the car was speeding, that policeman then called ahead to Constable Peabody, who was standing guard where a roadblock was placed. The plan worked! They caught someone driving at twelve miles an hour— William McAdoo, the police commissioner of New York City!

Although too much speed on the road is not a good thing, there is one time when you hope things move fast. When you pray for the help of the Lord, you hope he will come to your aid immediately. Like one of the writers of Psalms, you might ask, "Don't hide from your servant; answer me quickly, for I am in deep trouble!" (Psalm 69:17). Leave the speeding to God, and you will be happy to see him hurrying to help you.

September

What colors mean danger?

Sustain me, and I will be rescued.
PSALM 119:117

When you see yellow and black stripes, do you think of bees and wasps? Other insects do—they have learned that wasps and bees can sting and injure, so they make sure to stay away from the colors yellow and black. We humans have copied the yellow and black colors in some of our warning signs to remind people that danger is nearby. Another color that warns creatures to stay away is red. In South America there is a poison dart frog with bright red and black markings. Each frog has enough poison in its skin to kill 1,500 people! All the other animals are reminded by the frog's red and black colors to stay away. Similarly, people chose the color red to shine from traffic lights when cars are supposed to stop. But we humans aren't the only ones who have copied the colors of danger. Hoverflies are harmless insects, but their colors are yellow and black like the wasp, so other insects stay away just because the hoverfly looks dangerous.

In the world God created, he thought of everything. He took care of even the smallest details, like giving his creatures a way to protect themselves and also a way to warn others to stay away. God gave us a way to protect ourselves too, and he tells us how in the Bible: by asking for his help. The Bible gives us an example of what to say: "Sustain me, and I will be rescued" (Psalm 119:117). As God's children, we don't have to wear certain colors to protect ourselves. We just need to turn to him, and we can be confident he will take care of our souls.

September

How did a group of detectives accidentally fingerprint themselves?

I look at the night sky and see the work of your fingers—
the moon and the stars you set in place.
PSALM 8:3

In 1982 an aquarium's glass cracked in a Japanese crime lab where detectives were studying ways to trap criminals. One evening the detectives decided to fix the glass. They emptied the aquarium and smeared on superglue to try to fill in the crack. When they came back to the office the next morning, they saw white fingerprints all over the glass. They examined the ingredients in the superglue they had been using and found that there was a liquid in it that stuck to the body oils on the ridges of fingerprints. As it dried, it made a plastic mold of the fingerprint itself. The detectives found that they could use that chemical to make invisible fingerprints show up on glass, rubber bands, plastic, cellophane, or aluminum foil if a criminal had touched any of those objects. By accidentally fingerprinting themselves, the detectives learned a new way to check for the fingerprints of others.

Did you know that in a way God has left his own fingerprints to show us the wondrous things he has done? A writer of the book of Psalms says, "I look at the night sky and see the work of your fingers—the moon and the stars you set in place" (Psalm 8:3). Just look around—you will see God's fingerprints everywhere in our world!

September

Why was Alka-Seltzer invented?

We should help others do what is right
and build them up in the Lord.
ROMANS 15:2

Tom Keene was the editor of a newspaper in Elkhart, Indiana. This young man was worried that his employees might get sick from the influenza epidemic in the late 1920s, so he required them all to dissolve some baking soda and aspirin in water and drink it. No one was out sick when Hub Beardsley, the owner of a medicine laboratory, was visiting the newspaper office, and Hub learned about the special water. He went back to his company and asked his chief chemist, Maurice Treener, to work on improving the mixture and making it appealing for the public, and that is how Alka-Seltzer was first sold in 1931. Many people since have used the tablets, dropped in water, and found that they work well on ordinary ailments like headaches and stomachaches, even if they don't keep the flu away.

"We should help others do what is right and build them up in the Lord" (Romans 15:2). Tom was certainly trying to build up the health of his coworkers and neighbors. Each of us should look around at the people in our lives to see if there is any way we can be of help, like raking their leaves or sweeping their front porches. The more friendly and interested you are in others, the more chances you have to tell them that Jesus loves them.

September

How was the catcher's mitt introduced to the game of baseball?

Strengthen those who have tired hands.
ISAIAH 35:3

The game was Harvard against the Fall River, Massachusetts, team in 1875. William "Gunner" McGunnigle was the catcher for Fall River, and he appeared at his position on that day wearing thick bricklayer's gloves, which helped to pad his hands. After that game, the catcher for Harvard went out and bought himself a pair of bricklayer's gloves too, but he slid a thin sheet of lead into the palm of each glove to protect his hands even further. By 1890, as pitchers were moving farther away from home plate and overhand pitching made throws more forceful, it became normal for a team to have one or two pitchers but many catchers, because so many catchers were getting injured. In 1891, sports manufacturers started producing several different types of catcher's mitts.

The Bible speaks about how we can "strengthen those who have tired hands" (Isaiah 35:3). Whose hands wouldn't feel tired after trying to stop a speeding baseball? Fortunately for catchers, a few enterprising players found a way to do just that—to make their hands stronger so they could do a better job for their team. Look for ways you, too, can strengthen those who are tired by giving them a helping hand.

September

Before the hair dryer, how did people in a hurry dry their hair?

Then the LORD God formed the man from the dust of the ground. He breathed the breath of life into the man's nostrils, and the man became a living person.

GENESIS 2:7

Before the hair dryer was invented, people just let the ordinary air in the house or air from the outdoors dry their hair. But if they didn't have hours to wait, what could they do? Believe it or not, many people used their vacuum cleaners! Back then, a vacuum cleaner had one end that sucked air in and another end that blew air out, and you could hook up the hose to either end. By attaching the hose to the blow-out area, you could dry your hair. In 1920 a big, heavy hair dryer was finally invented, but it took thirty more years until a handheld dryer was available.

We can control the air a little bit with hair dryers or vacuum cleaners. But God did something with air that humans could never do. The Bible says, "Then the LORD God formed the man from the dust of the ground. He breathed the breath of life into the man's nostrils, and the man became a living person" (Genesis 2:7). The power of people is tiny compared to the power of God.

October
1

Have you ever used a Glo-Sheet for your homework?

Once you were full of darkness, but now you have light from the Lord. So live as people of light! For this light within you produces only what is good and right and true.
EPHESIANS 5:8-9

Thanks to a ten-year-old named Becky Schroeder, you can. Becky was trying to do her homework in the car when it began getting dark outside. Becky wished she had a way to light up her paper. That's when she got her idea. After a trip to the hardware store with her dad, Becky had a bucket of phosphorescent paint, which she took into the bathroom and painted onto a clipboard over and over again, turning the light off and on to test it. Her parents remember her running out of the bathroom saying, "It works! I'm writing in the dark!" When NASA read about Becky and her Glo-Sheet clipboard, they wrote her a letter to see if she was a former employee since her idea was so much like a project of theirs. They were really surprised to find out she was a child! In 1971 Becky was the youngest girl ever to be granted a U.S. patent, and she was also named Ohio Inventor of the Year. Many people bought Becky's glowing clipboard, which lit up the paper on top, including ambulance drivers who worked in the dark and photographers who needed to write in their darkrooms. Becky offered light-activated models and also electric-operated ones. Becky truly had a bright idea!

As you know, it's difficult to get anything accomplished in the dark. But when there's some light to guide you, it's possible to be productive and get many things done. The Bible describes what it's like to live in the light spiritually when it says, "Once you were full of darkness, but now you have light from the Lord. So live as people of light! For this light within you produces only what is good and right and true" (Ephesians 5:8-9). Try to live as if you're constantly under a Glo-Sheet so the whole world can see what you're accomplishing for Christ.

October

What can be shocking about your teeth?

I will praise the LORD at all times.
I will constantly speak his praises.
PSALM 34:1

Maybe you don't have cavities yourself, but you probably know some-one who has silver or gold fillings in his or her teeth. Whenever a piece of metal, like aluminum foil, touches those fillings, it sets up conditions for electricity to travel through the teeth. The last ingredient to add is a chemical with weak acid in it, like orange juice, or even saliva. When everything hits at the same time, it creates a kind of battery in your mouth, which sends a small current through your teeth. The electricity hits the nerves of your teeth and causes you to feel a little shocking surprise.

There may not be anything you can do about having something shocking inside your mouth, but you can certainly prevent something shocking from coming out of it! Your words can be hurtful for people to hear, so you need to be careful about what you say. How can you make sure that your words are always pleasing before God? The Bible has a simple answer: "I will praise the LORD at all times. I will constantly speak his praises" (Psalm 34:1).

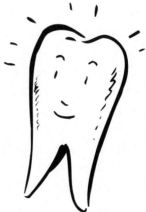

October
3

How do you take your tea?

Let us, your servants, see you work again;
let our children see your glory.
PSALM 90:16

Customs in the early days of America were constantly being shared and taught as people from different countries traveled here. When tea first became available in the American colonies in the 1600s, many housewives were not sure how to serve it. In those days tea came in the form of loose leaves, not in tea bags. Instead of using the leaves to make hot tea to drink as we do today, they boiled the leaves, threw out the water, and served the leaves with sugar on top.

When new things are taught to us, they can often be confusing. That's because we're only human, and we're trying to learn from other humans. But when God shows us something, he makes it very clear so we can learn more about him. "Let us, your servants, see you work again; let our children see your glory" (Psalm 90:16). God knows that life with him is the most important thing you will ever learn about, so he makes his Word very clear. Then everyone can understand it and live by it.

October 4

Which president of the United States had an important job even in high school?

The wages of sin is death, but the free gift of God is eternal life through Christ Jesus our Lord.
ROMANS 6:23

President Ronald Reagan took a summer job as a lifeguard during his high school years and beyond, beginning in 1927. He took this job seriously and devoted himself to doing it the best he could. There is proof that he succeeded in his goal. By the end of his lifeguarding career, seventy-seven people had been rescued by the man who would go on to be president.

Watching over swimmers and saving their lives is a wonderful gift for someone to give. Christians, however, look beyond the help of humans for ultimate saving, which comes from the Lord. As a child of God, you have something even better than a lifesaver in the water. Jesus will be your Life Savior, making sure that your soul is secure and that you will spend eternity with him. The Bible says, "The wages of sin is death, but the free gift of God is eternal life through Christ Jesus our Lord" (Romans 6:23). You will not drown in sin when Jesus is watching over your soul.

October

Which invention was most appreciated when someone sat on it?

Encourage each other with these words.
1 THESSALONIANS 4:18

Foam rubber is soft and spongy. Inventor E. A. Murphy used an egg whisk, and later a food mixer, to concoct the first foam rubber. With the help of another inventor, W. H. Chapman, he poured it into molds when the liquid mixture turned into gel. And how was foam rubber useful? In 1931, the first product to be made of foam rubber was motorcycle seats. Next, foam rubber was used to cushion the seats in the new Shakespeare Memorial Theater in Shakespeare's hometown in England. Seats for buses, and then mattresses for beds, came later. Even the most doubtful about E. A. Murphy's idea were pleasantly surprised when they actually sat on it.

Finding out that foam rubber was comfortable was a surprising and welcome discovery. It is a wonderful gift to be able to make someone more comfortable. But the best gift of all is being able to ease someone's mind and soul about what will happen to them for eternity. After telling about Christ's death and resurrection, the Bible says, "Encourage each other with these words" (1 Thessalonians 4:18). It's nice to offer someone a soft place to sit, but it's so much more comforting when you can tell someone about the assurance of sitting side by side with God in heaven. Earth provides nothing that will feel as good as that!

October

Where are you when you're "under the weather"?

He climbed into the boat, and the wind stopped.
MARK 6:51

When you are under the weather, you don't feel well. The expression comes from "under the weather bow," which is the side of a ship that is beaten the worst by the waves of bad weather. Sailors also used that term to describe seasickness. When the ship is tossing, you can feel nauseous in your stomach. The word *nausea* comes from the Greek word *naus*, which means "ship."

Whenever you are not feeling well, ask Jesus to comfort you. He will know best how to do that. The Bible tells us what Jesus once did when his friends were in a rocking boat: "He climbed into the boat, and the wind stopped" (Mark 6:51). Jesus will stay beside you in your time of discomfort.

October 7

Is this a self-service stable?

God will provide.
GENESIS 22:8

In the 1800s in England, an inventor wanted to get horses to take care of themselves. He devised a complicated system of pulleys attached to a floor that kept moving because of a continuous belt. The plan was for the horse to obediently walk along on its own while different machines fed, watered, and cleaned both the horse and the stable. But the invention never really took off, because that was just about the time in history when the car came along to replace the horse as a means of transportation.

No matter what we think will help us most, God knows what is best for us and for the other creatures he has made. The Bible tells us, "God will provide" (Genesis 22:8). That doesn't mean he will give us everything we ask of him, but it does mean he will always hear our prayers with love.

October

Where do the sunset's colors come from?

Red sky at night means fair weather tomorrow; red sky in the morning means foul weather all day.
MATTHEW 16:2-3

When the sun begins to go down in the sky as it gets close to setting, the light appears to change from yellow to red and orange. Why does that happen? As the sun's light gets closer to the earth's horizon, it is traveling a long way through dusty air. The air is thicker and absorbs the light, and the red and orange colors become more brilliant.

We are not the only people who try to figure out the weather. People in all times all over the world think about how the weather will affect their days. The Bible tells us an opinion people had about the weather back in Jesus' day: "Red sky at night means fair weather tomorrow; red sky in the morning means foul weather all day" (Matthew 16:2-3). But even if the weather changes, God will never change!

October

What's the first thing the inventor of elastic thought it could be used for?

Don't store up treasures here on earth,
where moths eat them and rust destroys them,
and where thieves break in and steal.
MATTHEW 6:19

Stretchy bands of elastic can be used for many things, most of them in clothing. They are helpful for holding pants and socks up, making sleeves fit on your arms, or making slippers expand for your feet. Elastic was invented in 1820 by Thomas Hancock. But his idea for what to do with his new invention was a little surprising—he thought the best use for elastic was to put it along the tops of pockets so thieves couldn't reach into them and steal what was inside!

People work hard to protect what they own from people who might want to take it away. But God shows you what's most important to keep. The Bible tells us, "Don't store up treasures here on earth, where moths eat them and rust destroys them, and where thieves break in and steal" (Matthew 6:19). God is telling you that when you give your heart to him, no one can take that away.

October

How smart is your goldfish?

God said, "Let us make human beings in our image, to be
like us. They will reign over the fish in the sea, the birds
in the sky, the livestock, all the wild animals on the earth,
and the small animals that scurry along the ground."
GENESIS 1:26

It has long been claimed that goldfish have only a three-second memory. But tests have proved that this is not true. In 2003, research on the memories of goldfish was done by the School of Psychology at the University of Plymouth. Researchers found that goldfish can remember things for at least three months and can tell the difference between different colors, sounds, and shapes. One test showed that the goldfish could be trained to push a lever to earn a food reward. Even when the lever was fixed to work for only one hour a day, the fish soon figured out how to make it work at the right time. Since we say that groups of fish swimming together are in a school, maybe they really are learning something there!

Fish are fascinating creatures, which is why some humans try to teach them things. This is all part of God's plan described in the Bible: "God said, 'Let us make human beings in our image, to be like us. They will reign over the fish in the sea, the birds in the sky, the livestock, all the wild animals on the earth, and the small animals that scurry along the ground'" (Genesis 1:26). God gave us animals not only to provide food for us but also to show us some of his creativity in making them.

October 11

Why do penguins have knees?

How precious is your unfailing love, O God! All humanity finds shelter in the shadow of your wings.
PSALM 36:7

Penguins need their knees to lower themselves onto their eggs and to walk. It's not easy to see a penguin's knees because they are covered by feathers to keep them warm. Penguins' legs are short and stubby. When swimming, penguins use their legs and feet to help them steer. In the water, their flipper-like wings provide the power. In fact, the penguin is the bird world's best swimmer, because its wings are more like flippers and have only very short feathers on them. Penguins are also world-champion divers. Other birds have hollow bones that allow them to fly. But penguins have solid bones, which keep their bodies heavy enough to make deep dives.

Just as God provided special wings for the penguin, he also promises to care for you. The Bible says, "How precious is your unfailing love, O God! All humanity finds shelter in the shadow of your wings" (Psalm 36:7). God is waiting to provide for all your needs, just as he does for the penguin. Run to his shelter, where you will be carefully watched over.

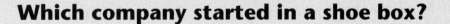

October

Which company started in a shoe box?

I will put my instructions deep within them,
and I will write them on their hearts.
JEREMIAH 31:33

In the early 1900s, a sixteen-year-old named J. C. Hall sold picture post-cards from around the world with his two older brothers. When he was eighteen, he moved from Nebraska to Kansas City, keeping his postcards in a shoe box while he opened his business of selling postcards. Five years later, after a fire destroyed all the products they had to sell, the Hall Brothers Company decided to start over, but this time J. C. created and sold his own cards. He believed people wanted to send greetings to each other in envelopes instead of just sending postcards. He also decided not to sell his cards out of closed drawers, which was the custom at the time. J. C. invented "Eye-Vision," which displayed cards in racks where customers could see them. The name of the company was changed to Hallmark. Historically, a hallmark was an official stamp put on gold or silver to guarantee that the metal was of good quality.

God understands our need for love and encouragement, and that's why we enjoy getting messages from each other. God has a message of his love for you too, but he doesn't need a card to send it to you. In fact, God has a more direct way to contact you. He says, "I will put my instructions deep within them, and I will write them on their hearts" (Jeremiah 31:33).

October

What are you doing when you "spill the beans"?

He knows the secrets of every heart.
PSALM 44:21

When people are supposed to keep a secret but they forget and tell it anyway, they might say, "Oops! I just spilled the beans!" What makes them say that? Long ago, the ancient Greeks had many secret clubs and organizations. When someone wanted to join, they were voted on by all of the members. Each member would walk by a container and drop in a white bean for a yes vote or a black bean for a no vote. Only the important officers of the club were supposed to know how many black beans there were. But once in a while someone would bump the container by mistake. Then the secret was known by everyone as the container tipped over and "spilled the beans."

Because God created us, he knows everything about us. When the Bible says that "he knows the secrets of every heart" (Psalm 44:21), it reminds us that God doesn't need to count beans before he can understand or discover something new about us. He has seen us inside and out since before we were born. That is why you can ask him for his help at any time. He already knows about your secrets, and when you invite him to come into your life, he can help you deal with whatever problem you're trying to hide. He wants you to be free from your burdens, so give them to him and trust that he will solve them in a way that will turn out to be the best for you.

October

What rumor about elephants is false?

I am leaving you with a gift—peace of mind and heart.
JOHN 14:27

Many stories have been told about elephants being afraid of mice. But that's not true. Elephants fear humans and big jungle cats. Elephants have been known to inspect little mice with their trunks, not to run from them. Another common misunderstanding about elephants is that they drink water through their trunks. That doesn't happen. The elephant sucks water into its trunk and then sprays the water into its mouth.

We often hear things or read things that are not true, like the wrong things people believe about elephants. As God's children, we need to carefully guard what we believe. If you are wondering what is true, ask Jesus to help you decide. He will give you wisdom that will help settle your mind. The Bible says, "I am leaving you with a gift—peace of mind and heart" (John 14:27). Accept the gift of Jesus and enjoy his peaceful rest.

October

What happened when a pig broke the law?

Oh, how great are God's riches and wisdom
and knowledge! How impossible it is for us to
understand his decisions and his ways!
ROMANS 11:33

In France in 1547, the laws of the land applied to people and animals in the same way. Once a mother pig, called a sow, and her six piglets were found guilty of beating a child. The sow was hanged, receiving the same harsh punishment an adult human would. But the piglets, it was decided, were to be set free because they were so young and their mother was such a bad influence.

It doesn't make much sense to expect animals to follow the same rules people do. God did not make animals to be the same as humans. This law seems odd to us because surely the lawmakers had noticed the differences between people and animals! When the Bible tells us about God, it says, "Oh, how great are God's riches and wisdom and knowledge! How impossible it is for us to understand his decisions and his ways!" (Romans 11:33). We will never be able to learn as much as God already knows. Ask him to explain to you what you need to understand, and he will find a way to do it.

October

How did Heinz 57 sauce get such a strange name?

God elevated [Jesus] to the place of highest honor
and gave him the name above all other names, that
at the name of Jesus every knee should bow.
PHILIPPIANS 2:9-10

Most people think there must be fifty-seven ingredients in this bottle of flavorful sauce. They would be surprised to find out that the number fifty-seven is really on the label because of some shoes! Henry John Heinz owned a food company, and one day while riding on a train, he saw a sign through the window that claimed a store had twenty-one styles of shoes. Mr. Heinz thought that having a number in the advertising was catchy, and he decided the name for his tasty sauce needed a number too. Just because he liked the sound of it and thought people would remember it, Mr. Heinz picked the number fifty-seven. It must have been a good choice—no one calls his sauce Heinz 21 by mistake.

Special names can be important in advertising because they remind you what's unique about a certain product. But the most special name on earth is Jesus Christ. He died on the cross so you could go to heaven one day. The Bible tells us, "God elevated [Jesus] to the place of highest honor and gave him the name above all other names, that at the name of Jesus every knee should bow" (Philippians 2:9-10). Always remember the name of Jesus; it's more important than any other name there is.

October

How did a dog almost cause the president of the United States to be shot?

All the LORD's promises prove true. He is a shield
for all who look to him for protection.
PSALM 18:30

The president was Gerald Ford; the dog was Liberty, his pet golden retriever; the place was the White House. One day in 1975, Liberty let President Ford know that it was time to go outside. So the president took Liberty down the elevator from the second floor and out the door of the Oval Office. President Ford didn't realize that he and Liberty were setting off a security alarm by walking outside. The Secret Service, assigned to guard the grounds of the White House, came running with their guns drawn to confront the trespasser and stop him from entering the White House. Imagine their surprise when they found the president and his dog instead!

The president relies on the Secret Service to protect him, and this story shows how diligently they try to shield him. But as a child of God, you are protected even more closely by your heavenly Father. We are told in the Bible, "All the LORD's promises prove true. He is a shield for all who look to him for protection" (Psalm 18:30). You have something even better than bodyguards to keep you safe; you have the all-powerful God as your own personal shield.

October 18

Is it true that some people never have dreams?

God gives rest to his loved ones.
PSALM 127:2

Everyone dreams. It seems that dreaming is a way for your brain to sort out your daytime thoughts during the night. Dreaming also acts as a "safety valve" to release tension, and it can express fears or wishes too. Most people spend about a fifth of their sleeping time dreaming. Scientists know this because they can measure the differences in your breathing, pulse rates, brain waves, and eye movements when you are dreaming and when you are not. Some people say they don't have dreams because they never remember them. But scientists have found otherwise. If people are woken up in the middle of a dream, they will remember they were having one.

Whether you are asleep or awake, as a child of God you have a special blessing. The Bible encourages us with these words: "God gives rest to his loved ones" (Psalm 127:2). You do not need to worry about dreams or feel afraid or be anxious about anything. God has taken care of all of that for you—you can trust him to love you deeply and care for you, whether it's day or night.

October **19**

Where did the snorkel come from?

When you give them your breath, life is created.
PSALM 104:30

When we use the word *snorkel*, we think of people putting on a face mask with a breathing tube attached so they can go explore the ocean and the creatures underwater. But the original use for snorkels started in Holland in 1938. The snorkel was invented so submarines could keep air coming into the ship and stay underwater longer. With the invention of radar, submarines were no longer able to remain undetected when they came up for air each night, so it was important for them to find a way to stay below the surface.

Now you know about the origin of the snorkel, but let's back up a step. What was the origin of the breath that goes into a snorkel? The Bible has a very clear answer: God. "When you give them your breath, life is created" (Psalm 104:30).

October

How did a frog help invent the battery?

He gives power to the weak and strength to the powerless.
ISAIAH 40:29

Experimenting on how electrical and nerve impulses move through the legs of frogs gave Luigi Galvani valuable information about how batteries might work. Later, other people used Luigi's work to continue making batteries, including Alessandro Volta, who is considered the inventor of the battery (and the person the word *volt* is named after), and Thomas Edison, who created a different kind of battery. Maybe you've wondered why C and D batteries are on store shelves but you haven't seen any plain A's or B's. Back in the days when radios were run only by battery, radios had two huge battery packs, called A and B. When newer kinds of batteries were invented, the letters *C* and *D* were used instead. Manufacturers have come back to using the letter *A*, but never by itself. Only AA, AAA, and AAAA are used for the smaller batteries that have been invented since the days of battery-powered radios.

It is always exciting to put a fresh battery into a machine that isn't working and watch it use the energy to begin performing beautifully. God wants us to experience that same kind of excitement when we invite his power into our lives. The Bible tells us, "He gives power to the weak and strength to the powerless" (Isaiah 40:29). And the best part is that when you get your energy from God, you never have to worry about it running out.

October 21

How many colors can we see?

I have seen your salvation, which you
have prepared for all people.
LUKE 2:30-31

A person with ordinary vision can distinguish about 150 different colors, tints, and shades. An expert with a highly trained eye for color can detect more than 100,000. Imagine the size and weight of a box of crayons that big!

There are many wondrous abilities God has given our eyes, but the most perfect vision you will ever have is when you see Jesus. The Bible tells us about the most exciting thing we can see: "I have seen your salvation, which you have prepared for all people" (Luke 2:30-31). All the colors of this world will seem faded compared to the glories of heaven.

October

What everyday problems can be solved with a candle, string, and nail polish?

Stand firm and keep a strong grip on the
teaching we passed on to you.
2 THESSALONIANS 2:15

Sometimes there are practical ways to solve small problems that will make a big difference. If you are worried that the address you just wrote on an envelope might get wet on your way out to the mailbox on a rainy day, try to find a white candle in the house before you go. Rub the flat end of the candle across the ink, and you will put a coat of wax over the ink that will keep it from running. When you are using a paint can and you want to have the same amount of paint on every brushful, tie a string or wire across the top of the open paint can, perhaps on the loops of the handle. Each time you dip the brush into the can, slide it across the string from the handle down to the bristles and the extra paint will drip back into the can. To keep your buttons from falling off, put a coat of clear nail polish across the crossed threads on the front and back of the button. These small suggestions can make your life easier in some pretty great ways.

Little household hints like these are good to remember, but they're not nearly as important as what the Bible teaches us. The Bible tells us, "Stand firm and keep a strong grip on the teaching we passed on to you" (2 Thessalonians 2:15). Never let go of what the Bible tells you. It's the best advice and help you'll ever get—for anything you want to fix.

October

How did pilots escape from their planes?

How much longer will you waver, hobbling between two opinions? If the LORD is God, follow him!

1 KINGS 18:21

In 1944 military planes were getting faster, and concerns were getting greater for the safety of the pilots. James Martin and his team were asked by the British Ministry of Aircraft Production to come up with a solution to keep the pilots safe. The result was an ejection seat. The idea was that the pilot's seat would have an explosive charge that would shoot it straight up, three hundred feet out of the plane, which would allow a parachute to open, even if the plane was parked on the ground. The canopy, or roof, of the cockpit would also be blown off to make room for the seat to fly out of the plane. In case of an emergency, the pilot could start a sequence of events by pulling a cord between his legs. If the pilot pulled another set of cords over his head, his face would be covered with a shield to protect him during the blast. Then the first charges would come to blow off the canopy. The seat would begin to eject, the parachute would be activated, and an oxygen supply would be provided and automatically turned on to help the pilot during ejection. The seat would be steadied and slowed, and the pilot would be released from the seat. Then the parachute would bring the pilot down, away from the plane and the seat. If the automatic system failed, the pilot could pull a rip cord to release a parachute. This ejection seat system was accepted and installed in military planes, and over the years it has saved more than eight thousand lives.

Pilots don't have much time to decide to activate their ejection seats. We don't know how much time we'll have to make important decisions in our lives either. Be wise and decide quickly to follow the Lord Jesus Christ. The Bible says, "How much longer will you waver, hobbling between two opinions? If the LORD is God, follow him!" (1 Kings 18:21).

October 24

What's so good about green?

Let the trees of the forest rustle with praise.
PSALM 96:12

Green in leaves is good! That shows that the leaves contain pigment, which will turn sunlight into energy for the tree. The gloss on tree leaves is like a clear protective coat that guards against damage from both the sun and the rain. Some trees stay green all year because they are hardy enough to survive winter weather. But for other trees, cooler air means it's time to start changing for the winter. The green leaves break down their energy-loaded pigment and send healthy chemicals back into the tree. When the green is gone from the leaves, yellow and red and orange pigments are left behind, which give the leaves their bright colors during the fall season.

Each season it seems that the trees are silently praising God for the gift of their colors. Celebrate with them, because we get to enjoy the colors too! And we can join the trees in praising God. The Bible tells us, "Let the trees of the forest rustle with praise" (Psalm 96:12).

October

When did an audience watch someone eat?

People do not live by bread alone; rather, we live by every word that comes from the mouth of the LORD.
DEUTERONOMY 8:3

Some of the kings in times past could consume such astonishingly huge meals that they would invite the public to watch! King Louis XIV of France ate most of his meals in front of a large audience. When King George II of Britain was in power, tickets were sold to the common folk so they could gather and observe the royal family eating their Sunday dinner.

God wants us to think of his Word as something so important to us that we can't live without it. Just as our bodies need food, our hearts and souls need nourishment from the Lord. The Bible says, "People do not live by bread alone; rather, we live by every word that comes from the mouth of the LORD" (Deuteronomy 8:3). Make every word in the Bible as special to you as every bite of food, and you will have a place at the Lord's table as well as at your own.

October

Who rode the first Ferris wheel?

If you fully obey the LORD your God and carefully keep all his commands that I am giving you today, the LORD your God will set you high above all the nations of the world.
DEUTERONOMY 28:1

Anyone who attended the 1893 Chicago World's Fair could take a trip on the gigantic Ferris wheel that had been built for the fair. Today most Ferris wheels have hanging seats in which two or three people can sit as the seats are lifted into the air and back down again while the wheel turns. But the first Ferris wheel at the fair had containers the size of buses, instead of small seats, for people to ride in. Each container could carry at least forty people. Altogether, that giant Ferris wheel gave rides to two thousand people at a time. And why was it called a Ferris wheel? George Ferris was the man who came up with the idea for the entertaining ride and knew how to make it work.

Imagine people's delight as they felt themselves rising high above the crowds when the wheel lifted their car! God has promised you an even bigger thrill. The Bible says, "If you fully obey the LORD your God and carefully keep all his commands that I am giving you today, the LORD your God will set you high above all the nations of the world" (Deuteronomy 28:1). God promises that he will refresh you if you are weary and help your soul soar high with hope. It is a much better ride to fly freely with the Lord than to just keep going around in Ferris wheel circles.

October 27

Why is all that stuff in your room called junk?

Don't forget to do good and to share with those in need.
HEBREWS 13:16

The word *junk* has ties to the sailing days of old. Several hundred years ago, when pieces of rope got frayed and couldn't be counted on to do the job anymore, they got a new name—junk—but they weren't thrown away. Pieces of junk were put in barrels together and used for another purpose. If the rope couldn't hold up sails anymore, it might be used to fill up a hole or soak up seawater. Eventually, all along the American shore in New England, stores began selling new and used accessories for sailing ships. Since old junk pieces could be bought there, it is believed that the stores were nicknamed junk stores and the owners were called junk dealers. Now anything that was used for one thing and is being kept in case it might be useful for something else someday is called junk.

Some people save everything, whether they have a use for it right now or not, in case they ever need it unexpectedly. But God has an even more amazing way of providing what we need. The Bible tells us, "Don't forget to do good and to share with those in need" (Hebrews 13:16). If you have some warm clothes that you could do without, go ahead and share them with someone who needs them. And if you see someone at school who is hungry, share your lunch with that person. God will make sure you have what you need when you need it. Don't trust your junk to protect you; God will provide what you need—to keep or to give away—in his best timing.

October

What code is used every time you buy something?

It is pleasant to see dreams come true.
PROVERBS 13:19

Bernard Silver heard a question one day that changed his life. He was a graduate student, and he listened to the president of a chain of food stores ask a dean, or head teacher, to figure out how to make pricing items easier. The dean did not want to work on this project, but Bernard did. Bernard asked another student, Joseph Woodland, to help, and together they experimented. They finally chose a complicated method for pricing that used Morse code along with some markings with patterned stripes on the sides of film. In 1949 they applied for their first patent for a code that used lines in circles, like a target. But stores didn't start using bar codes until 1967, and by then they had changed to a straight-line design. Scanners that used lasers appeared in the 1970s. There are four kinds: glass-top readers, gun readers, wand readers, and swipe readers. They all take pictures of the bar code, and the computer in the cash register turns the bars into a number.

Bernard and Joseph really wanted to solve the pricing mystery, and they did it! God is very gracious to us, allowing us to feel the satisfaction of accomplishing something. The Bible describes the feeling this way: "It is pleasant to see dreams come true" (Proverbs 13:19). The sweetness of getting a job done is one of the best rewards here on earth. God designed it that way.

October

What can you learn about trunks and tusks?

He never left them without evidence of himself and his goodness. For instance, he sends you rain and good crops and gives you food and joyful hearts.

ACTS 14:17

An elephant's nose is called a trunk because it resembles the trunk of a tree. There aren't any bones inside an elephant's trunk, but there are about ten thousand muscles. The elephant can spray water, greet other elephants, eat, and move obstacles with its trunk, even though it is really just a very long nose with grippers at the end. An elephant's tusk is the largest tooth in the animal kingdom, and it grows bigger throughout the elephant's lifetime. Each tusk, made of ivory, may reach ten feet in length and 125 pounds, and each elephant has two of them! Elephants use their tusks to defend themselves, dig up plants and roots, and move or push things.

The elephant, with its ability to supply itself with food and protection, depends completely on God's wisdom to meet its needs. We have a God whose goodness can be seen in the natural world and in our own lives. "He never left them without evidence of himself and his goodness. For instance, he sends you rain and good crops and gives you food and joyful hearts" (Acts 14:17). What a good God we have!

October

What's the story behind the equals sign?

The meaning of Jesus Christ's death was made as clear to you as if you had seen a picture of his death on the cross.
GALATIANS 3:1

We have all added two and two, and used the equals sign to show that the total is four. But who decided which sign we would use, and why did he pick it? Robert Recorde was a very smart child, and in 1557, when he was grown up, he wrote a book about algebra and mathematics. He made up the equals sign from his own imagination. Instead of always writing "is equal to," he chose to have two sideways lines of the same length. People saw the equals sign for the first time when they read his book. These two lines, one above the other, have been accepted as the equals symbol ever since.

The equals sign is a meaningful symbol for people who are doing addition. For God's people, the cross is the most meaningful symbol on earth. Jesus Christ died on the cross, and that is how he saved you. The Bible tells us, "The meaning of Jesus Christ's death was made as clear to you as if you had seen a picture of his death on the cross" (Galatians 3:1). Because of what Jesus did for you on the cross, you are able to be God's child and go to heaven someday. Every time you see a cross, it is a symbol to remind you how special you are to God.

October

What should you know about the hair on your head?

Blessings crown the head of the righteous.
PROVERBS 10:6, NIV

You may have heard some myths about hair. Some people say that cutting your hair makes it grow back more quickly. But getting a haircut makes absolutely no difference in whether your hair grows faster or slower. And some people believe that if you pull one hair out of your head, ten will grow back. That isn't true either. Only one hair can grow out of each of the hair bulbs in your scalp at a time. If it were true that you could grow hair back more thickly by pulling it out first, you would see a lot of men walking around yanking at the hair next to their bald spots.

People tend to spend a lot of time being concerned about how their hair looks to others. But that doesn't matter so much when you think about what the Bible says about your head. Even if you are having a "bad hair day," you can count on this promise from the Bible: "Blessings crown the head of the righteous" (Proverbs 10:6, NIV).

November **1**

Could you read by the light of a beetle?

The LORD, my God, lights up my darkness.
PSALM 18:28

Strangely enough, you could see well enough to read if you held this light-filled beetle close to your book. The Jamaican click beetle is about two inches long and emits a constant light instead of a blinking one, like the firefly does. These beetles use their light to look for other beetles like themselves. If you put about forty of them together, their light would be as bright as a candle's.

God knows that our eyes don't work well in the dark, and he has provided many ways for us to find light even when it is night. The same is true when it comes to our spiritual eyes. Before we become God's children, we can't see the wonder of his world and the brightness of the future he has planned for us in heaven. But when we accept Jesus Christ into our hearts, God's majesty and power become clear to us. The Bible says, "The LORD, my God, lights up my darkness" (Psalm 18:28). God takes care of our eyes, but he takes even more special care of our souls. He wants us to carry the light of his promises within us so we can see ourselves in the bright light of his love.

November 2

Do oysters climb trees?

The LORD God made all sorts of trees grow up
from the ground—trees that were beautiful
and that produced delicious fruit.
GENESIS 2:9

On many Caribbean islands there are mangrove trees with living oysters on their trunks. How did that happen? The trees grow in lagoons and swamps, which is where the oysters normally live. When the tide rises, the oysters rise with it and attach themselves to the lower parts of the tree trunks. Then the tide gets low again, but the oysters stay where they are, making a decoration for the mangrove trees.

God created an interesting variety of trees, and he also made the oysters you can find in some of those trees! The Bible says, "The LORD God made all sorts of trees grow up from the ground—trees that were beautiful and that produced delicious fruit" (Genesis 2:9). It is amazing to think of all the different creations God used to display his endless imagination.

November

Why was it called a stagecoach?

Praise the LORD, everything he has created,
everything in all his kingdom.
PSALM 103:22

A stagecoach was a vehicle people rode in when taking long cross-country trips that required many days of travel. There were many stops along the way, so the trip was made in stages, or parts, and that's why it was called a stagecoach. The most famous stagecoach makers were Lewis Downing and his partner, Stephen Abbot. In 1825 they made the Concord stagecoach, which was very luxurious for the time. The stagecoach rested on cowhide straps to make the ride smoother, and it had windows with leather curtains, as well as flat tops, where luggage could be stored. Later, when the steam buggy and the locomotive offered new ways to travel, the stagecoach wasn't the most popular way to travel anymore.

You can imagine how thrilled people must have been to have a more comfortable way to travel as they went across the country in a stagecoach. They must have been truly thankful for the blessing of smoother, cleaner accommodations than they were used to. As they made their way across the country, perhaps they noticed new parts of God's world that they hadn't seen before. We can say the same thing about the way we travel today—which is much improved over the stagecoach. The Bible says: "Praise the LORD, everything he has created, everything in all his kingdom" (Psalm 103:22). As you travel, praise the Lord for all the places you see, because they are all part of his Kingdom.

November 4

How close is the thunderstorm?

The clouds poured down rain; the thunder rumbled
in the sky. Your arrows of lightning flashed.
PSALM 77:17

Every minute there are two thousand thunderstorms and six thousand flashes of lightning in different places on earth. Lightning is a big spark of electricity, and it is drawn to the ground like a magnet draws metal. Thunder is the boom that happens when hot lightning makes the air around it expand too fast. Lightning and thunder actually happen at exactly the same time, but it takes sound longer to reach your ears than it takes light to reach your eyes. Sound takes five seconds to travel one mile. You can estimate how far away a thunderstorm is by using the "one-thousand rule." Start counting when you see the lightning: one one-thousand, two one-thousand, and so on, and stop when you hear the thunder. Then divide the number you stopped on by five. For example, if you counted to ten one-thousand, the storm would be two miles away. If you counted to twenty one-thousand, the storm would be four miles away. But when you are counting, make sure you pay attention to where you are for safety reasons. If the storm is very close and you are outside, go inside for shelter. If there is no building nearby, try to find a car, van, or truck to sit in with all the windows completely closed. Avoid water, metal objects, high ground, and trees. If you are inside during a thunderstorm, stay away from electrical appliances, telephones, headsets, water, windows, and doors. Remember, you want to watch the storm, not be hurt by it!

Weather is fascinating for us to watch, because it is something we can't control at all. God designed it, and he has shown his might and knowledge by creating things we would have no idea how to make ourselves. The Bible teaches us where the weather comes from when it says, "The clouds poured down rain; the thunder rumbled in the sky. Your arrows of lightning flashed" (Psalm 77:17). There is obviously nothing random or man-made about that!

November

What do the numbers on baseball uniforms mean?

Share each other's burdens, and in this
way obey the law of Christ.
GALATIANS 6:2

The first numbers went on the sleeves of baseball uniforms for the Cincinnati Reds in 1883 because the scorecard sellers wanted them there. But players objected because they thought the numbers made them look like convicts. The fans didn't like the numbers either, because they didn't understand the system and thought that the lower the number was, the better the player. So off came the numbers until 1929. That year the New York Yankees and the Cleveland Indians sewed permanent numbers on the backs of their jerseys, and the numbers stood for the batting order. It was just a few years later that every team had numbers on their backs, but the numbers no longer represented the batting order. Eventually last names were added as well. In the 1960s, a special jersey came along. It belonged to number 17, Carlos May, and the date of his birthday showed up on his back. Why? The back of his jersey read, "May 17"—the day he was born!

Baseball players had a hard time deciding what would work best on their uniforms, but eventually the problems were straightened out and no longer bothered them. The Bible gives us good advice about facing our problems: "Share each other's burdens, and in this way obey the law of Christ" (Galatians 6:2). Often, having a friend beside you during rough times makes things seem easier.

November

What famous library was started with eleven wagons full of books?

People are like grass; their beauty is like a flower in
the field. The grass withers and the flower fades.
But the word of the Lord remains forever.
1 PETER 1:24-25

It was the early 1800s, and the United States had a problem. During the War of 1812, the British burned the United States Capitol building in Washington DC and destroyed all the books collected in the building. The legislators no longer had a library. Usually books were collected from many places over a long period of time, so it would take many months to replace the books. But Thomas Jefferson, who had a lot of books but not a lot of money, came up with a way to help himself and his country at the same time. He sold his own collection of 6,500 volumes for $23,950 to America to start the new Library of Congress in Washington DC.

It takes a lot of books to gather information about our world. Fortunately for us, we only need one book to learn about God. This book, the Bible, tells us everything we need to know to live a life that is pleasing to God. And nothing like fire or flood or time can take away the truths of the Bible. The Bible promises, "People are like grass; their beauty is like a flower in the field. The grass withers and the flower fades. But the word of the Lord remains forever" (1 Peter 1:24-25).

November 7

How did an octopus trick the aquarium keepers each night?

They lie awake at night, hatching sinful plots. Their actions are never good. They make no attempt to turn from evil.
PSALM 36:4

The public aquarium in a New England town was dark and quiet for the night. When the workers came back in the morning, one of their aquariums was missing many of the fish that should have been there. The following night, the same thing happened. Fish were disappearing—but what was happening to them? It took weeks before the answer was discovered. In the same room as the mystery aquarium, there was another aquarium that was home to an octopus. The aquarium keepers finally found that each night the octopus was opening the top of its aquarium and making its way to the fish tank to have a huge dinner. Scientists have tested the octopus with puzzles and mazes, and they have found that the octopus is as smart as a pet cat.

Have you ever noticed how some people decide to do evil things at night, a little like the octopus did? It might seem easier to hide those things when it's dark and no one is paying attention. The Bible says, "They lie awake at night, hatching sinful plots. Their actions are never good. They make no attempt to turn from evil" (Psalm 36:4). But even if no one else sees, God's light always exposes what is right and wrong.

November

What's the difference between brown eggs and white eggs?

Everyone who belongs to Christ will be given new life.
1 CORINTHIANS 15:22

The color of the shell is the only thing different! Believe it or not, the color of the eggs can often be determined by what color the hen's earlobes are. That's right! Hens that have darker colored earlobes usually lay brown eggs, and hens that have white earlobes usually lay white eggs. But if the eggs of any kind of hen are allowed to hatch, the chicks all come out yellow.

Eggs can mean new life. Asking Jesus into your heart means new life for you, too. God promises, "Everyone who belongs to Christ will be given new life" (1 Corinthians 15:22). You will break out of your old self just like a chick breaks out of an egg, and you will experience a freedom you never knew existed before.

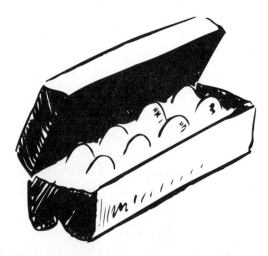

November

What is one of an animal's best weapons of protection?

All the animals of the forest are mine, and I own the cattle on a thousand hills. I know every bird on the mountains, and all the animals of the field are mine.
PSALM 50:10-11

Believe it or not, it's the animal's coloring. Many animals and insects are designed to blend into their surroundings so that predators are less likely to see them. When you think of examples of how creatures resemble nature, there are many to choose from. Butterflies look like leaves and flowers, and white polar bears blend into the snow. An insect called a praying mantis looks like a twig, and a copperhead snake looks like the dead leaves it hides in.

God provided a way for animals to stay protected from their enemies. He didn't leave out even the smallest detail as he planned how each animal would look, hunt, or live. In the Bible God describes his loving heart toward all of his creation: "All the animals of the forest are mine, and I own the cattle on a thousand hills. I know every bird on the mountains, and all the animals of the field are mine" (Psalm 50:10-11). God thinks of everything, and we can trust everything he thinks!

November

How did White House press conferences get started?

These gates lead to the presence of the
LORD, and the godly enter there.
PSALM 118:20

Bad weather began the tradition. When Theodore Roosevelt was president, he was looking outside a White House window one day and noticed that members of the press were waiting outside in the rain, wet and cold. At that time, it was the custom for reporters to wait by the gates to the White House and ask people who were going in or coming out what the latest news was. On that particular day, President Roosevelt invited the reporters to come inside, where he set aside a large room for them to get in out of the rain. From that day forward, the press became important in the eyes of America and reporters have had special access to the president.

The reporters had to wait for an invitation to go into the White House and be near the president. But you have access to someone much more important, and the invitation is always open to you. When you are in God's presence, you get much more than just a story to put in a newspaper. The Bible says, "These gates lead to the presence of the LORD, and the godly enter there" (Psalm 118:20). Being a Christian means that you don't get left outside of God's heavenly Kingdom and the reward he has waiting for you.

11

November

How did help arrive in a hurry?

"LORD, help!" they cried in their trouble, and
he saved them from their distress.
PSALM 107:19

In 1792, soldiers who were wounded in battle had only a first aid kit to help them. Then a French surgeon named Dominique Larrey arranged what was called the "flying ambulance." This was a group of paramedics who went to the aid of injured soldiers, bringing medical supplies and a lightweight vehicle to get them to a hospital. Later Dominique was promoted to chief surgeon of the French army, and he organized field hospitals, which were right near the battlefield.

The ambulance could get to people in trouble faster than anything else had been able to before, but nothing made by humans can be faster than God. Whenever we're in a bad situation, we can call out to the Great Healer for help. The Bible says, "'LORD, help!' they cried in their trouble, and he saved them from their distress" (Psalm 107:19).

November 12

How do you stop a toddler from spilling?

Like newborn babies, you must crave pure spiritual milk so that you will grow into a full experience of salvation.
1 PETER 2:2

When she was eleven, Alexia Abernathy needed an idea for a state-wide invention competition she wanted to enter. She thought about the problems she saw around her. She knew her babysitter had a messy one. Food was constantly spilling when her babysitter's two-year-old son, Charles, tried to eat from his bowl while walking around. Alexia understood that children at that age want to be independent and feed themselves, so she did some concentrating. The result was a new way of allowing toddlers to feed themselves without making such a mess. Alexia took a bigger bowl that had a snap-on top and put Charles's small bowl inside it. Then she cut a hole in the lid of the big bowl that Charles could reach into. If his little bowl tipped, the food spilled into the big bowl, not onto the floor. She called it the Oops! Proof No-Spill Feeding Bowl. With her dad's help, she found a company that would sell her product nationwide. Alexia's invention helped children only nine years younger than she was!

When babies are hungry, they don't need a toy or a nap. They need food. That's how God wants us to long for him. He doesn't want us to be satisfied until we are sure that we are his children. Keep running after God, asking him to feed you with his love. The Bible says, "Like newborn babies, you must crave pure spiritual milk so that you will grow into a full experience of salvation" (1 Peter 2:2).

November

What helmet was dangerous to wear?

Put on salvation as your helmet, and take the
sword of the Spirit, which is the word of God.
EPHESIANS 6:17

The idea was invented in 1916 by Albert Pratt. He started with a helmet
and then built a real gun into it. There was a tube from the trigger to
a mouthpiece. The soldier was supposed to blow into the mouthpiece,
which would send air into the tube. The force of the air would then fire
the gun. But this idea was too full of ifs to be a good one: *if* the soldier
could blow hard enough to send a powerful blast of air through the
tube, and *if* the air could actually set off the trigger of the gun, and *if*
the gun didn't misfire and blow up the helmet, then perhaps it might
work. There probably weren't many volunteers who wanted to be a part
of the experiments for this invention!

Fortunately for all of us, there's a much more reliable kind of helmet
that everyone can wear. The Bible tells us, "Put on salvation as your
helmet, and take the sword of the Spirit, which is the word of God"
(Ephesians 6:17). This helmet of salvation gives us much more protection than any other kind of helmet could ever give us!

November 14

What was strange about
early basketball courts?

I am giving you these instructions so you will enjoy a long life.
DEUTERONOMY 4:40

In the early days of the game of basketball, the courts often had some strange obstacles. A court might be designed to twist around a pillar or another large object if it happened to be in the way. On some courts, basketballs that went out-of-bounds were still considered in play, so the players had to climb into the stands and struggle with the spectators to get the ball back. Some basketball courts had ropes strung around the edges of them, so the players just bounced off the ropes as if they were boxing instead. Finally, in 1903, basketball courts were given the straight, marked boundaries that became the standard court for the game.

When there are no rules or the rules are unclear, things get confusing and are often unfair. No one really knows the right way to behave. The Bible tells us God's solution: "I am giving you these instructions so you will enjoy a long life" (Deuteronomy 4:40). When you know what to expect, things go much more smoothly.

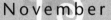

November

Could a cow cure you?

I am the LORD who heals you.
EXODUS 15:26

Thomas Beddoes, an English doctor in the late 1700s, had an idea for how best to cure his patients of all the illnesses they suffered. He believed that if people breathed in air that had first been purified by the presence of animals, they would get better. So whenever the doctor came to call, he left a cow in the sickroom. Not surprisingly, this "cure" didn't work.

Doctors have helped many people get well, and they've come a long way since the days of putting cows in sickrooms. But even so, their abilities can only go so far. In the end, our trust must rest with God. The Bible says, "I am the LORD who heals you" (Exodus 15:26). When you don't feel well, ask God to comfort you. He loves to take care of you, body and soul.

November

How does the sea otter make itself a snack?

The LORD rescued me.
PSALM 118:13

The sea otter stays busy collecting food because it eats as much as a third of its weight in food every day. The first thing a sea otter does is dive under the water, sometimes as far as three hundred feet deep. With one paw, it grabs a rock. With the other paw, it grabs a clam or an abalone. Do otters eat rocks? No, but they do use them to prepare their meals. When the otter swims up to the surface of the water, it flips over onto its back. It places the rock on its stomach, holding it with one paw. With the other paw, which holds the clam, the otter begins to bash the clam snack against the rock. Eventually the shell breaks open, and the otter gobbles the tasty treat that's inside.

Sometimes things just seem to go right, and our tasks are easy. Other times we don't have the right tools, and our jobs seem a lot harder to accomplish. But no matter what kind of experience we're facing, we know that as God's children we don't have to tackle these challenges on our own. Our Father is with us every step of the way. The Bible says it simply, truthfully, and best: "The LORD rescued me" (Psalm 118:13).

November 17

How can you tell if it's a drought?

The generous will prosper; those who refresh
others will themselves be refreshed.
PROVERBS 11:25

Sometimes an area can be experiencing a drought even though it just rained! A drought does not mean it has been too long since it rained. It means that the rain the plants and animals have gotten is not enough to meet their needs. In some places, like New Orleans, Louisiana, a drought can happen if they've gotten only sixty inches of rain instead of the sixty-four they usually get.

As humans, we need water to live. But the Bible reminds us that there are souls that need to be watered too—the souls that are thirsting for Jesus. The Bible says, "The generous will prosper; those who refresh others will themselves be refreshed" (Proverbs 11:25). If you spend time trying to give a blessing to others, you will be blessed also.

November 18

How did paper money become popular?

I don't have any silver or gold for you.
But I'll give you what I have.
ACTS 3:6

In Europe in the Middle Ages, it was the custom for people to keep gold and jewelry in vaults in the basements of goldsmiths' shops. Paper receipts were given to those who brought in their valuables, and they could get them back at any time by handing the goldsmith the receipt. Soon it became inconvenient to go to the vault every time money was needed, and people didn't want to have to carry their gold around. So the rich began to just use the receipts from the goldsmiths' shops to prove that they could afford to buy something, and this became the accepted way to do business.

God's children know that money is not the solution to every problem—the Lord is. We are to give others whatever we can that will make their lives easier. The Bible teaches us how to think about riches when it says, "I don't have any silver or gold for you. But I'll give you what I have" (Acts 3:6). Christ gave his life, so the least we can do is share what we've been given with others.

Why do women wear wedding rings?

I will honor you. . . . I will make you like a signet ring
on my finger, says the LORD, for I have chosen you.
HAGGAI 2:23

Back in biblical times, many Hebrew men wore signet rings, which were easy to identify as theirs. Each ring had some symbol on it—many times an initial—that showed who the ring belonged to. The man could send his ring with his servant or employee, and the worker would show the ring to prove that his boss had given him the authority to take care of his business for him. In the same way, when a woman wore her husband's ring, it was a way of proving to everyone that her husband trusted her to be his partner. She could say what her husband needed, and people would listen to her with respect. Eventually that tradition changed slightly, and women started wearing rings of their own to show they were married.

God has given us the authority to be his messengers, much like the people who used to receive signet rings. We have the privilege of being chosen by him to do his work here on earth. In the Bible, God says, "I will honor you. . . . I will make you like a signet ring on my finger, says the LORD, for I have chosen you" (Haggai 2:23).

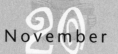

November

How does a hollow tree keep growing anyway?

To everyone who is victorious I will give fruit
from the tree of life in the paradise of God.
REVELATION 2:7

A tree has wood in the middle that is wrapped by bark on the outside, kind of like a tough skin for the tree. When insects or birds make holes in the bark or wind knocks branches down, leaving holes in the bark, fungi or worms that eat wood can get inside the tree through those holes and destroy the wood. Then the tree is left hollow in the middle. But sometimes an amazing thing happens. Even though most of the tree is empty, tiny tubes still run up and down the trunk, very close to the inside of the bark. Those tubes stretch from the soil to bring water to leaves that still grow from the branches, and they carry sap, which helps build new wood. So even though a tree may have a big hole inside, it can still continue to live and grow.

Every tree is special, because God created it. As caretakers of God's creation, we enjoy seeing things grow and stay healthy. But there is one tree that is more special than any other, and one day we will see it. Jesus tells us, "To everyone who is victorious I will give fruit from the tree of life in the paradise of God" (Revelation 2:7). We don't know yet what that tree will look like, but we can be sure it will be awesome to see.

November

What food do you eat that has the wrong name?

We escaped like a bird from a hunter's trap.
The trap is broken, and we are free!
PSALM 124:7

A bird called the guinea fowl was first eaten in Africa; then it was brought to the country of Turkey; and finally the English served the tasty bird and named it the turkey-cock, since it came to England from that country. Later, when the English went to North America, they thought they saw turkey-cock birds and began eating them and calling them turkeys. After some time, it was discovered that these two birds were not the same at all. And that is why our American bird is still called a turkey, even though it had never been in Turkey at all! Every year at the White House, the president "pardons" a turkey from being cooked for Thanksgiving Day. The fortunate turkey is sent to live on a farm for the rest of its life.

Like the turkey at the White House, we have been pardoned, or set free, too. "We escaped like a bird from a hunter's trap. The trap is broken, and we are free!" (Psalm 124:7). That verse describes what happens when we ask Jesus to be our Savior. We receive a pardon for all our sins and an invitation to spend eternity with God in heaven.

November

Why does a cat raise the fur on its back when it's frightened?

I prayed to the LORD, and he answered
me. He freed me from all my fears.
PSALM 34:4

A cat's fur has tiny follicles that hold each hair in place. These follicles are located right next to the cat's skin. When a cat gets scared, the muscles near the follicles tighten up, which causes the fur in each follicle to stand up. When its fur is raised, the cat looks larger, which helps it scare away enemies. The cat's back also arches to make other animals think it is powerful and fierce. A cat also tries to be tough by hissing and making a low noise in its throat.

Fortunately, we don't have to hiss or arch our backs when we are frightened, because we have a better way available to us. The Bible tells us what to do: "I prayed to the LORD, and he answered me. He freed me from all my fears" (Psalm 34:4). God does not want us to feel afraid—he will protect us and keep us safe.

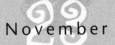

November

Where can you find a pearl?

The blessing of the LORD makes a person rich.
PROVERBS 10:22

Pearls are formed inside oyster shells. The oyster has a soft body, and when it opens its shell, sometimes sand or some other scratchy object gets inside. The oyster grows a smoothing substance, called nacre. It surrounds the piece of sand to keep it from irritating the oyster's body. Layers of this hard substance build up over time, and it becomes a pearl.

An oyster looks very ordinary on the outside, but it makes a beautiful, valuable pearl on the inside. That's how it is for God's children. No matter what kind of house you live in or what clothes you wear, those are just what is on the outside. On the inside, in your heart, is the best treasure. The Bible tells us, "The blessing of the LORD makes a person rich" (Proverbs 10:22).

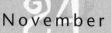

November 24

Why did a book salesman start selling perfume instead?

[God] uses us to spread the knowledge of
Christ everywhere, like a sweet perfume.

2 CORINTHIANS 2:14

In the 1870s, David McConnell sold books door-to-door to earn money for college. When women bought a book from him, he gave them a small gift of perfume. He realized that they were more interested in the perfume than in the books they had just bought, so he decided to sell perfumes and beauty products door-to-door instead. He called his new business, started in 1886, the California Perfume Company. More than forty years later, it became the Avon Company and was well known for the way the products were sold person-to-person rather than in stores. More than one hundred years later, Avon products are still sold much the same way.

David's customers were happy with their tiny gifts of perfume. God gives us the gift of eternal life, and that is infinitely more valuable than perfume. The truth is that the Good News about Jesus is the best smell there is. The Bible says that God "uses us to spread the knowledge of Christ everywhere, like a sweet perfume" (2 Corinthians 2:14).

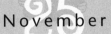

November

Which car was also the name of an article of clothing?

Jesus found a young donkey and rode on it, fulfilling the prophecy that said: "Don't be afraid, people of Jerusalem. Look, your King is coming, riding on a donkey's colt."
JOHN 12:14-15

The name was first given to an area in France and then to the distinctive article of clothing the people in this region wore—a hood with a visor. Next the name referred to fancy horse-drawn carriages that were made in that region. This type of carriage had an enclosed area for the passengers and a separate section with a hood for the driver. Finally, when elegant cars with drivers up front were designed, people used that same name. What was it? That part of France, those special hoods, the carriages, and finally the modern chauffeur-driven automobile were all referred to by the same name—limousine.

Limousines are long and roomy and filled with lots of special additions inside. People who ride in limousines are noticed by everyone and are often treated with importance because the cars are so fancy. Jesus didn't want people to admire him because of his mode of transportation or any other possession. He chose to be born in a stable where animals were kept, and when he entered the city of Jerusalem, he chose to ride through on a lowly donkey. The Bible describes it this way: "Jesus found a young donkey and rode on it, fulfilling the prophecy that said: 'Don't be afraid, people of Jerusalem. Look, your King is coming, riding on a donkey's colt'" (John 12:14-15). Jesus doesn't want anyone to hesitate to come to him. He wants everyone, including you, to feel comfortable and trust that he is never too important to care about you.

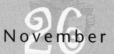

November

What's the background of the blackboard?

Wisdom is far more valuable than rubies.
Nothing you desire can compare with it.
PROVERBS 8:11

Reverend Samuel Read Hall was a schoolteacher for many years. Then in 1823 he started the Concord Academy, the first school in the United States dedicated to teaching teachers the best ways to teach. That is when Reverend Hall also revealed his invention of the blackboard. It was a smoothed-down, simple pine board that was painted black. Writing on the board with chalk enabled teachers to show the whole class the same information at the same time.

In the course of your lifetime, you will no doubt have many good teachers. Some you'll find in school, some may be your parents, and some may be relatives or friends or mentors who teach you a skill. God wants us to realize that "wisdom is far more valuable than rubies. Nothing you desire can compare with it" (Proverbs 8:11). Think of it this way. If you just have a certain number of rubies, eventually you will run out of them. But wisdom keeps serving you for your entire life.

What made the soap float?

Though your sins are like scarlet, I will make
them as white as snow. Though they are red like
crimson, I will make them as white as wool.
ISAIAH 1:18

The story has been told that Ivory Soap was invented by accident. An employee who was mixing up a batch of what was called White Soap went to lunch and forgot to turn off the churning soap machines. When he came back he realized his mistake, but it didn't seem to have hurt the soap any, so it was shipped out with all the other batches. But then people started asking for the new White Soap that floated. The customers who bought from the lunchtime batch found that the soap floated in the bathwater. That was because the extra churning added extra bubbles in the soap, which made it lighter than water. The Procter and Gamble Company decided to keep making the soap with added bubbles. But later, according to Procter and Gamble, some inventor's notes were discovered that revealed that maybe James Gamble had always intended for White Soap to float. No one knows for sure. But what is known is that Henry Procter got the name for the soap from listening to his minister in church, who read this verse from the Scriptures: "All thy garments smell of myrrh . . . out of the ivory palaces" (Psalm 45:8, KJV). And that is when he decided that the name should be changed to Ivory Soap.

The best part about soap is that you're clean after you use it. And the best part about Jesus is that you're clean on the inside after you ask him to come into your life. The Bible says, "Though your sins are like scarlet, I will make them as white as snow. Though they are red like crimson, I will make them as white as wool" (Isaiah 1:18). Being with Jesus is the only way to be spotless in your heart.

November

Where is it really difficult to get sick in the winter?

He forgives all my sins and heals all my diseases.
PSALM 103:3

The best place to stay healthy is the North Pole. It's very rare to get the flu or a cold or any viruses or germs there. The usual disease-causing micro-organisms cannot survive there to be spread from person to person. It is just too cold for the germs to survive.

To Jesus, the hurts his children receive to their spirits are even more important than the illnesses of their bodies. That is why the Bible tells us that "he forgives all my sins and heals all my diseases" (Psalm 103:3). Take all your troubles to the Lord, and he will take care of your hurts.

November

Do all birds fly?

In his grace, God has given us different
gifts for doing certain things well.
ROMANS 12:6

Believe it or not, just because we call it a bird doesn't always mean it can fly. Any bird that flies has huge chest muscles that are much larger than the rest of its body so it can flap its wings hard enough to carry it into the air. But some birds don't have big muscles in their chests, and they must stay on the ground. Big birds like the ostrich and the penguin have wings, but their wings don't work well enough to get them off the ground.

Our heavenly Father designed every creature—he gave each one the ability to do different things in different ways. God gave every person unique talents too. There are things you can do that others can't. Maybe you are able to dance or memorize things well or solve math problems without much trouble. Whatever you are good at, God designed you that way. The Bible reminds us, "In his grace, God has given us different gifts for doing certain things well" (Romans 12:6).

November

Why did people wear pouches around their waists?

Better to have little, with fear for the LORD, than
to have great treasure and inner turmoil.
PROVERBS 15:16

In the beginning, it seemed like a good idea. These pouches, which were like small bags, were invented so people could have an easy place to keep their money. The pouch just hung from a string that was tied on like a belt. The problems were that thieves could easily reach the pouches they saw and people had to remember to add the pouches to their wardrobes every day. To make it harder for robbers to attack, people began wearing the pouches *inside* their pants. But that created a new complication—it was very difficult for the owner to reach his own money. So slits were made in the side of pants, allowing the owner to open his money bag more easily. Then came the idea that the pouch should be sewn onto the inside of the pants, so people wouldn't forget to take it with them. Finally, in the seventeenth century, the pouches themselves were abandoned, and pockets replaced them.

People give a lot of thought to protecting their possessions. That's not a bad idea, but the Bible tells us there's something even more important: "Better to have little, with fear for the LORD, than to have great treasure and inner turmoil" (Proverbs 15:16). If you allow the Lord to keep track of what belongs to you, you will see what he thinks is most important for you to have. He cares about your heart, not about your wealth or what you own.

December 1

Which cake mix was named after a traveling salesman?

Your name, O LORD, endures forever; your fame,
O LORD, is known to every generation.
PSALM 135:13

You've probably seen Duncan Hines cake mixes in the grocery store or even in your own cupboard. But Duncan Hines wasn't a baker or a cook of any kind. He was an author who wrote about food cooked by others. In 1928 Duncan Hines was a salesman who traveled all over the United States, and he began taking notes about every restaurant he ate at along the way. He became famous in 1936 for writing a book that told traveling Americans which restaurants along the roadways served the best food. Soon the restaurants that were praised in Duncan's book began to hang signs out front that said, "Recommended by Duncan Hines." People trusted Duncan's opinion about which foods were the most enjoyable to eat. After ten years of writing about restaurants, Duncan Hines was considered a food specialist, and that is why he gave permission for his name to be used on boxes of baked goods. As soon as people saw the name Duncan Hines, they wanted the cake mixes that he liked enough to put his name on.

Do you think Duncan Hines liked being famous for cakes or for being a writer? Is it better to be a famous athlete or a famous pianist or a famous teacher? The truth is, there are about as many ways to be famous as there are human beings on earth. But there would be only one winner in a contest for "most famous person on earth and in heaven." The Bible says, "Your name, O LORD, endures forever; your fame, O LORD, is known to every generation" (Psalm 135:13). Jesus Christ will always be the most famous winner of our hearts and souls.

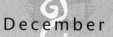

December 2

Why does a toadstool care about its posture?

As long as the earth remains, there will be planting and harvest, cold and heat, summer and winter, day and night.
GENESIS 8:22

A toadstool is a mushroom that has a stem with a round cap on top. But have you ever looked underneath a toadstool's hat? If you look closely, you'll find many gills, or frilly sections of the toadstool, that line up closely to each other. Between the gills are millions of tiny seedlike spores, which eventually drop down through the spaces and are carried away by the wind to make new toadstools. What you may not know is that the toadstool's most important job is to always be paying attention to gravity! The gills need to be lined up exactly with the ground, making it easy for the spores to drop down. If the toadstool leans in either direction, the gills will quickly adjust themselves until they perfectly match the slant of the earth below again. A tilting toadstool will be constantly aligning itself.

There are so many wonderful living things that God created for the earth, and each plant and animal seems to hold a special surprise when you take the time to look carefully. God has a plan for each of his creations, just as he has a plan for each of his children. The Bible tells us, "As long as the earth remains, there will be planting and harvest, cold and heat, summer and winter, day and night" (Genesis 8:22). Try to find new surprises wherever you look. If you made a list of them, you could keep on writing forever!

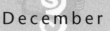

December

How did a twelve-year-old find a huge fossil?

Patient endurance is what you need now,
so that you will continue to do God's will.
HEBREWS 10:36

Mary Anning grew up in a family without much money. She lived in England, near some cliffs called Lyme Regis. These cliffs held fossils that her family would dig up and sell to tourists. Mary's father died in 1810, when Mary was eleven, but she continued to look for fossils to sell to help support her family. When Mary was twelve, she and her brother made a gigantic discovery. They saw the outline of a very large fossil in the cliffs. They thought it was a four-foot-long alligator. But within a year of chipping away rock, Mary had exposed and excavated another twenty-six feet of fossil! The fossil was an ichthyosaur, a large extinct reptile. This was the first of several major fossils that Mary found. She was able to support her family by selling the fossils and to help scientists learn how she found and recovered the fossils. She was called the "Princess of Paleontology."

Mary and her family showed a lot of patience as they dug out the fossils. We all need patience too, whether we're doing schoolwork, waiting in line, or counting down the days until a big event. The Bible says, "Patient endurance is what you need now, so that you will continue to do God's will" (Hebrews 10:36).

December 4

How much sleep is just right?

People who work hard sleep well.
ECCLESIASTES 5:12

When you are asleep, your body has time to get refreshed and your mind has a chance to catch up on all the thoughts you had during the day. Adults in 1900 slept about nine hours every night, but six to seven hours became the normal amount for adults as time went on. If you're between the ages of seven and twelve, doctors say you need around ten to eleven hours. Newborn babies sleep up to twenty hours out of twenty-four, with plenty of short wake-up times added in. They need a lot of sleep because their bodies are growing so fast. As for animals and insects, the koala bear sleeps twenty-two hours a day, the elephant sleeps only two hours, and the ant sleeps just a few minutes.

There is nothing like a good night's sleep to end a busy day. Do your best from morning until night, and then you'll be able to say, "People who work hard sleep well" (Ecclesiastes 5:12).

December 5

Which popular drink had no liquid in it?

God loved the world so much that he gave his
one and only Son, so that everyone who believes
in him will not perish but have eternal life.
JOHN 3:16

When this drink was first invented, it was a liquid in a corked bottle and was called Fruit Smack, with flavors of cherry, grape, orange, lemon-lime, raspberry, and strawberry. It was Edwin Perkins's creation, but he soon realized how expensive it was to mail to people who ordered it, and there was also the problem of the glass bottles breaking. Edwin had been experimenting and inventing things since he was young, and he was able to remove the liquid and make the drink into a powder in 1927, much like the Jell-O mixture he admired so much. His powder could easily be mailed in small packets, which is the way this drink has been sold since. In 1950 his company made a million packets a day! The name was changed from Fruit Smack to one that the whole country learned to recognize—it became Kool-Aid!

Kool-Aid was invented to be sent through the mail. What's the best thing that anybody's ever sent to you in the mail? No matter what's been brought to you by a mail truck, it will never be better than what God has sent to you and everyone else in the world. The Bible tells us, "God loved the world so much that he gave his one and only Son, so that everyone who believes in him will not perish but have eternal life" (John 3:16). You can receive God's gift any time you want to, and you don't have to pay even a penny for it.

December

How many faces can you make?

Let your face smile on us, LORD.
PSALM 4:6

Believe it or not, someone counted them! There are forty different muscles in your face. You can arrange those muscles 340 ways by pushing, pulling, squeezing, or stretching them, which means that you can make five thousand different expressions with your face! That's a good thing, because the looks you make with your face can be understood all over the world, no matter what language the people who see them speak. If you make a frown, everyone can see that you're not happy. If you raise your eyebrows, you are asking a question. People everywhere can share their feelings using their faces, without saying a word.

It is interesting to study faces and to decide what the expressions mean. But no face could ever be more precious for God's children to see than the face of our Lord. This is one of our greatest requests: "Let your face smile on us, LORD" (Psalm 4:6). There can be no doubt about the joy his face brings us!

December

What was the start of the stapler?

Praise the Lord; praise God our savior! For
each day he carries us in his arms.
PSALM 68:19

The earliest stapler appeared in offices in 1914, but it was not very easy to use. Staples came wrapped in paper, and each time the stapler was pressed, a new staple had to be pushed through the paper surrounding it. If the staples came out of the stapler at all, many of them were bent before they even got a chance to do their job. Finally, in 1922, someone came up with a better idea. The Boston Wire Stitcher Company, which later became Bostitch, had a solution that worked. They were responsible for the idea of gluing all the staples together in a row, which meant that the staples didn't get caught in their own paper wrappers anymore.

Have you ever had one of those days when the tool you need most gets broken or you lose your favorite pen or you miss your favorite TV show? Or maybe the dog throws up on the carpet, your sister is wearing your socks, and there's going to be liver for dinner tonight. Jesus knows what those kind of days feel like. But he also knows that none of those things are as important as choosing to follow God anyway. He will help you keep your patience, overcome obstacles, and remain kind even when you don't want to. The Bible tells us how God responds when we have tough days: "Praise the Lord; praise God our savior! For each day he carries us in his arms" (Psalm 68:19).

December

Which finger is the most important?

All of you together are Christ's body,
and each of you is a part of it.
1 CORINTHIANS 12:27

You use your hands to do many things, and your hands need your fingers to get things done. But one finger is the most helpful of all: your thumb. Without a thumb, you couldn't tie a bow. You couldn't catch a baseball. You couldn't pick up a grain of sand. The thumb can do things that your other fingers can't do. Your thumb is the only finger that can directly touch the tips of the other fingers on the same hand. And your thumb is the only finger that can stretch to touch the opposite side of your palm. Try an experiment. Tape your thumb across your palm so that you are not able to move it. Now see how many other activities are difficult—or impossible—to do without it.

Just as God designed each part of your body to perform certain activities, like lifting or walking or thinking, he calls each of his children to be a part of spreading the word about Jesus Christ. We each have a special job to accomplish. The Bible says, "All of you together are Christ's body, and each of you is a part of it" (1 Corinthians 12:27).

December

9

What else can you ski on besides snow?

[God] changes rivers into deserts, and
springs of water into dry, thirsty land.
PSALM 107:33

In 1922, people were only skiing in the winter—on snow. But teenager Ralph Samuelson wondered if it was possible to ski on water, too. So he decided to find out if it could be done. The first challenge was what to use for skis. The first day, Ralph tried his snow skis, and he sank. The next day, he tried wooden slats from a barrel, and he sank. Next were eight-foot-long pine boards with curled tips. Those worked best, but they cracked, so he had the local blacksmith reinforce them with metal. Through all the test runs, kids lined up along the shore of the Lake City Marina in Minneapolis to laugh at Ralph's failures. But day after day, he wouldn't give up. He finally found the right type of rope to hold on to and then the right way to stand on his skis so the speedboat could pull him up onto the water. At last he had accomplished his goal—he was waterskiing! He spent many years giving exhibits of skiing tricks near his home and then in Florida. In 1966 he was officially named the "father of waterskiing."

When we think about all the work Ralph Samuelson did just to conquer the water, we realize how powerless humans really are compared to the majesty of God. The Bible says that God "changes rivers into deserts, and springs of water into dry, thirsty land" (Psalm 107:33). God is all-powerful. You are far better off going to the source of all power for help than trying to do things all on your own. Want to conquer fear? Go to Jesus and he will help you. Want to be wiser? Go to Jesus and he will teach you. Want to be a better person? Go to Jesus and he will show you how. The answer to all you need will always be Jesus.

December

Why did all New Yorkers stay inside one morning?

The very essence of your words is truth; all your
just regulations will stand forever.
PSALM 119:160

James Gordon Bennett was the publisher of the *New York Herald* newspaper, and one night he bragged to his friends that he could make the people of New York do anything he wanted them to. He claimed he would prove it the next morning by keeping them all off the streets, which were always busy. Sure enough, there was no one outside the next morning. How did James keep everyone at home? He ordered a story printed on the front page of his paper about dangerous zoo animals that had escaped and were roaming around the city hurting people. Everyone who read the paper stayed inside, until they began to realize that the story was only a trick. Then life slowly went back to normal, and everyone started up with their busy schedules again.

Sometimes things you read or hear about can turn out to be false or misleading or just someone's opinion. But that's not true about what you read in the Bible. The Bible is where you will find the Word of God, which is described this way: "The very essence of your words is truth; all your just regulations will stand forever" (Psalm 119:160). God would never play a joke on you or tell a lie or try to make you do something just to show how powerful he is. You will never read anything in the Bible that you later find out was just a trick.

December 11

How did Spam get its name?

I rejoice in your word like one who discovers a great treasure.
PSALM 119:162

What do you do with several thousand pounds of pork shoulder that you have no plans for? In 1927 the Hormel meatpacking plant found out about a new idea from an executive: the pork could be chopped up, and then the ham and some spices could be added into a can with a clear gelatin that encased all the food products. A contest was held, offering a one-hundred-dollar prize, to give the new invention a catchier name than Hormel Spiced Ham, which was the original name. A Hormel executive's brother won with his idea of *Spam*, taking the "sp" from "spiced" and the "am" from "ham." People have eaten Spam since it was introduced in 1937, at a rate of about 122 million cans a year. Because Spam seemed to be everywhere and was included in many different meals, a skit was performed on TV in the 1970s in which everything on a menu had Spam in it. Later, because people poked fun at Spam for being eaten in so many ways, *spam* was also the word chosen for unwanted e-mails that are sent to people's computers.

The Hormel company didn't realize that the leftover ham it had would become such a treasure. That surprise doesn't even come close to the treasure of following Jesus Christ. The Bible says, "I rejoice in your word like one who discovers a great treasure" (Psalm 119:162). When you follow the words of Jesus, you find a way to live that you will treasure forever.

December

What made the paper bag popular?

Anyone who believes in God's Son has eternal life.
JOHN 3:36

The first paper bag machine made a bag that was large but was shaped like an envelope at the bottom, so it didn't open wide or hold much. Then along came Margaret Knight, who improved the paper bag in the 1870s by creating a machine that made the bags square and flat on the bottom. Suddenly people found that the bags could hold much more and were easier and more efficient to use. A small change made a very big difference!

When you decide to accept Jesus Christ into your life by believing in him, God will cause a change that's much greater and more useful than any improvement to a paper bag could be. The Bible promises, "Anyone who believes in God's Son has eternal life" (John 3:36). What could be a more important change in your life than that?

December

Why did remote controls make watching TV harder at first?

Teach us to number our days aright,
that we may gain a heart of wisdom.
PSALM 90:12, NIV

It took a while to make a television remote control that worked well. Here are some of the problems encountered along the way. The first remote control, operated by radio waves, sometimes changed the channel on your neighbor's TV when it changed yours, or let your neighbor change *your* channel in the middle of your favorite show. Definitely not a successful idea! The next experiment was a remote control that used a cable. The trouble was that people kept tripping over the cable wire that stretched across the room from the remote control in your hand to the TV—a solution that was too dangerous. Another idea was the wireless remote control. Believe it or not, ordinary sunshine could change a channel just like the remote control could, so all day long, the sun was in charge of your TV. The last unsuccessful remote control used ultrasound, which produced a high-pitched sound that made dogs bark—and just the clinking of silverware during dinner could change the channel as well. There were many plans that failed before a workable answer was finally found.

What a lot of effort went into changing the number of a TV channel! The Bible advises us to pay more attention to a different number. It tells us to ask God to "teach us to number our days aright, that we may gain a heart of wisdom" (Psalm 90:12, NIV). When we count days instead of TV channels, we are learning how we can live our lives more fully.

December

Why are the teeth of animals so different from ours?

[God] gives food to the wild animals and
feeds the young ravens when they cry.
PSALM 147:9

A walrus sticks its tusks into the ice to pull its body out of the water. A parrot fish's teeth are set all the way down its throat so it can chew its food on the way to its stomach. Rodents, like mice and hamsters and squirrels, have to chew constantly to help wear down their teeth, or the teeth will grow too big for their mouths. Many herbivores (animals that eat only plants), such as cows, don't have any upper teeth in the front of their mouths. They use their lips and gums and tongues to pull plants into their mouths and then push the plants to the back of their mouths, where the molars chew them. People don't need to do all those tasks animals do, so our teeth are much better suited to our human mouths than any of these animal teeth would be.

When God takes care of his creation, he thinks of everything. Not only did he design animals' mouths to be excellent tools for them, but he also takes care of their other needs. The Bible tells us, "He gives food to the wild animals and feeds the young ravens when they cry" (Psalm 147:9). It is astounding to think that God can keep track of what each creature needs and when it needs it. He loves us much more than the animals, so we can trust that he is taking even better care of our needs—often before we even know we need something.

December

What makes soda fizzy?

How joyful are those who fear the LORD and
delight in obeying his commands.
PSALM 112:1

When you are going to drink a soda, there are bubbles in it as you open it up. Have you ever wondered why they are there? They are added to your soda on purpose. At the factory, carbon dioxide, which stays in the form of bubbles, is forced into your drink. As you open it, the bubbles are released again and come out.

The next time you have a bubbly drink, imagine that each bubble is a little celebration for you from God. He is happy that you are his child! The Bible says, "How joyful are those who fear the LORD and delight in obeying his commands" (Psalm 112:1). Try to count your "bubble blessings" if you can—there will probably be way more than you can keep track of.

December

Why would a bird spit?

My God is my rock, in whom I find protection.
He is my shield, the power that saves me, and
my place of safety. He is my refuge, my savior,
the one who saves me from violence.
2 SAMUEL 22:3

A small bird called a swift has an unusual way of protecting its eggs. It spits on them! You might be wondering how that could help, but the missing clue is that the swift's saliva is sticky like glue. The swift covers its eggs with saliva, and they become glued to the nest. That way the eggs won't fall out when a strong wind blows, and no other creatures can steal the eggs from the nest—they won't move. The swift also glues the pieces of its nest together so the nest becomes one of the strongest in the bird world. Why doesn't the swift's saliva glue its own beak shut? That's the best part! The saliva doesn't turn to glue until it dries.

Just as the swift protects its baby birds, the Lord protects his children. The Bible tells us what God is like: "My God is my rock, in whom I find protection. He is my shield, the power that saves me, and my place of safety. He is my refuge, my savior, the one who saves me from violence" (2 Samuel 22:3). You can feel safe and secure knowing that God will never let you fall once you are in the circle of his heavenly arms.

December 17

What's worse than a snowsuit?

She has no fear of winter for her household,
for everyone has warm clothes.
PROVERBS 31:21

Children couldn't have enjoyed being dressed for winter in Victorian times (during the 1800s in England). First, their chests were smeared with lots of goose grease to keep them warm. Next, they put on their underclothes, which were sewn shut (except for the button flaps in the seat) until spring. There were no baths throughout the winter. In America, children almost suffered the same treatment. In Pennsylvania in 1840, there was a law that some people tried to pass that would have required American children to follow the same types of customs. Fortunately, it didn't pass.

Since indoor heating systems didn't exist hundreds of years ago like they do today, parents had to find other ways to keep their children warm through the winter. No matter how old you are, it's always a good idea to be prepared so you can carry out your responsibilities. The Bible tells what a woman who is prepared is like: "She has no fear of winter for her household, for everyone has warm clothes" (Proverbs 31:21). When you think ahead and make plans—for example, making sure your dog has fresh water before you leave the house—you can be confident you've done the best job you could.

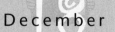

December

Why do fireflies blink?

The way of the righteous is like the first gleam of dawn,
which shines ever brighter until the full light of day.
PROVERBS 4:18

Fireflies are also called lightning bugs, and they use the lights in their bodies to send messages. They tell other fireflies who they are and warn all other creatures to stay away. There is a special chemical that reacts inside the firefly's abdomen that allows it to light up and blink off and on for the rest of the world to see.

The Bible says, "The way of the righteous is like the first gleam of dawn, which shines ever brighter until the full light of day" (Proverbs 4:18). When you walk through a bunch of fireflies that are twinkling at night, you get a little glimpse of the excitement of knowing that the Lord is leading you with his loving glow.

December 19

What miniature toy did almost every boy wish for in the 1950s?

Character strengthens our confident hope of salvation.
And this hope will not lead to disappointment. For we
know how dearly God loves us, because he has given
us the Holy Spirit to fill our hearts with his love.
ROMANS 5:4-5

The most popular wish boys made was to have an electric toy train set of their own. In 1953, the Lionel Corporation, which made trains, was the largest toy manufacturer in the world, with two thousand employees. The trains they made came with many choices. Some had engines with pretend smoke coming out of the smokestacks, others had real working windshield wipers, and of course there were engines that whistled. Some trains had milk cars with milkmen to load tiny milk cans onto the train. If a button was pressed, it would open the door of the cattle car, and the cattle would come out of the train and into a corral. To try to appeal to little girls, Lionel made train cars that were pink, blue, yellow, and purple in 1957. But most girls didn't like them, so in 1959 the toy company stopped making trains for girls. The inventor of the electric toy train, Joshua Lionel Cowen, made his first train when he was just seven years old. He carved it out of wood and put a small steam engine in it, but it didn't work well and blew up instead. Joshua also invented the funny electric flowerpot you can read about on December 24, and he invented the first electric doorbell for houses.

Everyone knows what it's like to wish for something. Most of our wishes are for things we've seen here on earth, like a toy or a house or special clothes. But our hearts should yearn to have something much greater. The Bible tells us, "Character strengthens our confident hope of salvation. And this hope will not lead to disappointment. For we know how dearly God loves us, because he has given us the Holy Spirit to fill our hearts with his love" (Romans 5:4-5). Anything we might own will never bring the same thrill as knowing we are children of God forever.

December

What can you prove with bare feet and a refrigerator?

The LORD is your security. He will keep your
foot from being caught in a trap.
PROVERBS 3:26

Try this experiment. Take off your shoes and socks, and stand in front of a closed refrigerator for fifteen seconds. Are your feet cooler, or is your forehead? Now open the refrigerator door, stand up close, and answer the same question. This time your feet should feel a rush of cool air that you really notice. Why? The air in the refrigerator is around 35 degrees, and cool air is always heavier than warm air. The cool air won't travel up and hit you in the face. It will go down to the bottom of the warm air outside the door, which means it will sweep over your feet instead.

God made certain laws about our earth to be consistently true, like the way cold air goes lower and heat rises. You can have confidence in the way God has planned things. You can also have confidence that God cares about your feet, your whole body, and your soul. A little cold air won't hurt your feet, but not following in the Lord's footsteps could get you into trouble. Keep believing in God's love for you, and do your best to please him each day. The Bible tells us, "The LORD is your security. He will keep your foot from being caught in a trap" (Proverbs 3:26). You can count on God to keep his promises.

December 21

How did a mousetrap catch a thief?

I have chosen the way of truth;
I have set my heart on your laws.
PSALM 119:30, NIV

In 1853, seventeen-year-old Jay Gould was going to New York to find someone who would help him sell a better mousetrap. His grandfather designed it but gave the mousetrap to Jay to see if he could make a fortune with it. When Jay got to New York City, he took a trolley to get to the business district. The mousetrap was on the seat beside him, inside a very expensive-looking wooden box. Jay went to the back of the trolley to look at all the gigantic buildings, and when he returned to his seat, the beautiful box was gone. The trolley driver told him that a man had just gotten off the bus with the box. Jay chased after the man, quickly pinning him to the ground and grabbing the box. Just then a policeman came by, and the thief started yelling that Jay was robbing him! The policeman took Jay and the other man to the station, and it was there that Jay won the fight. Jay was the only one who could say what was in the box, proving that he was the owner. And the thief was shocked to learn that the fancy box held not jewels or gold but only one very plain and practical invention.

What really saved the day for Jay was being able to tell the truth about what was inside the fancy box. It's amazing what rewards can come when you do not lie. The Bible tells us the best way to live: "I have chosen the way of truth; I have set my heart on your laws" (Psalm 119:30, NIV). Try to pay attention to what you say each day, and strive to be truthful. It is a quality that makes people trust you, and it also makes God happy.

D e c e m b e r

Can you explain the sneeze, please?

The Spirit of God has made me, and the
breath of the Almighty gives me life.
JOB 33:4

There are lots of reasons people sneeze. The sneeze is a reflex, or reaction, to an irritant that is bothering the nerve endings in the mucous membrane of your nose. Irritants can be just about anything—infection or pollen or dust or any number of other things that might fly up your nose. The sneeze tries very forcefully to blow that awful thing out, and it travels at one hundred miles per hour! But have you ever noticed that going out in bright sunlight can also make you sneeze? Called the photic sneeze reflex, it happens to about a fourth of all people. Of course, even at 1.7 miles a minute, your sneeze will never blow out the sun!

Sneezing can be annoying, but it's a sign that you're alive, and that's something to be thankful for. The Bible says, "The Spirit of God has made me, and the breath of the Almighty gives me life" (Job 33:4). Whether you're breathing in or sneezing out, remember that God has more for you to do on this earth, because he is sustaining you by giving you breath.

December

Why do mirrors get foggy?

Guard me as you would guard your own eyes.
Hide me in the shadow of your wings.
PSALM 17:8

When the mirror in the bathroom fogs up and you can't see yourself, what causes this? It is a mixture of hot and cold. Your shower creates warm, steamy air that fills the bathroom. Then the air comes into contact with the still-cold mirror. When warm steam hits something cool, it cools down itself and turns into very tiny drops of water. The drops make a smeary, foggy appearance on the mirror. Technically, steam is a gas that turns into a liquid, and that process is called condensation. The same thing happens when a dentist puts a mirror into your mouth. When your warm breath hits the surface, it creates a foggy layer over the small mirror.

The next time you see a foggy mirror, imagine you are frightened and need a place to hide. Look how the fog makes it hard to see. When you really are frightened, run to Jesus. He will cover you and protect you even better than the fog could hide you. The Bible says, "Guard me as you would guard your own eyes. Hide me in the shadow of your wings" (Psalm 17:8). Trust Jesus to be your safe place.

December 24

What invention grew out of a funny electric flowerpot?

The Word gave life to everything that was created, and his life brought light to everyone. The light shines in the darkness, and the darkness can never extinguish it.

JOHN 1:4-5

The answer is the flashlight! First came the invention of electricity, and then the battery was invented. A man named Joshua Cowen decided to make an electric flowerpot just for fun. He put a tube with a battery and a light inside a fake flowerpot so it lit up a fake flower. But people didn't really like this funny invention. What they wished for was a useful way to carry a light with them wherever they were going. Conrad Hubert came up with the solution in 1898. The new invention was called a "flash light" because it didn't stay on very long. But with the improvement of batteries, that problem was solved. Every flashlight came in a handmade paper container reinforced with fiber. To get people familiar with using flashlights, they were given away for free to New York City policemen. The policemen liked them, and the flashlight eventually became a popular tool for everyone.

It's very helpful to be able to see where you are going. As God's child, you receive a special gift that we celebrate at Christmas—Jesus Christ, the Light of the World! The Bible tells us, "The Word gave life to everything that was created, and his life brought light to everyone. The light shines in the darkness, and the darkness can never extinguish it" (John 1:4-5). Let each sparkling light you see remind you of the excitement of the coming of Jesus!

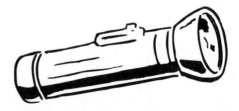

December 25

How did animal crackers become a Christmas present?

The Savior—yes, the Messiah, the Lord—has been
born today in Bethlehem, the city of David!
LUKE 2:11

Cookies in the shapes of animals were first made in England. In 1902 the Nabisco company decided to bake animal crackers in the United States, after adding eighteen new types of animals. The cookies were called Barnum's Animals, in honor of the popular Barnum and Bailey Circus. All twenty-two types of animals were packed in a small box that looked like an animal cage from the circus. The box had a string attached to use as a handle. This made the box a fun toy so kids could pretend it was a purse, but that's not why the handle was added. The animal crackers were first offered for sale right before Christmas, and the handle turned the box into an ornament that parents could hang on the Christmas tree.

Although animal crackers were an enjoyable Christmas gift, nothing can compare to the gift God gave the world for Christmas. This is the day we celebrate the birth of the baby Jesus. The Bible tells us, "The Savior—yes, the Messiah, the Lord—has been born today in Bethlehem, the city of David!" (Luke 2:11). The first Christmas was a special part of God's plan. He brought Jesus into the world so we could be with him in heaven by choosing to follow him. There has never been, and never will be, a better gift than that!

December

Why would potato farmers be interested in jellyfish?

I am the light of the world. If you follow me,
you won't have to walk in darkness, because
you will have the light that leads to life.

JOHN 8:12

Scientists tried adding the protein that makes a jellyfish glow into the cells of a potato. What they got was a potato that glows yellow when it needs to be watered. The glow alerts monitors out in the field to send a signal to the farmer, who then knows it's time to spray the potato patch.

Jesus said, "I am the light of the world. If you follow me, you won't have to walk in darkness, because you will have the light that leads to life" (John 8:12). Isn't it exciting for God's children when the light of Jesus comes shining into their hearts? It is even more special than discovering a potato that can light up.

December 27

What inspired the baby mobile?

It is the LORD who provides the sun to light the day
and the moon and stars to light the night.
JEREMIAH 31:35

Go into almost any store that sells baby cribs, and you'll find that most of the cribs have a swinging, swaying, twirling colorful gadget attached to them. When this hanging object is wound up, it begins to move in a circle above the baby's head to entertain the baby. It's called a mobile (because it moves), and it was Alexander Calder who created the original idea and found a way to make it work. Alexander was an artist, but he also studied engineering. He said that the solar system was his inspiration for how to make the little shapes move around one another. "I work from a large, live model!" he exclaimed.

Alexander must have spent a lot of time studying the skies to get his idea for the baby mobile. There's no better place to come up with ideas than from God's creation! The Bible says, "It is the LORD who provides the sun to light the day and the moon and stars to light the night" (Jeremiah 31:35). It's a compliment to God's creativity when we come up with ideas of our own that reflect his amazing handiwork.

December

How can you help someone who is fainting?

Have you never heard? Have you never understood?
The LORD is the everlasting God, the Creator of all
the earth. He never grows weak or weary.
ISAIAH 40:28

In movies and on TV shows, actors usually fall straight backward when they're supposed to be fainting, because that is more interesting to watch than what really happens. People who are truly fainting fall to the side or fall forward. If you notice that someone is about to faint, you should get beside or in front of the person if you can. Then you can help hold him or her up or at least stop the person from crashing directly to the ground.

Because we are human, our bodies get weak and may even faint. But you never need to worry about God losing his strength that way. The Bible says, "Have you never heard? Have you never understood? The LORD is the everlasting God, the Creator of all the earth. He never grows weak or weary" (Isaiah 40:28). God wants to hold you up and help you along when you feel weak. Ask him to be your Lord today!

What game inspired the merry-go-round?

Are any of you happy? You should sing praises.
JAMES 5:13

In Italy in the seventeenth century, athletes played sports and games in a tournament called a *carosello*. The game that inspired the merry-go-round, or carousel, was one in which someone rode a galloping horse around a circular track. The idea was for the rider to try to poke his spear through a ring and collect the ring on his spear at the same time he was riding around the track. That is why on the earliest carousels there was always a brass ring hanging nearby that the riders on the wooden horses tried to grab as the carousel went around and around. Later the carousel came to America and also came to be known as the merry-go-round. The brass ring is usually not included anymore, but riding on the pretend horses is still a lot of fun.

Riding a merry-go-round can be lots of fun. God wants us to enjoy ourselves. And one of the ways we can show we're happy is to sing. The Bible says about Christians, "Are any of you happy? You should sing praises" (James 5:13). The next time you are having a wonderful time, sing!

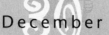

December

What's proof of a dutiful dog?

Remember and obey all the commands of the LORD.
NUMBERS 15:39

There is a story of a mixed-breed dog that loved candy. One day the dog noticed a bowl of candy on a table next to where the dog's master was sitting. The owner watched while the dog snuck over to the bowl and took a piece of candy. But the dog knew it wasn't supposed to eat the treat. It took the candy back to the rug by the fireplace and played with it for a moment, never looking its master in the eye. Finally the dog gave a big sigh, walked back to the candy dish on the table, and dropped the wrapped candy back into the bowl.

It's not always easy to be obedient and follow the rules, but it's the right thing to do. The Bible says, "Remember and obey all the commands of the LORD" (Numbers 15:39). Imagine how happy the dog's owner was when the dog returned the candy, and then think how much greater the joy of Jesus is when you make the choice to follow his commands.

December 31

Why do evergreens stay green all year long?

You have been born again, but not to a life that will quickly end. Your new life will last forever because it comes from the eternal, living word of God.

1 PETER 1:23

Evergreens have thin, needle-shaped leaves instead of circular, flat ones. Since water soaks up into trees from their roots and then evaporates through their leaves, the trees with fatter leaves lose more water. Trees are able to keep more water by dropping off the big leaves when the fall season comes. But evergreen needles have a waxy coating and don't lose much water, so they stay attached to their trees and bushes through all the seasons. Since evergreens keep their leaves, they are able to store up chlorophyll (the substance that gives them their green color) until warmer weather returns.

It makes us happy to see trees that stay green all the time. But there's even more joy in knowing that you will live eternally in heaven with God. The Bible says, "You have been born again, but not to a life that will quickly end. Your new life will last forever because it comes from the eternal, living word of God" (1 Peter 1:23). The tree is just evergreen, but a decision to ask Jesus to be the Lord of your life is everlasting.

Notes

JANUARY 1
Where did the first calendar come from?
Andrew Dunn, *The Children's Atlas of Scientific Discoveries and Inventions* (Brookfield, CT: Millbrook Press, 1997).

JANUARY 2
When were ducks in the Olympics?
Steve Riach, *Amazing but True Sports Stories* (Kansas City, MO: Hallmark Books, 2004).

JANUARY 3
How did a three-year-old inspire the invention of a camera?
Roger Bridgman, *1,000 Inventions and Discoveries* (New York: DK Publishing, 2002).
Rodney Carlisle, *Scientific American Inventions and Discoveries: All the Milestones in Ingenuity—from the Discovery of Fire to the Invention of the Microwave Oven* (Hoboken, NJ: Wiley & Sons, 2004).
Andrea Chesman, ed., *The Inventive Yankee: From Rockets to Roller Skates, 200 Years of Yankee Inventors and Inventions* (Dublin, NH: Yankee Books, 1989).
Norman King, *The Almanac of Fascinating Beginnings: From the Academy Awards to the Xerox Machine* (Secaucus, NJ: Carol Publishing Group, 1994).

JANUARY 4
Why would you need a big boat to help build a road?
Rodney Carlisle, *Scientific American Inventions and Discoveries: All the Milestones in Ingenuity—from the Discovery of Fire to the Invention of the Microwave Oven* (Hoboken, NJ: Wiley & Sons, 2004).
Sharon Bertsch McGrayne, *Blue Genes and Polyester Plants: 365 More Surprising Scientific Facts, Breakthroughs, and Discoveries* (New York: Wiley & Sons, 1997).
Steve Parker, *53½ Things That Changed the World and Some That Didn't* (New York: Simon and Schuster, 1992).

JANUARY 5
Why won't your ballpoint pen write, even when it has plenty of ink?
Ty Reynolds, ed., *That's a Good Question 6* (Calgary, Alberta: Script Publishing, 1995).

JANUARY 6
What's in your kitchen that used to be locked in a safe?
Rodney Carlisle, *Scientific American Inventions and Discoveries: All the Milestones in Ingenuity—from the Discovery of Fire to the Invention of the Microwave Oven* (Hoboken, NJ: Wiley & Sons, 2004).
Charlotte Foltz Jones, *Accidents May Happen: Fifty Inventions Discovered by Mistake* (New York: Delacorte Press, 1996).
Bill McLain, *What Makes Flamingos Pink: A Colorful Collection of Q and A's for the Unquenchably Curious* (New York: HarperCollins, 2001).

JANUARY 7
Take a toothpick, some cotton, and a baby's ear, and what do you get?
Johnny Acton, Tania Adams, and Matt Packer, *Origin of Everyday Things* (New York: Sterling, 2006).
Stephen van Dulken, *American Inventions: A History of Curious, Extraordinary, and Just Plain Useful Patents* (New York: New York University Press, 2004).

JANUARY 8
How do iguanas skydive?
Bruce Witherspoon, *The Great Big Book of Astounding Facts: A Compendium of Everything You Never Knew You Needed to Know* (New York: Bristol Park Books, 1993).

JANUARY 9
When did a mirror take the place of a person?
Don L. Wulffson, *The Kid Who Invented the Popsicle, and Other Surprising Stories about Inventions* (New York: Cobblehill Books/ Dutton, 1997).

JANUARY 10
When did a president play a joke on his guests?
Paul Boller, *Presidential Anecdotes* (New York: Oxford University Press, 1981).
David Hardy, *What a Mistake!* (Secaucus, NJ: Octopus Books, 1987).

JANUARY 11
Which food product tasted much better the older it got?
Charlotte Foltz Jones, *Accidents May Happen: Fifty Inventions Discovered by Mistake* (New York: Delacorte Press, 1996).
Charles Panati, *Panati's Extraordinary Origins of Everyday Things* (New York: Harper and Row, 1987).

JANUARY 12
What do we eat that has a smile on it?
Phil Gates, *Nature Got There First* (New York: Kingfisher, 1995).
Charlotte Foltz Jones, *Eat Your Words: A Fascinating Look at the Language of Food* (New York: Delacorte Press, 1999).
Christopher Maynard, *Why Are Pineapples Prickly? Questions Children Ask about Food* (New York: DK Publishing, 1997).
Mitchell Symons, *The Other Book . . . of the Most Perfectly Useless Information* (New York: HarperCollins, 2006).

JANUARY 13
Why do cows seem sloppy and slow?
Steve Murrie and Matthew Murrie, *Every Minute on Earth: Fun Facts That Happen Every 60 Seconds* (New York: Scholastic, 2007).
Mike O'Connor, *Why Don't Woodpeckers Get Headaches? and Other Bird Questions You Know You Want to Ask* (Boston: Beacon Press, 2007).

JANUARY 14
Why did people suddenly want a mouse in their homes?
Johnny Acton, Tania Adams, and Matt Packer, *Origin of Everyday Things* (New York: Sterling, 2006).
Roger Bridgman, *1,000 Inventions and Discoveries* (New York: DK Publishing, 2002).
David E. Brown, *Inventing Modern America: From the Microwave to the Mouse* (Cambridge, MA: MIT Press, 2002).
Ty Reynolds, ed., *That's a Good Question 6* (Calgary, Alberta: Script Publishing, 1995).

JANUARY 15
Which sea creature couldn't survive without its powerful eyes?
Phil Gates, *Nature Got There First* (New York: Kingfisher, 1995).

JANUARY 16
What tricks can a crow perform?
Bruce Witherspoon, *The Great Big Book of Astounding Facts: A Compendium of Everything You Never Knew You Needed to Know* (New York: Bristol Park Books, 1993).

JANUARY 17
Who would want to go where the burglars are?
Johnny Acton, Tania Adams, and Matt Packer, *Origin of Everyday Things* (New York: Sterling, 2006).

JANUARY 18
What invention did a kindergartener think of and build?
Steven Caney, *Steven Caney's Invention Book* (New York: Workman Publishing, 1985).
Rodney Carlisle, *Scientific American Inventions and Discoveries: All the Milestones in Ingenuity—from the Discovery of Fire to the Invention of the Microwave Oven* (Hoboken, NJ: Wiley & Sons, 2004).
Arlene Erlbach, *The Kids' Invention Book* (Minneapolis: Lerner Publishing Group, 1997).
Norman King, *The Almanac of Fascinating Beginnings: From the Academy Awards to the Xerox Machine* (Secaucus, NJ: Carol Publishing Group, 1994).

JANUARY 19
Why does the woodpecker hit its own head?
Phil Gates, *Nature Got There First* (New York: Kingfisher, 1995).
Steve Murrie and Matthew Murrie, *Every Minute on Earth: Fun Facts That Happen Every 60 Seconds* (New York: Scholastic, 2007).
Mike O'Connor, *Why Don't Woodpeckers Get Headaches? and Other Bird Questions You Know You Want to Ask* (Boston: Beacon Press, 2007).

JANUARY 20
What was Blibber-Blubber?
Johnny Acton, Tania Adams, and Matt Packer, *Origin of Everyday Things* (New York: Sterling, 2006).
Lee Wardlaw, *Bubblemania: The Chewy History of Bubble Gum* (New York: Aladdin, 1997).

JANUARY 21
What can a snake's teeth tell you?
Bruce Witherspoon, *The Great Big Book of Astounding Facts: A Compendium of Everything You Never Knew You Needed to Know* (New York: Bristol Park Books, 1993).

JANUARY 22
How did the first artificial snow on a ski slope get there?
Andrea Chesman, ed., *The Inventive Yankee: From Rockets to Roller Skates, 200 Years of Yankee Inventors and Inventions* (Dublin, NH: Yankee Books, 1989).

JANUARY 23
Which animal attacks by running backward?
Phil Gates, *Nature Got There First* (New York: Kingfisher, 1995).

JANUARY 24
Buffalo don't fly, so what are "buffalo wings"?
Charlotte Foltz Jones, *Eat Your Words: A Fascinating Look at the Language of Food* (New York: Delacorte Press, 1999).

JANUARY 25
How was a teapot responsible for waking people up each morning?
Roger Bridgman, *1,000 Inventions and Discoveries* (New York: DK Publishing, 2002).
Jilly MacLeod, *Great Inventions* (Mankato, MN: Creative Education, 1997).

JANUARY 26
What makes snow crunchy?
Mark Eubank, *The Weather Detectives: Fun-Filled Facts, Experiments, and Activities for Kids!* (Layton, UT: G. Smith, Publisher, 2004).
Terry Martin, *Why Does Lightning Strike? Questions Children Ask about the Weather* (New York: DK Publishing, 1996).
Mitchell Symons, *The Other Book . . . of the Most Perfectly Useless Information* (New York: HarperCollins, 2006).

JANUARY 27
Where did the sports term first string *come from?*
Don Wulffson and Pam Wulffson, *Abracadabra to Zombie: More than 300 Wacky Word Origins* (New York: Dutton Children's Books/Penguin, 2003).

JANUARY 28
Oranges and lemons: to stamp or to sticker?
Ty Reynolds, ed., *That's a Good Question 6* (Calgary, Alberta: Script Publishing, 1995).

JANUARY 29
Is talking easier for men or women?
Bruce Witherspoon, *The Great Big Book of Astounding Facts: A Compendium of Everything You Never Knew You Needed to Know* (New York: Bristol Park Books, 1993).

JANUARY 30
How could a mom cuddle her baby without using her hands?
Susan Casey, *Women Invent! Two Centuries of Discoveries That Have Shaped Our World* (Chicago: Chicago Review Press, 1997).

Catherine Thimmesh, *Girls Think of Everything: Stories of Ingenious Inventions by Women* (New York: Houghton Mifflin, 2000).

JANUARY 31
What car was the first car Henry Ford built?
Wes Hardin, *Henry Ford Museum: An ABC of American Innovation* (New York: Harry N. Abrams, 1997).
David Rubel, *The United States in the 19th Century* (New York: Scholastic, 1996).
Mitchell Symons, *The Other Book . . . of the Most Perfectly Useless Information* (New York: HarperCollins, 2006).

FEBRUARY 1
How did a mistake and a teacher inspire the invention of the paper towel?
Don L. Wulffson, *The Kid Who Invented the Popsicle and Other Surprising Stories about Inventions* (New York: Cobblehill Books/Dutton, 1997).

FEBRUARY 2
Which piece of clothing always has a buttonhole without a matching button?
Lesley Scott and Brenda Apsley, *315 Children's Questions and Answers* (New York: Derrydale Books, 1985).

FEBRUARY 3
Why were there so many toothbrushes in the White House?
James Humes, *Which President Killed a Man? Tantalizing Trivia and Fun Facts about Our Chief Executives and First Ladies* (New York: McGraw-Hill, 2003).

FEBRUARY 4
What is inside an apple?
Christopher Maynard, *Why Are Pineapples Prickly? Questions Children Ask about Food* (New York: DK Publishing, 1997).

FEBRUARY 5
What was so special about rubber gloves?
Don L. Wulffson, *The Kid Who Invented the Popsicle and Other Surprising Stories about Inventions* (New York: Cobblehill Books/Dutton, 1997).

FEBRUARY 6
Why is bread in the shape it's in?
David Feldman, *Why Do Pirates Love Parrots?* (New York: HarperCollins, 2006).

FEBRUARY 7
How did one man make laughter his life's work?
Don Wulffson, *Toys! Amazing Stories behind Some Great Inventions* (New York: Henry Holt, 2000).

FEBRUARY 8
What are some things you can count on about money?
Lesley Scott and Brenda Apsley, *315 Children's Questions and Answers* (New York: Derrydale Books, 1985).
Barbara Seuling, *You Can't Count a Billion Dollars, and Other Little-Known Facts about Money* (Garden City, NY: Doubleday, 1979).

FEBRUARY 9
Why do we say "o'clock"?
James Meyers, *The Best Amazing Question and Answer Book* (New York: Playmore, Inc. Publishers, 1987).

FEBRUARY 10
Why did people put Bubble Wrap on their walls?
Johnny Acton, Tania Adams, and Matt Packer, *Origin of Everyday Things* (New York: Sterling, 2006).
Roger Bridgman, *1,000 Inventions and Discoveries* (New York: DK Publishing, 2002).

FEBRUARY 11
How does sand help eggs hatch?
Animals in Action (Alexandria, VA: Time-Life Books, 1988).

FEBRUARY 12
How can you tell a moth and a butterfly apart?
Jane Parker Resnick, Rebecca L. Grambo, and Tony Tallarico, *The Big Book of Questions and Answers* (Boston: Kidsbooks, 2002).

FEBRUARY 13
How did the spicy sauce horseradish get its name?
Don Wulffson and Pam Wulffson, *Abracadabra to Zombie: More than 300 Wacky Word Origins* (New York: Dutton Children's Books/Penguin, 2003).

FEBRUARY 14
Which finger is closest to the heart?
Don L. Wulffson, *The Kid Who Invented the Popsicle, and Other Surprising Stories about Inventions* (New York: Cobblehill Books/Dutton, 1997).

FEBRUARY 15
How old was the inventor of the scooter?
Don L. Wulffson, *The Kid Who Invented the Popsicle, and Other Surprising Stories about Inventions* (New York: Cobblehill Books/Dutton, 1997).

FEBRUARY 16
Why was 1908 such a happy year for dogs?
Linda Schmittroth, ed., *Eureka! Scientific Discoveries & Inventions That Shaped the World*, vol. 2, (New York: International Thomson Publishing, 1995).

FEBRUARY 17
When could you talk by telephone to the president of the United States?
James Humes, *Which President Killed a Man? Tantalizing Trivia and Fun Facts about Our Chief Executives and First Ladies* (New York: McGraw-Hill, 2003).
Richard Lederer, *Presidential Trivia: The Feats, Fates, Families, Foibles, and Firsts of Our American Presidents* (Layton, UT: Gibbs Smith, 2007).
Barbara Taylor, *I Wonder Why Zippers Have Teeth, and Other Questions about Inventions* (New York: Kingfisher, 1995).

FEBRUARY 18
How did LEGOs get their name?
Gil Asakawa and Leland Rucker, *The Toy Book* (New York: Knopf, 1991).

Allyn Freeman and Bob Golden, *Why Didn't I Think of That? Bizarre Origins of Ingenious Inventions We Couldn't Live Without* (New York: Wiley & Sons, 1997).

Deborah Jaffé, *The History of Toys: From Spinning Tops to Robots* (Stroud, England: Sutton, 2006).

Andrew McClary, *Toys with Nine Lives: A Social History of American Toys* (North Haven, CT: Linnet Books, 1997).

Steve Murrie and Matthew Murrie, *Every Minute on Earth: Fun Facts That Happen Every 60 Seconds* (New York: Scholastic, 2007).

Steve Parker, *53½ Things That Changed the World and Some That Didn't* (New York: Simon and Schuster, 1992).

Don Wulffson, *Toys! Amazing Stories behind Some Great Inventions* (New York: Henry Holt, 2000).

FEBRUARY 19
What makes flamingos so pink?
Terry Martin, *Why Are Zebras Black and White? Questions Children Ask about Color* (New York: DK Publishing, 1996).

Bill McLain, *What Makes Flamingos Pink? A Colorful Collection of Q and A's for the Unquenchably Curious* (New York: HarperCollins, 2001).

John Mitchinson and John Lloyd, *The Book of General Ignorance* (New York: Harmony Books/Random House, 2007).

Mike O'Connor, *Why Don't Woodpeckers Get Headaches? and Other Bird Questions You Know You Want to Ask* (Boston: Beacon Press, 2007).

FEBRUARY 20
What's in your closet that took the place of a hook?
Stephen van Dulken, *American Inventions: A History of Curious, Extraordinary, and Just Plain Useful Patents* (New York: New York University Press, 2004).

Don L. Wulffson, *The Kid Who Invented the Trampoline: More Surprising Stories about Inventions* (New York: Dutton Children's Books/Penguin, 2001).

FEBRUARY 21
What do the keys to the city open?
George Stimpson, *Why Do Some Shoes Squeak? And 568 Other Popular Questions Answered* (New York: Bell Publishing, 1984).

FEBRUARY 22
How did a bottle turn into a rubber band?
Don Wulffson, The *Invention of Ordinary Things* (New York: Lothrop, Lee, and Shepard Books, 1981).

FEBRUARY 23
What's the story behind the letters j and w in our alphabet?
Don Wulffson and Pam Wulffson, *Abracadabra to Zombie: More than 300 Wacky Word Origins* (New York: Dutton Children's Books/Penguin, 2003).

FEBRUARY 24
What was a fly bat, and why was it invented?
Harry Harris, *Good Old-Fashioned Yankee Ingenuity: Unsung Triumphs of American Invention* (Chelsea, MA: Scarborough House, 1990).

Don L. Wulffson, *The Kid Who Invented the Popsicle, and Other Surprising Stories about Inventions* (New York: Cobblehill Books/Dutton, 1997).

FEBRUARY 25
Do mice have anything to do with an athlete's muscles?
James Meyers, *The Best Amazing Question and Answer Book* (New York: Playmore, Inc. Publishers, 1987).

FEBRUARY 26
Why did babies wear pieces of shower curtains?
Linda Schmittroth, ed., *Eureka! Scientific Discoveries & Inventions That Shaped the World*, vol. 2, (New York: International Thomson Publishing, 1995).

FEBRUARY 27
Can you name that cheese, please?
The Galahad Treasury of Trivia (New York: Galahad Books, 1979).

FEBRUARY 28
What happens to the missing leap year birthdays?
Lesley Scott and Brenda Apsley, *315 Children's Questions and Answers* (New York: Derrydale Books, 1985).

George Stimpson, *Why Do Some Shoes Squeak? And 568 Other Popular Questions Answered* (New York: Bell Publishing, 1984).

MARCH 1
Why do we call it a Caesar salad?
Charlotte Foltz Jones, *Eat Your Words: A Fascinating Look at the Language of Food* (New York: Delacorte Press, 1999).

MARCH 2
What happened to all the cars?
Bruce Witherspoon, *The Great Big Book of Astounding Facts: A Compendium of Everything You Never Knew You Needed to Know* (New York: Bristol Park Books, 1993).

MARCH 3
How much salt could you earn in a day?
Charlotte Foltz Jones, *Eat Your Words: A Fascinating Look at the Language of Food* (New York: Delacorte Press, 1999).

MARCH 4
Which American candy was named after someone's daughter?
Allyn Freeman and Bob Golden, *Why Didn't I Think of That? Bizarre Origins of Ingenious Inventions We Couldn't Live Without* (New York: Wiley & Sons, 1997).

Norman King, *The Almanac of Fascinating Beginnings: From the Academy Awards to the Xerox Machine* (Secaucus, NJ: Carol Publishing Group, 1994).

Don Wulffson and Pam Wulffson, *Abracadabra to Zombie: More than 300 Wacky Word Origins* (New York: Dutton Children's Books/Penguin, 2003).

MARCH 5
What in the world was a "Dial-a-Fish"?
Arlene Erlbach, *The Kids' Invention Book* (Minneapolis: Lerner Publishing Group, 1997).

MARCH 6
When was there a garage sale on the lawn of the White House?
Paul Boller, *Presidential Anecdotes* (New York: Oxford University Press, 1981).

James Humes, *Which President Killed a Man? Tantalizing Trivia and Fun Facts about Our Chief Executives and First Ladies* (New York: McGraw-Hill, 2003).

MARCH 7
What did Vaseline have to do with oil wells?
Allyn Freeman and Bob Golden, *Why Didn't I Think of That? Bizarre Origins of Ingenious Inventions We Couldn't Live Without* (New York: Wiley & Sons, 1997).

David Lindsay, *House of Invention: The Secret Life of Everyday Products* (New York: Lyons Press, 2000).

Stephen van Dulken, *American Inventions: A History of Curious, Extraordinary, and Just Plain Useful Patents* (New York: New York University Press, 2004).

MARCH 8
What's the best way to tell time on a ship?
Elaine Israel, ed., *The World Almanac for Kids 2001* (New York: The World Almanac Education Group, 2000).

MARCH 9
Can you imagine a bicycle with ten seats?
Wes Hardin, *Henry Ford Museum: An ABC of American Innovation* (New York: Harry N. Abrams, 1997).

MARCH 10
What don't you know about the ladybug?
Jacqui Bailey, *Amazing Animal Facts* (New York: DK Publishing, 2003).

Phil Gates, *Nature Got There First* (New York: Kingfisher, 1995).

MARCH 11
Do large or small hailstones cause the most damage?
Rhoda Blumberg and Lela Blumberg, *The Simon and Schuster Book of Facts and Fallacies* (New York: Simon and Schuster, 1983).

MARCH 12
What was the first book ever printed?
Andrew Dunn, *The Children's Atlas of Scientific Discoveries and Inventions* (Brookfield, CT: Millbrook Press, 1997).

MARCH 13
What was the one place the bus used to stop?
Don Wulffson and Pam Wulffson, *Abracadabra to Zombie: More than 300 Wacky Word Origins* (New York: Dutton Children's Books/Penguin, 2003).

MARCH 14
Why don't spiders get stuck in their own webs?
Jane Parker Resnick, Rebecca L. Grambo, and Tony Tallarico, *The Big Book of Questions and Answers* (Boston: Kidsbooks, 2002).

MARCH 15
How did three men change the world of medicine?
Roger Bridgman, *1,000 Inventions and Discoveries* (New York: DK Publishing, 2002).

Elaine Israel, ed. *The World Almanac for Kids 2001* (New York: The World Almanac Education Group, 2000).

Steve Parker, *53½ Things That Changed the World and Some That Didn't* (New York: Simon and Schuster, 1992).

Steve Tomecek, *What a Great Idea! Inventions That Changed the World* (New York: Scholastic Nonfiction, 2003).

David Wallechinsky, *The People's Almanac Presents the Twentieth Century: History with the Boring Parts Left Out* (New York: Overlook Press, 1999).

Don L. Wulffson, *The Kid Who Invented the Popsicle, and Other Surprising Stories about Inventions* (New York: Cobblehill Books/Dutton, 1997).

MARCH 16
What odd ideas made terrible inventions?
Jilly MacLeod, *Great Inventions* (Mankato, MN: Creative Education, 1997).

Stephen van Dulken, *American Inventions: A History of Curious, Extraordinary, and Just Plain Useful Patents* (New York: New York University Press, 2004).

MARCH 17
What's one way to catch a criminal?
Tim Wood, *What They Don't Teach You about History: Hundreds of Peculiar and Fascinating Facts* (Hemel Hempstead, Great Britain: Simon and Schuster, 1990).

MARCH 18
What city is home to the most bats?
Jacqui Bailey, *Amazing Animal Facts* (New York: DK Publishing, 2003).

Jenny E. Tesar, *America's Top 10 Curiosities* (Woodbridge, CT: Blackbirch Press, 1998).

MARCH 19
How did an eleven-year-old help change history?
David E. Brown, *Inventing Modern America: From the Microwave to the Mouse* (Cambridge, MA: MIT Press, 2002).

MARCH 20
Which covered wagon was the best in the west?
Richard Ammon, *Conestoga Wagons* (New York: Holiday House, 2000).

Tim McNeese, *Conestogas and Stagecoaches* (New York: Maxwell Macmillan International, 1993).

MARCH 21
Why is it easier to walk than to stand still?
David Feldman, *Why Do Pirates Love Parrots?* (New York: HarperCollins, 2006).

MARCH 22
Which animal builds its own haystack?
Mark Eubank, *The Weather Detectives: Fun-Filled Facts, Experiments, and Activities for Kids!* (Layton, UT: G. Smith, Publisher, 2004).

MARCH 23
What if there were bread at the end of your pencil?
Rodney Carlisle, *Scientific American Inventions and Discoveries: All the Milestones in Ingenuity—from the Discovery of Fire to the Invention of the Microwave Oven* (Hoboken, NJ: Wiley & Sons, 2004).
Linda Schmittroth, ed., *Eureka! Scientific Discoveries & Inventions That Shaped the World*, vol. 2, (New York: International Thomson Publishing, 1995).
Don L. Wulffson, *The Kid Who Invented the Trampoline: More Surprising Stories about Inventions* (New York: Dutton Children's Books/ Penguin, 2001).

MARCH 24
What if you learned your ETAs instead of your ABCs?
Bruce Witherspoon, *The Great Big Book of Astounding Facts: A Compendium of Everything You Never Knew You Needed to Know* (New York: Bristol Park Books, 1993).

MARCH 25
Why was the money on the move?
Bruce Witherspoon, *The Great Big Book of Astounding Facts: A Compendium of Everything You Never Knew You Needed to Know* (New York: Bristol Park Books, 1993).

MARCH 26
How did a trail lead to trivia?
Don Wulffson and Pam Wulffson, *Abracadabra to Zombie: More than 300 Wacky Word Origins* (New York: Dutton Children's Books/Penguin, 2003).

MARCH 27
Why was the hopperdozer invented?
W. R. Runyan, *Whiffletrees and Goobers: 1,001 Fun and Fabulous Forgotten Words and Phrases* (New York: Skyhorse Publishing, 2007).

MARCH 28
Which lizard swims in the sand?
Bruce Witherspoon, *The Great Big Book of Astounding Facts: A Compendium of Everything You Never Knew You Needed to Know* (New York: Bristol Park Books, 1993).

MARCH 29
How many times would you chew?
Bruce Witherspoon, *The Great Big Book of Astounding Facts: A Compendium of Everything You Never Knew You Needed to Know* (New York: Bristol Park Books, 1993).

MARCH 30
What makes the starfish special?
Jane Parker Resnick, Rebecca L. Grambo, and Tony Tallarico, *The Big Book of Questions and Answers* (Boston: Kidsbooks, 2002).

MARCH 31
Where did the "Happy Birthday" song come from?
Kevin Davis, *Look What Came from the United States* (New York: F. Watts, 1999).

Norman King, *The Almanac of Fascinating Beginnings: From the Academy Awards to the Xerox Machine.* (Secaucus, NJ: Carol Publishing Group, 1994).
Don Wulffson and Pam Wulffson, *Abracadabra to Zombie: More than 300 Wacky Word Origins* (New York: Dutton Children's Books/Penguin, 2003).

APRIL 1
What's so crooked about croquet?
Don L. Wulffson, *The Kid Who Invented the Popsicle, and Other Surprising Stories about Inventions* (New York: Cobblehill Books/Dutton, 1997).

APRIL 2
Who was P. T. Barnum?
P. T. Barnum, *Struggles and Triumphs* (Hartford: J. B. Burr, 1869).
Andrea Chesman, ed., *The Inventive Yankee: From Rockets to Roller Skates, 200 Years of Yankee Inventors and Inventions* (Dublin, NH: Yankee Books, 1989).
David Rubel, *The United States in the 19th Century* (New York: Scholastic, 1996).

APRIL 3
What was an electric sink?
Daniel Cohen, *The Last Hundred Years, Household Technology* (New York: M. Evans, 1982).

APRIL 4
Which cure for a disease actually made it worse?
Steve Parker, *53½ Things That Changed the World and Some That Didn't* (New York: Simon and Schuster, 1992).

APRIL 5
Why are Campbell's soup cans red and white?
Erin Barrett and Jack Mingo, *Not Another Apple for the Teacher! Hundreds of Fascinating Facts from the World of Teaching* (Berkeley, California: Conari Press/Red Wheel Weiser, 2002).
Bill McLain, *What Makes Flamingos Pink: A Colorful Collection of Q and A's for the Unquenchably Curious* (New York: HarperCollins, 2001).
Steve Murrie and Matthew Murrie, *Every Minute on Earth: Fun Facts That Happen Every 60 Seconds* (New York: Scholastic, 2007).
Ty Reynolds, ed., *That's a Good Question 6* (Calgary, Alberta: Script Publishing, 1995).
Don Wulffson and Pam Wulffson, *Abracadabra to Zombie: More than 300 Wacky Word Origins* (New York: Dutton Children's Books/Penguin, 2003).

APRIL 6
Why count the chirps of crickets?
Mark Eubank, *The Weather Detectives: Fun-Filled Facts, Experiments, and Activities for Kids!* (Layton, UT: G. Smith, Publisher, 2004).
Robert Wolke, *What Einstein Didn't Know* (Secaucus, NJ: Carol Publishing Group, 1997).

APRIL 7
Why would a beetle stand on its head?
Jane Parker Resnick, Rebecca L. Grambo, and Tony Tallarico, *The Big Book of Questions and Answers* (Boston: Kidsbooks, 2002).

APRIL 8
Does a bird really "eat like a bird"?
Rhoda Blumberg and Lela Blumberg, *The Simon and Schuster Book of Facts and Fallacies* (New York: Simon and Schuster, 1983).

APRIL 9
How did mirrors help fight a war?
The Galahad Treasury of Trivia (New York: Galahad Books, 1979).

APRIL 10
Why don't bones break as easily while you're young?
Bruce Witherspoon, *The Great Big Book of Astounding Facts: A Compendium of Everything You Never Knew You Needed to Know* (New York: Bristol Park Books, 1993).

APRIL 11
When was there a surprise family reunion?
Bruce Witherspoon, *The Great Big Book of Astounding Facts: A Compendium of Everything You Never Knew You Needed to Know* (New York: Bristol Park Books, 1993).

APRIL 12
Which invention was created to pay a debt?
Johnny Acton, Tania Adams, and Matt Packer, *Origin of Everyday Things* (New York: Sterling, 2006).
David Rubel, *The United States in the 19th Century* (New York: Scholastic, 1996).
Don L. Wulffson, *The Kid Who Invented the Trampoline: More Surprising Stories about Inventions* (New York: Dutton Children's Books/ Penguin, 2001).

APRIL 13
What extremely unusual thing happened to President Andrew Jackson—twice?
Thomas Ayres, *That's Not in My American History Book* (Austin, TX: Taylor Trade Publishing, 2000).

APRIL 14
Why aren't all rivers straight?
Bill Nye, *Bill Nye the Science Guy's Consider the Following* (New York: Disney Press, 1995).

APRIL 15
How were people able to buy extra time?
Joel Levy, *Really Useful: The Origins of Everyday Things* (Willowdale, ON: Firefly Books, 2002).
Jane Wilcox, *Why Do We Use That?* (New York: F. Watts, 1996).
Don L. Wulffson, *The Kid Who Invented the Trampoline: More Surprising Stories about Inventions* (New York: Dutton Children's Books/ Penguin, 2001).

APRIL 16
What's so nutty about the nuthatch?
Mike O'Connor, *Why Don't Woodpeckers Get Headaches? and Other Bird Questions You Know You Want to Ask* (Boston: Beacon Press, 2007).

APRIL 17
What's wrong with the way we draw raindrops?
Jane Parker Resnick, Rebecca L. Grambo, and Tony Tallarico, *The Big Book of Questions and Answers* (Boston: Kidsbooks, 2002).

APRIL 18
Where did the name motel come from?
Johnny Acton, Tania Adams, and Matt Packer, *Origin of Everyday Things* (New York: Sterling, 2006).
David Rubel, *The United States in the 19th Century* (New York: Scholastic, 1996).

APRIL 19
How long can a sermon be?
Bruce Witherspoon, *The Great Big Book of Astounding Facts: A Compendium of Everything You Never Knew You Needed to Know* (New York: Bristol Park Books, 1993).

APRIL 20
What huts were popular in the 1940s?
Andrea Chesman, ed., *The Inventive Yankee: From Rockets to Roller Skates, 200 Years of Yankee Inventors and Inventions* (Dublin, NH: Yankee Books, 1989).

APRIL 21
What do bats and dolphins have in common?
Jane Parker Resnick, Rebecca L. Grambo, and Tony Tallarico, *The Big Book of Questions and Answers* (Boston: Kidsbooks, 2002).

APRIL 22
Why do we feel cold when we're wet?
Barbara Taylor, *I Wonder Why Soap Makes Bubbles, and Other Questions about Science* (New York: Kingfisher, 1994).

APRIL 23
How was a bird responsible for starting Guinness World Records?
Joel Levy, *Really Useful: The Origins of Everyday Things* (Willowdale, ON: Firefly Books, 2002).
Don L. Wulffson, *The Kid Who Invented the Trampoline: More Surprising Stories about Inventions* (New York: Dutton Children's Books/ Penguin, 2001).

APRIL 24
Why did a hearing aid weigh sixteen pounds?
Rodney Carlisle, *Scientific American Inventions and Discoveries: All the Milestones in Ingenuity—from the Discovery of Fire to the Invention of the Microwave Oven* (Hoboken, NJ: Wiley & Sons, 2004).
Don L. Wulffson, *The Kid Who Invented the Popsicle, and Other Surprising Stories about Inventions* (New York: Cobblehill Books/Dutton, 1997).

APRIL 25
Have you ever wondered why we blink?
Steve Murrie and Matthew Murrie, *Every Minute on Earth: Fun Facts That Happen Every 60 Seconds* (New York: Scholastic, 2007).
Mitchell Symons, *The Other Book . . . of the Most Perfectly Useless Information* (New York: HarperCollins, 2006).

APRIL 26
What's the largest living thing on earth?
John Mitchinson and John Lloyd, *The Book of General Ignorance* (New York: Harmony Books/ Random House, 2007).

APRIL 27
Eaten any Twinkle Fingers lately?
Don L. Wulffson, *The Kid Who Invented the Popsicle, and Other Surprising Stories about Inventions* (New York: Cobblehill Books/ Dutton, 1997).
Carolyn Wyman, *I'm a Spam Fan: America's Best-Loved Foods* (Stamford, CT: Longmeadow Press, 1993).

APRIL 28
What tales does a squirrel's tail tell?
Bill McLain, *What Makes Flamingos Pink: A Colorful Collection of Q and A's for the Unquenchably Curious* (New York: HarperCollins, 2001).

APRIL 29
What sparked the idea for the first fire hose?
Don L. Wulffson, *The Kid Who Invented the Trampoline: More Surprising Stories about Inventions* (New York: Dutton Children's Books/ Penguin, 2001).

APRIL 30
How was a little electricity tamed?
Roger Bridgman, *1,000 Inventions and Discoveries* (New York: DK Publishing, 2002).
Linda Schmittroth, ed., *Eureka! Scientific Discoveries & Inventions That Shaped the World*, vol. 2, (New York: International Thomson Publishing, 1995).

MAY 1
What was the best way to park a covered wagon?
Christy Maganzini, *Cool Math: Math Tricks, Amazing Math Activities, Awesome Math Factoids, and More* (New York: Price Stern Sloan, 1997).

MAY 2
Where could you shop for items from around the world?
Allan Fowler, *World's Fairs and Expos* (Chicago: Children's Press, 1991).

MAY 3
Who first declared war on germs?
Roger Bridgman, *1,000 Inventions and Discoveries* (New York: DK Publishing, 2002).
Steve Parker, *53½ Things That Changed the World and Some That Didn't* (New York: Simon and Schuster, 1992).
Steve Tomecek, *What a Great Idea! Inventions That Changed the World* (New York: Scholastic Nonfiction, 2003).
Peter Turvey, *Inventors and Ingenious Ideas* (New York: Franklin Watts, 1992).

MAY 4
Why would you give someone a "white elephant"?
Marvin Terban, *In a Pickle, and Other Funny Idioms* (New York: Clarion Books, 1983).

MAY 5
What kind of jar could make you jump?
Roger Bridgman, *1,000 Inventions and Discoveries* (New York: DK Publishing, 2002).

MAY 6
Why was everyone talking about the temperature?
Jane Parker Resnick, Rebecca L. Grambo, and Tony Tallarico, *The Big Book of Questions and Answers* (Boston: Kidsbooks, 2002).

MAY 7
What did Wilt the Stilt do to make basketball history?
Bruce Witherspoon, *The Great Big Book of Astounding Facts: A Compendium of Everything You Never Knew You Needed to Know* (New York: Bristol Park Books, 1993).

MAY 8
Do all mosquitoes bite?
Rhoda Blumberg and Lela Blumberg, *The Simon and Schuster Book of Facts and Fallacies* (New York: Simon and Schuster, 1983).

MAY 9
Could the tortoise really beat the hare?
The Galahad Treasury of Trivia (New York: Galahad Books, 1979).

MAY 10
How many offspring are springing off?
Bruce Witherspoon, *The Great Big Book of Astounding Facts: A Compendium of Everything You Never Knew You Needed to Know* (New York: Bristol Park Books, 1993).

MAY 11
How does a sponge hold so much water with all those holes?
Jane Parker Resnick, Rebecca L. Grambo, and Tony Tallarico, *The Big Book of Questions and Answers* (Boston: Kidsbooks, 2002).

MAY 12
What tricky words can you use to stump your friends?
The Galahad Treasury of Trivia (New York: Galahad Books, 1979).

MAY 13
Can lightning strike twice?
The Galahad Treasury of Trivia (New York: Galahad Books, 1979).

MAY 14
Why did people bounce up and down in the 1920s?
Johnny Acton, Tania Adams, and Matt Packer, *Origin of Everyday Things* (New York: Sterling, 2006).

MAY 15
What got grown-ups practicing their painting?
Johnny Acton, Tania Adams, and Matt Packer, *Origin of Everyday Things* (New York: Sterling, 2006).

MAY 16
Which bird prefers to live underground?
Jane Parker Resnick, Rebecca L. Grambo, and Tony Tallarico, *The Big Book of Questions and Answers* (Boston: Kidsbooks, 2002).

MAY 17
How fast was the Pony Express?
Andrea Chesman, ed., *The Inventive Yankee: From Rockets to Roller Skates, 200 Years of Yankee Inventors and Inventions* (Dublin, NH: Yankee Books, 1989).
Bill McLain, *What Makes Flamingos Pink: A Colorful Collection of Q and A's for the Unquenchably Curious* (New York: HarperCollins, 2001).
Mitchell Symons, *The Other Book . . . of the Most Perfectly Useless Information* (New York: HarperCollins, 2006).

MAY 18
What was so sweet about Milton Hershey?
Betty Burford, *Chocolate by Hershey: A Story about Milton S. Hershey* (Minneapolis: Carolrhoda Books, 1994).
Steve Murrie and Matthew Murrie, *Every Minute on Earth: Fun Facts That Happen Every 60 Seconds* (New York: Scholastic, 2007).

MAY 19
What's the sweetest place on earth?
Betty Burford, *Chocolate by Hershey: A Story about Milton S. Hershey* (Minneapolis: Carolrhoda Books, 1994).
Steve Murrie and Matthew Murrie, *Every Minute on Earth: Fun Facts That Happen Every 60 Seconds* (New York: Scholastic, 2007).

MAY 20
What's so great about these two states?
George Stimpson, *Why Do Some Shoes Squeak? And 568 Other Popular Questions Answered* (New York: Bell Publishing, 1984).

MAY 21
What was the big breakthrough for whipped cream?
Charles Panati, *Panati's Extraordinary Origins of Everyday Things* (New York: Harper and Row, 1987).

MAY 22
Which brand of coffee was named after a hotel?
Noah McCullough, *The Essential Book of Presidential Trivia* (New York: Random House, 2006).

MAY 23
What's unusual about "home sweet home" for these animals?
John Nicholson, *Animal Architects* (Crows Nest, NSW: Allen & Unwin, 2003).

MAY 24
Does each tree grow only one kind of leaf?
Rhoda Blumberg and Lela Blumberg, *The Simon and Schuster Book of Facts and Fallacies* (New York: Simon and Schuster, 1983).

MAY 25
What's going on when you yawn?
Mary Elting, *Answers and More Answers* (New York: Grosset and Dunlap, 1974).

MAY 26
Are the Pennsylvania Dutch really Dutch?
Carroll Calkins, ed., *The Story of America* (Pleasantville, NY: The Reader's Digest Association, 1975).

James Meyers, *The Best Amazing Question and Answer Book* (New York: Playmore, Inc. Publishers, 1987).

MAY 27
What question started the Quadro Jump?
Susan Casey, *Women Invent! Two Centuries of Discoveries That Have Shaped Our World* (Chicago: Chicago Review Press, 1997).

MAY 28
How does a newspaper machine know what day it is?
David Feldman, *Why Do Pirates Love Parrots?* (New York: HarperCollins, 2006).

MAY 29
How do some books travel the world?
Margriet Ruurs, *My Librarian Is a Camel: How Books Are Brought to Children around the World* (Honesdale, PA: Boyds Mills Press, 2005).

MAY 30
How was the first sports drink connected to alligators?
Erin Barrett and Jack Mingo, *Not Another Apple for the Teacher! Hundreds of Fascinating Facts from the World of Teaching* (Berkeley, CA: Conari Press/Red Wheel Weiser, 2002).

MAY 31
When could doing your homework get you into trouble?
David Hardy, *What a Mistake!* (Secaucus, NJ: Octopus Books, 1987).

JUNE 1
What was so wonderful about the wheelbarrow?
Roger Bridgman, *1,000 Inventions and Discoveries* (New York: DK Publishing, 2002).
Charise Mericle Harper, *Imaginative Inventions: The Who, What, Where, When, and Why of Roller Skates, Potato Chips, Marbles, and Pie (and More!)* (Boston: Little Brown, 2001).

JUNE 2
How did Canada get its name?
Don Wulffson and Pam Wulffson, *Abracadabra to Zombie: More than 300 Wacky Word Origins* (New York: Dutton Children's Books/Penguin, 2003).

JUNE 3
Where could you catch dinner without leaving the kitchen?
The Galahad Treasury of Trivia (New York: Galahad Books, 1979).

JUNE 4
What happened to the caboose?
David Feldman, *Why Do Pirates Love Parrots?* (New York: HarperCollins, 2006).

JUNE 5
Why would people eat oysters only during the months spelled with an r?
Robert L. Shook, *The Book of Why* (Maplewood, NJ: Hammond, 1983).

JUNE 6
What does D-day mean?
Ty Reynolds, ed., *That's a Good Question 6* (Calgary, Alberta: Script Publishing, 1995).

JUNE 7
What color are goldfish?
Bruce Witherspoon, *The Great Big Book of Astounding Facts: A Compendium of Everything You Never Knew You Needed to Know* (New York: Bristol Park Books, 1993).

JUNE 8
How do you speak to an alligator egg?
Bruce Witherspoon, *The Great Big Book of Astounding Facts: A Compendium of Everything You Never Knew You Needed to Know* (New York: Bristol Park Books, 1993).

JUNE 9
What was on the menu for the king?
Tim Wood, *What They Don't Teach You about History: Hundreds of Peculiar and Fascinating Facts* (Hemel Hempstead, Great Britain: Simon and Schuster, 1990).

JUNE 10
Why did two sea creatures become buddies?
Bruce Witherspoon, *The Great Big Book of Astounding Facts: A Compendium of Everything You Never Knew You Needed to Know* (New York: Bristol Park Books, 1993).

JUNE 11
What are some inventions that never became popular?
Judith St. George, *So You Want to Be an Inventor?* (New York: Scholastic, 2003).

JUNE 12
How do mother animals and their babies keep track of each other?
Mary Elting, *Answers and More Answers* (New York: Grosset and Dunlap, 1974).

JUNE 13
How does the automatic store door know you want to come in?
Catherine Ripley, *Do the Doors Open by Magic? and Other Supermarket Questions* (Toronto: Greey de Pencier Books, 1995).

JUNE 14
Why do fruits and flowers have such bright colors?
Terry Martin, *Why Are Zebras Black and White? Questions Children Ask about Color* (New York: DK Publishing, 1996).

JUNE 15
What made air-conditioning cool?
Roger Bridgman, *1,000 Inventions and Discoveries* (New York: DK Publishing, 2002).
Bryan Bunch, *The History of Science and Technology: A Browser's Guide to the Great Discoveries, Inventions, and the People Who Made Them from the Dawn of Time to Today* (Boston: Houghton Mifflin, 2004).
Norman King, *The Almanac of Fascinating Beginnings: From the Academy Awards to the Xerox Machine* (Secaucus, NJ: Carol Publishing Group, 1994).

Charles Panati, *Panati's Extraordinary Origins of Everyday Things* (New York: Harper and Row, 1987).

JUNE 16
Is it true that fish can't drown?
Rhoda Blumberg and Lela Blumberg, *The Simon and Schuster Book of Facts and Fallacies* (New York: Simon and Schuster, 1983).

JUNE 17
Why are marbles so marvelous?
Charise Mericle Harper, *Imaginative Inventions: The Who, What, Where, When, and Why of Roller Skates, Potato Chips, Marbles, and Pie (and More!)* (Boston: Little Brown, 2001).
Richard Lederer, *Presidential Trivia: The Feats, Fates, Families, Foibles, and Firsts of Our American Presidents* (Layton, UT: Gibbs Smith, 2007).

JUNE 18
How did a bridge provide entertainment for travelers?
Lawrence Pringle, *"The Earth Is Flat" and Other Great Mistakes* (New York: William Morrow and Company, 1983).

JUNE 19
Why do moths get so close to lights?
Anthony Addison, ed., *The Children's Book of Questions and Answers* (London: Treasure Press, 1987).
John Mitchinson and John Lloyd, *The Book of General Ignorance* (New York: Harmony Books/ Random House, 2007).

JUNE 20
What's the biggest flower in the world?
James Meyers, *The Best Amazing Question and Answer Book* (New York: Playmore, Inc. Publishers, 1987).

JUNE 21
Which is the oldest vegetable on earth?
The Galahad Treasury of Trivia (New York: Galahad Books, 1979).

JUNE 22
How does a kaleidoscope work?
Roger Bridgman, *1,000 Inventions and Discoveries* (New York: DK Publishing, 2002).

JUNE 23
What can you do in case of fire?
Susan Casey, *Women Invent! Two Centuries of Discoveries That Have Shaped Our World* (Chicago: Chicago Review Press, 1997).

JUNE 24
What's a Cracker Jack?
Harry Harris, *Good Old-Fashioned Yankee Ingenuity: Unsung Triumphs of American Invention* (Chelsea, MI: Scarborough Press, 1990).
Charlotte Foltz Jones, *Accidents May Happen: Fifty Inventions Discovered by Mistake* (New York: Delacorte Press, 1996).
Norman King, *The Almanac of Fascinating Beginnings: From the Academy Awards to the Xerox Machine.* (Secaucus, NJ: Carol Publishing Group, 1994).

Don Wulffson and Pam Wulffson, *Abracadabra to Zombie: More than 300 Wacky Word Origins* (New York: Dutton Children's Books/Penguin, 2003).

JUNE 25
How do owls hunt at night?
Anthony Addison, ed., *The Children's Book of Questions and Answers* (London: Treasure Press, 1987).
Jacqui Bailey, *Amazing Animal Facts* (New York: DK Publishing, 2003).
John Mitchinson and John Lloyd, *The Book of General Ignorance* (New York: Harmony Books/Random House, 2007).

JUNE 26
What country helped inspire Lincoln Logs?
Gil Asakawa and Leland Rucker, *The Toy Book* (New York: Knopf, 1991).
Deborah Jaffé, *The History of Toys: From Spinning Tops to Robots* (Stroud, England: Sutton, 2006).
Andrew McClary, *Toys with Nine Lives: A Social History of American Toys* (North Haven, CT: Linnet Books, 1997).
Stephen van Dulken, *American Inventions: A History of Curious, Extraordinary, and Just Plain Useful Patents* (New York: New York University Press, 2004).

JUNE 27
Do humans copy animals' homes?
Phil Gates, *Nature Got There First* (New York: Kingfisher, 1995).

JUNE 28
What was a Pig Stand, and what could you do there?
Johnny Acton, Tania Adams, and Matt Packer, *Origin of Everyday Things* (New York: Sterling, 2006).

JUNE 29
How did one man build a gigantic castle all by himself—twice?
Bill McLain, *What Makes Flamingos Pink: A Colorful Collection of Q and A's for the Unquenchably Curious* (New York: HarperCollins, 2001).

JUNE 30
What bird uses a spear to catch its dinner?
Phil Gates, *Nature Got There First* (New York: Kingfisher, 1995).

JULY 1
What does it mean to be there "with bells on"?
Richard Ammon, *Conestoga Wagons* (New York: Holiday House, 2000).

JULY 2
Why does a baseball field have a raised pitcher's mound?
Andrea Chesman, ed., *The Inventive Yankee: From Rockets to Roller Skates, 200 Years of Yankee Inventors and Inventions* (Dublin, NH: Yankee Books, 1989).
David Feldman, *Why Do Pirates Love Parrots?* (New York: HarperCollins, 2006).

JULY 3
How could a loud band help with a bad tooth?
Tim Wood, *What They Don't Teach You about History: Hundreds of Peculiar and Fascinating Facts* (Hemel Hempstead, Great Britain: Simon and Schuster, 1990).

JULY 4
What are some little-known secrets of the Statue of Liberty?
Bill McLain, *Do Fish Drink Water? Puzzling and Improbable Questions and Answers* (New York: William Morrow and Company, 1999).

JULY 5
Can your cat talk?
Bill McLain, *Do Fish Drink Water? Puzzling and Improbable Questions and Answers* (New York: William Morrow and Company, 1999).

JULY 6
How did Abraham Lincoln make fun of how he looked?
James Humes, *Which President Killed a Man? Tantalizing Trivia and Fun Facts about Our Chief Executives and First Ladies* (New York: McGraw-Hill, 2003).
Richard Lederer, *Presidential Trivia: The Feats, Fates, Families, Foibles, and Firsts of Our American Presidents* (Layton, UT: Gibbs Smith, 2007).
Noah McCullough, *The Essential Book of Presidential Trivia* (New York: Random House, 2006).

JULY 7
How did an accident that caused broken glass end up protecting people?
Don L. Wulffson, *The Kid Who Invented the Popsicle, and Other Surprising Stories about Inventions* (New York: Cobblehill Books/Dutton, 1997).

JULY 8
Which insect flies faster than all the rest?
Jane Parker Resnick, Rebecca L. Grambo, and Tony Tallarico, *The Big Book of Questions and Answers* (Boston: Kidsbooks, 2002).

JULY 9
When was a typewriter used for something else?
The Galahad Treasury of Trivia (New York: Galahad Books, 1979).

JULY 10
When did it become a good idea to jump?
Roger Bridgman, *1,000 Inventions and Discoveries* (New York: DK Publishing, 2002).
Bryan Bunch, *The History of Science and Technology: A Browser's Guide to the Great Discoveries, Inventions, and the People Who Made Them from the Dawn of Time to Today* (Boston: Houghton Mifflin, 2004).
Gillian Clements, *The Picture History of Great Inventors* (New York: A. Knopf, 1993).
Harry Harris, *Good Old-Fashioned Yankee Ingenuity: Unsung Triumphs of American Invention* (Chelsea, MI: Scarborough House, 1990).

JULY 11
What was worth more upside down than right side up?
The Galahad Treasury of Trivia (New York: Galahad Books, 1979).

JULY 12
How did a simple cloth become known as a handkerchief?
Don Wulffson and Pam Wulffson, *Abracadabra to Zombie: More than 300 Wacky Word Origins* (New York: Dutton Children's Books/Penguin, 2003).

JULY 13
Why was a toilet also made into an aquarium?
Patricia Lauber, *What You Never Knew about Tubs, Toilets, and Showers* (New York: Simon and Schuster, 2001).
Steve Parker, *53½ Things That Changed the World and Some That Didn't* (New York: Simon and Schuster, 1992).
Steve Parker, *The Flying Bedstead, and Other Ingenious Inventions* (New York: Kingfisher, 1995).
Barbara Taylor, *I Wonder Why Zippers Have Teeth, and Other Questions about Inventions* (New York: Kingfisher, 1995).
Peter Turvey, *Inventions: Inventors and Ingenious Ideas* (New York: F. Watts, 1992).
Jane Wilcox, *Why Do We Use That?* (New York: F. Watts, 1996).

JULY 14
Why do snakes have forked, or split, tongues?
Jacqui Bailey, *Amazing Animal Facts* (New York: DK Publishing, 2003).
Sharon Bertsch McGrayne, *Blue Genes and Polyester Plants: 365 More Surprising Scientific Facts, Breakthroughs, and Discoveries* (New York: Wiley & Sons, 1997).

JULY 15
Why do baby teeth fall out?
Jane Parker Resnick, Rebecca L. Grambo, and Tony Tallarico, *The Big Book of Questions and Answers* (Boston: Kidsbooks, 2002).

JULY 16
Where on earth can you see the Atlantic Ocean and the Pacific Ocean at the same time?
James Meyers, *The Best Amazing Question and Answer Book* (New York: Playmore, Inc. Publishers, 1987).

JULY 17
What invention was more than skin deep?
Susan Casey, *Women Invent! Two Centuries of Discoveries That Have Shaped Our World* (Chicago: Chicago Review Press, 1997).

JULY 18
Why do you get thirsty?
Jane Parker Resnick, Rebecca L. Grambo, and Tony Tallarico, *The Big Book of Questions and Answers* (Boston: Kidsbooks, 2002).

JULY 19
Why did clothes dryers need windows in the front?
Linda Schmittroth, ed., *Eureka! Scientific Discoveries & Inventions That Shaped the World*, vol. 2, (New York: International Thomson Publishing, 1995).

JULY 20
What do a snail and an engine have in common?
Phil Gates, *Nature Got There First* (New York: Kingfisher, 1995).

JULY 21
When was it very inconvenient to listen to a stereo system?
Don L. Wulffson, *The Kid Who Invented the Trampoline: More Surprising Stories about Inventions* (New York: Dutton Children's Books/Penguin, 2001).

JULY 22
Why was a tree named after a president of the United States?
Richard Lederer, *Presidential Trivia: The Feats, Fates, Families, Foibles, and Firsts of Our American Presidents* (Layton, UT: Gibbs Smith, 2007).

JULY 23
How did a shoe polish gimmick turn into a tangled-up game?
Don Wulffson, *Toys! Amazing Stories behind Some Great Inventions* (New York: Henry Holt, 2000).

JULY 24
How did a stoplight experiment end up catching speeders?
Andrea Chesman, ed., *The Inventive Yankee: From Rockets to Roller Skates, 200 Years of Yankee Inventors and Inventions* (Dublin, NH: Yankee Books, 1989).

JULY 25
Which word never existed?
Richard Shenkman and Kurt Reiger, *One-Night Stands with American History: Odd, Amusing, and Little-Known Incidents* (New York: Morrow, 1980).

JULY 26
Why did people want to sit on top of a flagpole?
Charles Panati, *Panati's Parade of Fads, Follies, and Manias: The Origins of Our Most Cherished Obsessions* (New York: HarperPerennial, 1991).

JULY 27
Are those birds really humming?
James Meyers, *The Best Amazing Question and Answer Book* (New York: Playmore, Inc. Publishers, 1987).
Steve Murrie and Matthew Murrie, *Every Minute on Earth: Fun Facts That Happen Every 60 Seconds* (New York: Scholastic, 2007).
Kathy Wollard, *How Come? Planet Earth* (New York: Workman Publishing, 1999).

JULY 28
What does a skateboard have to do with the ocean?
Gil Asakawa and Leland Rucker, *The Toy Book* (New York: Knopf, 1991).
Harry Harris, *Good Old-Fashioned Yankee Ingenuity: Unsung Triumphs of American Invention* (Chelsea, MI: Scarborough House, 1990).
Deborah Jaffé, *The History of Toys: From Spinning Tops to Robots* (Stroud, England: Sutton, 2006).
Charles Panati, *Panati's Parade of Fads, Follies, and Manias: The Origins of Our Most Cherished Obsessions* (New York: HarperPerennial, 1991).

JULY 29
How did a young person name a former planet?
Dennis B. Fradin, *With a Little Luck: Surprising Stories of Amazing Discoveries* (New York: Dutton Children's Books, 2006).
Marc McCutcheon, *The Kid Who Named Pluto: And the Stories of Other Extraordinary Young People in Science* (San Francisco: Chronicle Books, 2004).

JULY 30
When were oysters used in court?
James Meyers, *The Best Amazing Question and Answer Book* (New York: Playmore, Inc. Publishers, 1987).

JULY 31
What would be a good reason to turn down an invitation to the White House?
Richard Lederer, *Presidential Trivia: The Feats, Fates, Families, Foibles, and Firsts of Our American Presidents* (Layton, UT: Gibbs Smith, 2007).

AUGUST 1
Seaweed is just a weed, right?
Rhoda Blumberg and Lela Blumberg, *The Simon and Schuster Book of Facts and Fallacies* (New York: Simon and Schuster, 1983).

AUGUST 2
Was there really such a thing as a "bat bomb"?
Tim Wood, *What They Don't Teach You about History: Hundreds of Peculiar and Fascinating Facts* (Hemel Hempstead, Great Britain: Simon and Schuster, 1990).

AUGUST 3
Are canaries supposed to bark?
The Galahad Treasury of Trivia (New York: Galahad Books, 1979).

AUGUST 4
What did a little girl discover in the cave?
Dennis B. Fradin, *With a Little Luck: Surprising Stories of Amazing Discoveries* (New York: Dutton Children's Books, 2006).
Patricia Lauber, *Painters of the Caves* (Washington, DC: National Geographic Society, 1998).
Lawrence Pringle, *"The Earth Is Flat" and Other Great Mistakes* (New York: William Morrow and Company, 1983).
Steve Tomacek, *What a Great Idea! Inventions That Changed the World* (New York: Scholastic Nonfiction, 2003).

AUGUST 5
Where does the world's smallest fish live?
The Galahad Treasury of Trivia (New York: Galahad Books, 1979).
George Stimpson, *Why Do Some Shoes Squeak? And 568 Other Popular Questions Answered* (New York: Bell Publishing, 1984).

AUGUST 6
What did a raisin start out as?
Anthony Addison, ed., *The Children's Book of Questions and Answers* (London: Treasure Press, 1987).
Christopher Maynard, *Why Are Pineapples Prickly? Questions Children Ask about Food* (New York: DK Publishing, 1997).

AUGUST 7
Why did people wear those wacky glasses?
Jilly MacLeod, *Great Inventions* (Mankato, MN: Creative Education, 1997).
Charles Panati, *Panati's Parade of Fads, Follies, and Manias: The Origins of Our Most Cherished Obsessions* (New York: HarperPerennial, 1991).

AUGUST 8
Why did a father encourage his children to play with food at the table?
Don Wulffson, *Toys! Amazing Stories behind Some Great Inventions* (New York: Henry Holt, 2000).

AUGUST 9
What kind of hats did the first baseball players wear?
Don L. Wulffson, *The Kid Who Invented the Popsicle, and Other Surprising Stories about Inventions* (New York: Cobblehill Books/ Dutton, 1997).

AUGUST 10
What do a deer and a dollar bill have in common?
Don Wulffson and Pam Wulffson, *Abracadabra to Zombie: More than 300 Wacky Word Origins* (New York: Dutton Children's Books/Penguin, 2003).

AUGUST 11
What were the rules of the road?
The Galahad Treasury of Trivia (New York: Galahad Books, 1979).

AUGUST 12
How do you know how "hot" spicy food really is?
Ty Reynolds, ed., *That's a Good Question 6* (Calgary, Alberta: Script Publishing, 1995).

AUGUST 13
Do sharks have metal detectors?
Phil Gates, *Nature Got There First* (New York: Kingfisher, 1995).

AUGUST 14
Where do the butterflies go?
Kathy Wollard, *How Come? Planet Earth* (New York: Workman Publishing, 1999).

AUGUST 15
What was so good about a cut?
Susan Casey, *Women Invent! Two Centuries of Discoveries That Have Shaped Our World* (Chicago: Chicago Review Press, 1997).

AUGUST 16
What does God know about you that you don't even know about yourself?
Steve Murrie and Matthew Murrie, *Every Minute on Earth: Fun Facts That Happen Every 60 Seconds* (New York: Scholastic, 2007).

AUGUST 17
How did a man who was blind make it safer for people to drive a car?
Joel Levy, *Really Useful: The Origins of Everyday Things* (Willowdale, ON: Firefly Books, 2002).

AUGUST 18
Which animal was chosen to be the first animal-shaped balloon?
Don L. Wulffson, *The Kid Who Invented the Popsicle, and Other Surprising Stories about Inventions* (New York: Cobblehill Books/Dutton, 1997).

AUGUST 19
How did a fifth grader invent a way to help people in wheelchairs?
Arlene Erlbach, *The Kids' Invention Book* (Minneapolis: Lerner Publishing Group, 1997).

AUGUST 20
Can you top this toy?
Gil Asakawa and Leland Rucker, *The Toy Book* (New York: Knopf, 1991).
Deborah Jaffé, *The History of Toys: From Spinning Tops to Robots* (Stroud, England: Sutton, 2006).
Andrew McClary, *Toys with Nine Lives: A Social History of American Toys* (North Haven, CT: Linnet Books, 1997).
Charles Panati, *Panati's Extraordinary Origins of Everyday Things* (New York: Harper and Row, 1987).
Don Wulffson, *Toys! Amazing Stories behind Some Great Inventions* (New York: Henry Holt, 2000).

AUGUST 21
What's the secret to scissors?
Phil Gates, *Nature Got There First* (New York: Kingfisher, 1995).

AUGUST 22
What mistake did President Truman find in the White House?
Richard Shenkman and Kurt Reiger, *One-Night Stands with American History: Odd, Amusing, and Little-Known Incidents* (New York: Morrow, 1980).

AUGUST 23
Which invention was called a "slide fastener"?
Johnny Acton, Tania Adams, and Matt Packer, *Origin of Everyday Things* (New York: Sterling, 2006).
Barbara Taylor, *I Wonder Why Zippers Have Teeth, and Other Questions about Inventions* (New York: Kingfisher, 1995).

AUGUST 24
What dessert was once called the "I-Scream Bar"?
Steven Caney, *Steven Caney's Invention Book* (New York: Workman Publishing, 1985).

AUGUST 25
Which trip would most people take only once?
Lawrence Pringle, *"The Earth Is Flat" and Other Great Mistakes* (New York: William Morrow and Company, 1983).

AUGUST 26
What made groups of soldiers turn blue?
Anita Sitarski, *Cold Light: Creatures, Discoveries, and Inventions That Glow* (Honesdale, PA: Boyds Mills Press, 2007).

AUGUST 27
Would you want to "go overboard"?
Teri Degler, *Scuttlebutt, and Other Expressions of Nautical Origin* (New York: H. Holt, 1989).

AUGUST 28
How does a rattlesnake protect itself?
Phil Gates, *Nature Got There First* (New York: Kingfisher, 1995).

AUGUST 29
How could there be a "folding bathtub"?
Daniel Cohen, *The Last Hundred Years: Household Technology* (New York: M. Evans, 1982).

AUGUST 30
How did a basketball player get the name "Chicken Man"?
Steve Riach, *Amazing but True Sports Stories* (Kansas City, MO: Hallmark Books, 2004).

AUGUST 31
How did pilots' uniforms help with the invention of the electric blanket?
Rodney Carlisle, *Scientific American Inventions and Discoveries: All the Milestones in Ingenuity—from the Discovery of Fire to the Invention of the Microwave Oven* (Hoboken, NJ: Wiley & Sons, 2004).
Norman King, *The Almanac of Fascinating Beginnings: From the Academy Awards to the Xerox Machine* (Secaucus, NJ: Carol Publishing Group, 1994).
Don L. Wulffson, *The Kid Who Invented the Popsicle, and Other Surprising Stories about Inventions* (New York: Cobblehill Books/Dutton, 1997).

SEPTEMBER 1
Is that real gold on top?
Mary Elting, *Answers and More Answers* (New York: Grosset and Dunlap, 1974).

SEPTEMBER 2
How has the Bible been important to presidents of the United States?
Richard Lederer, *Presidential Trivia: The Feats, Fates, Families, Foibles, and Firsts of Our American Presidents* (Layton, UT: Gibbs Smith, 2007).

SEPTEMBER 3
What made a chair fit for a king?
Steve Parker, *53½ Things That Changed the World and Some That Didn't* (New York: Simon and Schuster, 1992).
Jane Wilcox, *Why Do We Use That?* (New York: F. Watts, 1996).

SEPTEMBER 4
What are those crab shells doing on the sand?
Rhoda Blumberg and Lela Blumberg, *The Simon and Schuster Book of Facts and Fallacies* (New York: Simon and Schuster, 1983).

SEPTEMBER 5
Who stuck to making gum?
Lee Wardlaw, *Bubblemania: The Chewy History of Bubble Gum* (New York: Aladdin, 1997).
Carolyn Wyman, *I'm a Spam Fan: America's Best-Loved Foods* (Stamford, CT: Longmeadow Press, 1993).

SEPTEMBER 6
Does everything with the word scotch in its name come from Scotland?
J. Allen Varasdi, *Myth Information: An Extraordinary Collection of 590 Popular Misconceptions, Fallacies, and Misbeliefs* (New York: Ballantine Books, 1989).

SEPTEMBER 7
What delightful drink was invented because someone ran out of ingredients?
Charles Panati, *Panati's Extraordinary Origins of Everyday Things* (New York: Harper and Row, 1987).
David Rubel, *The United States in the 19th Century* (New York: Scholastic, 1996).

SEPTEMBER 8
What's the connection between tall buildings and boats?
Rodney Carlisle, *Scientific American Inventions and Discoveries: All the Milestones in Ingenuity—from the Discovery of Fire to the Invention of the Microwave Oven* (Hoboken, NJ: Wiley & Sons, 2004).
Teri Degler, *Scuttlebutt, and Other Expressions of Nautical Origin* (New York: H. Holt, 1989).
Olivia A. Isil, *When a Loose Cannon Flogs a Dead Horse There's the Devil to Pay: Seafaring Words in Everyday Speech* (Camden, ME: International Marine, 1996).
Norman King, *The Almanac of Fascinating Beginnings: From the Academy Awards to the Xerox Machine* (Secaucus, NJ: Carol Publishing Group, 1994).
Steve Parker, *53½ Things That Changed the World and Some That Didn't* (New York: Simon and Schuster, 1992).

SEPTEMBER 9
Why won't you find a cashew in its shell?
J. Allen Varasdi, *Myth Information: An Extraordinary Collection of 590 Popular Misconceptions, Fallacies, and Misbeliefs* (New York: Ballantine Books, 1989).

SEPTEMBER 10
How do you teach a parrot to talk?
The Galahad Treasury of Trivia (New York: Galahad Books, 1979).

SEPTEMBER 11
Which spelling mistake created an embarrassing story in the newspaper?
Richard Shenkman and Kurt Reiger, *One-Night Stands with American History: Odd, Amusing, and Little-Known Incidents* (New York: Morrow, 1980).

SEPTEMBER 12
Who is Big Ben?
Robert L. Shook, *The Book of Why* (Maplewood, NJ: Hammond, 1983).
J. Allen Varasdi, *Myth Information: An Extraordinary Collection of 590 Popular Misconceptions, Fallacies, and Misbeliefs* (New York: Ballantine Books, 1989).

SEPTEMBER 13
What old idea made a new kind of pen?
Barbara Taylor, *I Wonder Why Zippers Have Teeth, and Other Questions about Inventions* (New York: Kingfisher, 1995).

SEPTEMBER 14
Which came first: the chicken or the egg?
John Mitchinson and John Lloyd, *The Book of General Ignorance* (New York: Harmony Books/Random House, 2007).

SEPTEMBER 15
Can squirrels fly?
Bill McLain, *What Makes Flamingos Pink: A Colorful Collection of Q and A's for the Unquenchably Curious* (New York: HarperCollins, 2001).

SEPTEMBER 16
Why were skates made of bones?
Roger Bridgman, *1,000 Inventions and Discoveries* (New York: DK Publishing, 2002).
James Meyers, *The Best Amazing Question and Answer Book* (New York: Playmore, Inc. Publishers, 1987).

SEPTEMBER 17
When can you see a rainbow?
The Galahad Treasury of Trivia (New York: Galahad Books, 1979).

SEPTEMBER 18
When was a watch first watched?
Roger Bridgman, *1,000 Inventions and Discoveries* (New York: DK Publishing, 2002).
Steve Parker, *53½ Things That Changed the World and Some That Didn't* (New York: Simon and Schuster, 1992).
Linda Schmittroth, ed., *Eureka! Scientific Discoveries & Inventions That Shaped the World*, vol. 2, (New York: International Thomson Publishing, 1995).
Don L. Wulffson, *The Kid Who Invented the Popsicle, and Other Surprising Stories about Inventions* (New York: Cobblehill Books/Dutton, 1997).

SEPTEMBER 19
What was one of the first video games?
Gil Asakawa and Leland Rucker, *The Toy Book* (New York: Knopf, 1991).
Bryan Bunch, *The History of Science and Technology: A Browser's Guide to the Great Discoveries, Inventions, and the People Who Made Them from the Dawn of Time to Today* (Boston: Houghton Mifflin, 2004).
Peter Turvey, *Inventors and Ingenious Ideas* (New York: Franklin Watts, 1992).

SEPTEMBER 20
Why doesn't a jellyfish match its name?
J. Allen Varasdi, *Myth Information: An Extraordinary Collection of 590 Popular Misconceptions, Fallacies, and Misbeliefs* (New York: Ballantine Books, 1989).

SEPTEMBER 21
Which toy has also been a whistling weapon, a weather watcher, and even a fish catcher?
Charlotte Foltz Jones, *Accidents May Happen: Fifty Inventions Discovered by Mistake* (New York: Delacorte Press, 1996).
Steve Parker, *53½ Things That Changed the World and Some That Didn't* (New York: Simon and Schuster, 1992).
David Rubel, *The United States in the 19th Century* (New York: Scholastic, 1996).
Don Wulffson, *Toys! Amazing Stories behind Some Great Inventions* (New York: Henry Holt, 2000).

SEPTEMBER 22
What's so fascinating about feathers?
Mike O'Connor, *Why Don't Woodpeckers Get Headaches? and Other Bird Questions You Know You Want to Ask* (Boston: Beacon Press, 2007).

SEPTEMBER 23
Where did Abraham Lincoln find the nine words he never forgot?
James Humes, *Which President Killed a Man? Tantalizing Trivia and Fun Facts about Our Chief Executives and First Ladies* (New York: McGraw-Hill, 2003).

SEPTEMBER 24
What's the story behind the glow-in-the-dark rock?
Anita Sitarski, *Cold Light: Creatures, Discoveries, and Inventions That Glow* (Honesdale, PA: Boyds Mills Press, 2007).

SEPTEMBER 25
Where do you hide a traffic policeman?
Andrea Chesman, ed., *The Inventive Yankee: From Rockets to Roller Skates, 200 Years of Yankee Inventors and Inventions* (Dublin, NH: Yankee Books, 1989).

SEPTEMBER 26
What colors mean danger?
Phil Gates, *Nature Got There First* (New York: Kingfisher, 1995).
Terry Martin, *Why Are Zebras Black and White? Questions Children Ask about Color* (New York: DK Publishing, 1996).

SEPTEMBER 27
How did a group of detectives accidentally fingerprint themselves?
Charlotte Foltz Jones, *Accidents May Happen: Fifty Inventions Discovered by Mistake* (New York: Delacorte Press, 1996).

SEPTEMBER 28
Why was Alka-Seltzer invented?
Harry Harris, *Good Old-Fashioned Yankee Ingenuity: Unsung Triumphs of American Invention* (Chelsea, MI: Scarborough House, 1990).
Norman King, *The Almanac of Fascinating Beginnings: From the Academy Awards to the Xerox Machine* (Secaucus, NJ: Carol Publishing Group, 1994).

SEPTEMBER 29
How was the catcher's mitt introduced to the game of baseball?
Andrea Chesman, ed., *The Inventive Yankee: From Rockets to Roller Skates, 200 Years of Yankee Inventors and Inventions* (Dublin, NH: Yankee Books, 1989).
Sally Cook, *Hey Batta Batta Swing! The Wild Old Days of Baseball* (New York: M. K. McElderry Books, 2007).

SEPTEMBER 30
Before the hair dryer, how did people in a hurry dry their hair?
Norman King, *The Almanac of Fascinating Beginnings: From the Academy Awards to the Xerox Machine* (Secaucus, NJ: Carol Publishing Group, 1994).
Don Wulffson and Pam Wulffson, *Abracadabra to Zombie: More than 300 Wacky Word Origins* (New York: Dutton Children's Books/Penguin, 2003).
Don L. Wulffson, *The Kid Who Invented the Popsicle, and Other Surprising Stories about Inventions* (New York: Cobblehill Books/Dutton, 1997).

OCTOBER 1
Have you ever used a Glo-Sheet for your homework?
Susan Casey, *Women Invent! Two Centuries of Discoveries That Have Shaped Our World* (Chicago: Chicago Review Press, 1997).
Catherine Thimmesh, *Girls Think of Everything: Stories of Ingenious Inventions by Women* (New York: Houghton Mifflin, 2000).
Tom Tucker, *Brainstorm! The Stories of Twenty American Kid Inventors* (New York: Farrar, Straus and Giroux, 1995).

OCTOBER 2
What can be shocking about your teeth?
Bill Nye, *Bill Nye the Science Guy's Consider the Following* (New York: Disney Press, 1995).

OCTOBER 3
How do you take your tea?
Tim Wood, *What They Don't Teach You about History: Hundreds of Peculiar and Fascinating Facts* (Hemel Hempstead, Great Britain: Simon and Schuster, 1990).

OCTOBER 4
Which president of the United States had an important job even in high school?
James Humes, *Which President Killed a Man? Tantalizing Trivia and Fun Facts about Our Chief Executives and First Ladies* (New York: McGraw-Hill, 2003).

OCTOBER 5
Which invention was most appreciated when someone sat on it?
Don L. Wulffson, *The Kid Who Invented the Popsicle, and Other Surprising Stories about Inventions* (New York: Cobblehill Books/Dutton, 1997).

OCTOBER 6
Where are you when you're "under the weather"?
Olivia A. Isil, *When a Loose Cannon Flogs a Dead Horse There's the Devil to Pay: Seafaring Words in Everyday Speech* (Camden, ME: International Marine, 1996).
Marvin Terban, *Mad as a Wet Hen! and Other Funny Idioms* (New York: Clarion Books, 1987).

OCTOBER 7
Is this a self-service stable?
Tim Wood, *What They Don't Teach You about History: Hundreds of Peculiar and Fascinating Facts* (Hemel Hempstead, Great Britain: Simon and Schuster, 1990).

OCTOBER 8
Where do the sunset's colors come from?
Terry Martin, *Why Are Zebras Black and White? Questions Children Ask about Color* (New York: DK Publishing, 1996).

OCTOBER 9
What's the first thing the inventor of elastic thought it could be used for?
Barbara Taylor, *I Wonder Why Zippers Have Teeth, and Other Questions about Inventions* (New York: Kingfisher, 1995).

OCTOBER 10
How smart is your goldfish?
John Mitchinson and John Lloyd, *The Book of General Ignorance* (New York: Harmony Books/Random House, 2007).

OCTOBER 11
Why do penguins have knees?
Anthony Addison, ed., *The Children's Book of Questions and Answers* (London: Treasure Press, 1987).
Mike O'Connor, *Why Don't Woodpeckers Get Headaches? and Other Bird Questions You Know You Want to Ask* (Boston: Beacon Press, 2007).

OCTOBER 12
Which company started in a shoe box?
Allyn Freeman and Bob Golden, *Why Didn't I Think of That? Bizarre Origins of Ingenious Inventions We Couldn't Live Without* (New York: Wiley & Sons, 1997).

OCTOBER 13
What are you doing when you "spill the beans"?
Charlotte Foltz Jones, *Eat Your Words: A Fascinating Look at the Language of Food* (New York: Delacorte Press, 1999).

OCTOBER 14
What rumor about elephants is false?
Rhoda Blumberg and Lela Blumberg, *The Simon and Schuster Book of Facts and Fallacies* (New York: Simon and Schuster, 1983).

OCTOBER 15
What happened when a pig broke the law?
Tim Wood, *What They Don't Teach You about History: Hundreds of Peculiar and Fascinating Facts* (Hemel Hempstead, Great Britain: Simon and Schuster, 1990).

OCTOBER 16
How did Heinz 57 sauce get such a strange name?
Richard Shenkman and Kurt Reiger, *One-Night Stands with American History: Odd, Amusing, and Little-Known Incidents* (New York: Morrow, 1980).

OCTOBER 17
How did a dog almost cause the president of the United States to be shot?
James Humes, *Which President Killed a Man? Tantalizing Trivia and Fun Facts about Our Chief Executives and First Ladies* (New York: McGraw-Hill, 2003).

OCTOBER 18
Is it true that some people never have dreams?
Rhoda Blumberg and Lela Blumberg, *The Simon and Schuster Book of Facts and Fallacies* (New York: Simon and Schuster, 1983).

OCTOBER 19
Where did the snorkel come from?
Roger Bridgman, *1,000 Inventions and Discoveries* (New York: DK Publishing, 2002).

OCTOBER 20
How did a frog help invent the battery?
Jill Hauser, *Gizmos and Gadgets: Creating Science Contraptions That Work (and Knowing Why)* (Charlotte, VT: Williamson Publishing, 1999).

Ty Reynolds, ed., *That's a Good Question 6* (Calgary, Alberta: Script Publishing, 1995).

OCTOBER 21
How many colors can we see?
The Galahad Treasury of Trivia (New York: Galahad Books, 1979).

OCTOBER 22
What everyday problems can be solved with a candle, string, and nail polish?
The Diagram Group, *How to Hold a Crocodile* (Willowdale, ON: Firefly Books, 2003).

OCTOBER 23
How did pilots escape from their planes?
Rodney Carlisle, *Scientific American Inventions and Discoveries: All the Milestones in Ingenuity—from the Discovery of Fire to the Invention of the Microwave Oven* (Hoboken, NJ: Wiley & Sons, 2004).

OCTOBER 24
What's so good about green?
Terry Martin, *Why Are Zebras Black and White? Questions Children Ask about Color* (New York: DK Publishing, 1996).

OCTOBER 25
When did an audience watch someone eat?
Tim Wood, *What They Don't Teach You about History: Hundreds of Peculiar and Fascinating Facts* (Hemel Hempstead, Great Britain: Simon and Schuster, 1990).

OCTOBER 26
Who rode the first Ferris wheel?
Bill McLain, *What Makes Flamingos Pink: A Colorful Collection of Q and A's for the Unquenchably Curious* (New York: HarperCollins, 2001).
Don Wulffson and Pam Wulffson, *Abracadabra to Zombie: More than 300 Wacky Word Origins* (New York: Dutton Children's Books/Penguin, 2003).

OCTOBER 27
Why is all that stuff in your room called junk?
Teri Degler, *Scuttlebutt, and Other Expressions of Nautical Origin* (New York: H. Holt, 1989).

OCTOBER 28
What code is used every time you buy something?
Johnny Acton, Tania Adams, and Matt Packer, *Origin of Everyday Things* (New York: Sterling, 2006).
Barbara Taylor, *I Wonder Why Zippers Have Teeth, and Other Questions about Inventions* (New York: Kingfisher, 1995).
Don L. Wulffson, *The Kid Who Invented the Popsicle, and Other Surprising Stories about Inventions* (New York: Cobblehill Books/Dutton, 1997).

OCTOBER 29
What can you learn about trunks and tusks?
Jacqui Bailey, *Amazing Animal Facts* (New York: DK Publishing, 2003).
David Feldman, *Why Do Pirates Love Parrots?* (New York: HarperCollins, 2006).
Jennifer Storey Gillis, *Tooth Truth: Fun Facts and Projects* (Pownal, VT: Storey Communications, 1996).

OCTOBER 30
What's the story behind the equals sign?
John Mitchinson and John Lloyd, *The Book of General Ignorance* (New York: Harmony Books/Random House, 2007).

OCTOBER 31
What should you know about the hair on your head?
Rhoda Blumberg and Lela Blumberg, *The Simon and Schuster Book of Facts and Fallacies* (New York: Simon and Schuster, 1983).

NOVEMBER 1
Could you read by the light of a beetle?
Anita Sitarski, *Cold Light: Creatures, Discoveries, and Inventions That Glow* (Honesdale, PA: Boyds Mills Press, 2007).

NOVEMBER 2
Do oysters climb trees?
Bruce D. Witherspoon, *The Great Big Book of Astounding Facts: A Compendium of Everything You Never Knew You Needed to Know* (New York: Bristol Park Books, 1993).

NOVEMBER 3
Why was it called a stagecoach?
Andrea Chesman, ed., *The Inventive Yankee: From Rockets to Roller Skates, 200 Years of Yankee Inventors and Inventions* (Dublin, NH: Yankee Books, 1989).
Tim McNeese, *Conestogas and Stagecoaches* (New York: Maxwell Macmillan International, 1993).
Don Wulffson and Pam Wulffson, *Abracadabra to Zombie: More than 300 Wacky Word Origins* (New York: Dutton Children's Books/Penguin, 2003).

NOVEMBER 4
How close is the thunderstorm?
Mark Eubank, *The Weather Detectives: Fun-Filled Facts, Experiments, and Activities for Kids!* (Layton, UT: G. Smith, Publisher, 2004).
Terry Martin, *Why Does Lightning Strike? Questions Children Ask about the Weather* (New York: DK Publishing, 1996).
Steve Murrie and Matthew Murrie, *Every Minute on Earth: Fun Facts That Happen Every 60 Seconds* (New York: Scholastic, 2007).

NOVEMBER 5
What do the numbers on baseball uniforms mean?
Sally Cook, *Hey Batta Batta Swing! The Wild Old Days of Baseball* (New York: M. K. McElderry Books, 2007).

NOVEMBER 6
What famous library was started with eleven wagons full of books?
James Humes, *Which President Killed a Man? Tantalizing Trivia and Fun Facts about Our Chief Executives and First Ladies* (New York: McGraw-Hill, 2003).
David Rubel, *The United States in the 19th Century* (New York: Scholastic, 1996).

NOVEMBER 7
How did an octopus trick the aquarium keepers each night?
Toney Allman, *From Octopus Eyes to Powerful Lenses* (Detroit, MI: KidHaven Press, 2007).

NOVEMBER 8
What's the difference between brown eggs and white eggs?
Rhoda Blumberg and Lela Blumberg, *The Simon and Schuster Book of Facts and Fallacies* (New York: Simon and Schuster, 1983).

NOVEMBER 9
What is one of an animal's best weapons of protection?
Martin Goldwyn, *How a Fly Walks Upside Down . . . and Other Curious Facts* (New York: Citadel Press, 1979).

NOVEMBER 10
How did White House press conferences get started?
Richard Lederer, *Presidential Trivia: The Feats, Fates, Families, Foibles, and Firsts of Our American Presidents* (Layton, UT: Gibbs Smith, 2007).

NOVEMBER 11
How did help arrive in a hurry?
Roger Bridgman, *1,000 Inventions and Discoveries* (New York: DK Publishing, 2002).

NOVEMBER 12
How do you stop a toddler from spilling?
Susan Casey, *Women Invent! Two Centuries of Discoveries That Have Shaped Our World* (Chicago: Chicago Review Press, 1997).

NOVEMBER 13
What helmet was dangerous to wear?
Jilly MacLeod, *Great Inventions* (Mankato, MN: Creative Education, 1997).

NOVEMBER 14
What was strange about early basketball courts?
Bruce Witherspoon, *The Great Big Book of Astounding Facts: A Compendium of Everything You Never Knew You Needed to Know* (New York: Bristol Park Books, 1993).

NOVEMBER 15
Could a cow cure you?
Tim Wood, *What They Don't Teach You about History: Hundreds of Peculiar and Fascinating Facts* (Hemel Hempstead, Great Britain: Simon and Schuster, 1990).

NOVEMBER 16
How does the sea otter make itself a snack?
Warren D. Thomas and Daniel Kaufman, *Dolphin Conferences, Elephant Midwives, and Other Astonishing Facts about Animals* (Los Angeles: Jeremy P. Tarcher, 1990).

NOVEMBER 17
How can you tell if it's a drought?
Rhoda Blumberg and Lela Blumberg, *The Simon and Schuster Book of Facts and Fallacies* (New York: Simon and Schuster, 1983).

NOVEMBER 18
How did paper money become popular?
David Louis, *More Fascinating Facts: 1,001 Astonishing Facts on Every Imaginable Subject* (New York: Ridge Press, 1979).

NOVEMBER 19
Why do women wear wedding rings?
Robert L. Shook, *The Book of Why* (Maplewood, NJ: Hammond, Inc., 1983).

NOVEMBER 20
How does a hollow tree keep growing anyway?
Mary Elting, *Answers and More Answers* (New York: Grosset and Dunlap, 1974).

NOVEMBER 21
What food do you eat that has the wrong name?
Charlotte Foltz Jones, *Eat Your Words: A Fascinating Look at the Language of Food* (New York: Delacorte Press, 1999).

NOVEMBER 22
Why does a cat raise the fur on its back when it's frightened?
Martin Goldwyn, *How a Fly Walks Upside Down . . . and Other Curious Facts* (New York: Citadel Press, 1979).

NOVEMBER 23
Where can you find a pearl?
Jane Parker Resnick, Rebecca L. Grambo, and Tony Tallarico, *The Big Book of Questions and Answers* (Boston: Kidsbooks, 2002).

NOVEMBER 24
Why did a book salesman start selling perfume instead?
Charlotte Foltz Jones, *Accidents May Happen: Fifty Inventions Discovered by Mistake* (New York: Delacorte Press, 1996).
Joel Levy, *Really Useful: The Origins of Everyday Things* (Willowdale, ON: Firefly Books, 2002).

NOVEMBER 25
Which car was also the name of an article of clothing?
Don Wulffson and Pam Wulffson, *Abracadabra to Zombie: More than 300 Wacky Word Origins* (New York: Dutton Children's Books/Penguin, 2003).

NOVEMBER 26
What's the background of the blackboard?
Andrea Chesman, ed., *The Inventive Yankee: From Rockets to Roller Skates, 200 Years of Yankee Inventors and Inventions* (Dublin, NH: Yankee Books, 1989).

NOVEMBER 27
What made the soap float?
Don Wulffson and Pam Wulffson, *Abracadabra to Zombie: More than 300 Wacky Word Origins* (New York: Dutton Children's Books/Penguin, 2003).

NOVEMBER 28
Where is it really difficult to get sick in the winter?
David Louis, *More Fascinating Facts: 1,001 Astonishing Facts on Every Imaginable Subject.* (New York: Ridge Press, 1979).

NOVEMBER 29
Do all birds fly?
Jane Parker Resnick, Rebecca L. Grambo, and Tony Tallarico, *The Big Book of Questions and Answers* (Boston: Kidsbooks, 2002).

NOVEMBER 30
Why did people wear pouches around their waists?
Don L. Wulffson, *The Kid Who Invented the Popsicle, and Other Surprising Stories about Inventions* (New York: Cobblehill Books/Dutton, 1997).

DECEMBER 1
Which cake mix was named after a traveling salesman?
Charles Panati, *Panati's Extraordinary Origins of Everyday Things* (New York: Harper and Row, 1987).
Carolyn Wyman, *I'm a Spam Fan: America's Best-Loved Foods* (Stamford, CT: Longmeadow Press, 1993).

DECEMBER 2
Why does a toadstool care about its posture?
Phil Gates, *Nature Got There First* (New York: Kingfisher, 1995).
Terry Martin, *Why Do Sunflowers Face the Sun?* (New York: DK Publishing, 1996).

DECEMBER 3
How did a twelve-year-old find a huge fossil?
Dennis B. Fradin, *With a Little Luck: Surprising Stories of Amazing Discoveries* (New York: Dutton Children's Books, 2006).

DECEMBER 4
How much sleep is just right?
Terry Martin, *Why Do We Laugh? Questions Children Ask about the Human Body* (New York: DK Publishing, 1996).
John Mitchinson and John Lloyd, *The Book of General Ignorance* (New York: Harmony Books/Random House, 2007).

DECEMBER 5
Which popular drink had no liquid in it?
Johnny Acton, Tania Adams, and Matt Packer, *Origin of Everyday Things* (New York: Sterling, 2006).

DECEMBER 6
How many faces can you make?
The Super Chunky Question and Answer Book (New York: Playmore, Inc., 1987).

DECEMBER 7
What was the start of the stapler?
Stephen van Dulken, *American Inventions: A History of Curious, Extraordinary, and Just Plain Useful Patents* (New York: New York University Press, 2004).

DECEMBER 8
Which finger is the most important?
The Super Chunky Question and Answer Book (New York: Playmore, Inc., 1987).

DECEMBER 9
What else can you ski on besides snow?
Jill Frankel Hauser, *Gizmos and Gadgets: Creating Science Contraptions That Work (and Knowing Why)* (Charlotte, VT: Williamson Pub., 1999).
Tom Tucker, *Brainstorm! The Stories of Twenty American Kid Inventors* (New York: Farrar, Straus and Giroux, 1995).

DECEMBER 10
Why did all New Yorkers stay inside one morning?
Richard Shenkman and Kurt Reiger, *One-Night Stands with American History: Odd, Amusing, and Little-Known Incidents* (New York: Morrow, 1980).

DECEMBER 11
How did Spam get its name?
Johnny Acton, Tania Adams, and Matt Packer, *Origin of Everyday Things* (New York: Sterling, 2006).
Don Wulffson and Pam Wulffson, *Abracadabra to Zombie: More than 300 Wacky Word Origins* (New York: Dutton Children's Books/Penguin, 2003).
Carolyn Wyman, *I'm a Spam Fan: America's Best-Loved Foods* (Stamford, CT: Longmeadow Press, 1993).

DECEMBER 12
What made the paper bag popular?
David Lindsay, *House of Invention: The Secret Life of Everyday Products* (New York: Lyons Press, 2000).
Catherine Thimmesh, *Girls Think of Everything: Stories of Ingenious Inventions by Women* (New York: Houghton Mifflin, 2000).

DECEMBER 13
Why did remote controls make watching TV harder at first?
Joel Levy, *Really Useful: The Origins of Everyday Things* (Willowdale, ON: Firefly Books, 2002).

DECEMBER 14
Why are the teeth of animals so different from ours?
Jennifer Storey Gillis, *Tooth Truth: Fun Facts and Projects* (Pownal, VT: Storey Communications, 1996).

DECEMBER 15
What makes soda fizzy?
Christopher Maynard, *Why Are Pineapples Prickly? Questions Children Ask about Food* (New York: DK Publishing, 1997).

DECEMBER 16
Why would a bird spit?
The Super Chunky Question and Answer Book (New York: Playmore, Inc., 1987).

DECEMBER 17
What's worse than a snowsuit?
Tim Wood, *What They Don't Teach You about History: Hundreds of Peculiar and Fascinating Facts* (Hemel Hempstead, Great Britain: Simon and Schuster, 1990).

DECEMBER 18
Why do fireflies blink?
Jane Parker Resnick, Rebecca L. Grambo, and Tony Tallarico, *The Big Book of Questions and Answers* (Boston: Kidsbooks, 2002).

DECEMBER 19
What miniature toy did almost every boy wish for in the 1950s?
Gil Asakawa and Leland Rucker, *The Toy Book* (New York: Knopf, 1991).

Charles Panati, *Panati's Parade of Fads, Follies, and Manias: The Origins of Our Most Cherished Obsessions* (New York: HarperPerennial, 1991).

DECEMBER 20
What can you prove with bare feet and a refrigerator?
Mark Eubank, *The Weather Detectives: Fun-Filled Facts, Experiments, and Activities for Kids!* (Layton, UT: G. Smith, Publisher, 2004).

DECEMBER 21
How did a mousetrap catch a thief?
Richard Shenkman and Kurt Reiger, *One-Night Stands with American History: Odd, Amusing, and Little-Known Incidents* (New York: Morrow, 1980).

DECEMBER 22
Can you explain the sneeze, please?
Steve Murrie and Matthew Murrie, *Every Minute on Earth: Fun Facts That Happen Every 60 Seconds* (New York: Scholastic, 2007).

DECEMBER 23
Why do mirrors get foggy?
Barbara Taylor, *I Wonder Why Soap Makes Bubbles, and Other Questions about Science* (New York: Kingfisher, 1994).

DECEMBER 24
What invention grew out of a funny electric flowerpot?
Joel Levy, *Really Useful: The Origins of Everyday Things* (Willowdale, ON: Firefly Books, 2002).

DECEMBER 25
How did animal crackers become a Christmas present?
Charise Mericle Harper, *Imaginative Inventions: The Who, What, Where, When, and Why of Roller Skates, Potato Chips, Marbles, and Pie (and More!)* (Boston: Little Brown, 2001).

DECEMBER 26
Why would potato farmers be interested in jellyfish?
Jane Parker Resnick, Rebecca L. Grambo, and Tony Tallarico, *The Big Book of Questions and Answers* (Boston: Kidsbooks, 2002).

DECEMBER 27
What inspired the baby mobile?
Jill Frankel Hauser, *Gizmos and Gadgets* (Charlotte, VT: Williamson Publishing, 1999).

DECEMBER 28
How can you help someone who is fainting?
Rhoda Blumberg and Lela Blumberg, *The Simon and Schuster Book of Facts and Fallacies* (New York: Simon and Schuster, 1983).

DECEMBER 29
What game inspired the merry-go-round?
Don L. Wulffson, *The Kid Who Invented the Popsicle, and Other Surprising Stories about Inventions* (New York: Cobblehill Books/ Dutton, 1997).

DECEMBER 30
What's proof of a dutiful dog?
Bruce Witherspoon, *The Great Big Book of Astounding Facts: A Compendium of Everything You Never Knew You Needed to Know* (New York: Bristol Park Books, 1993).

DECEMBER 31
Why do evergreens stay green all year long?
Jane Parker Resnick, Rebecca L. Grambo, and Tony Tallarico, *The Big Book of Questions and Answers* (Boston: Kidsbooks, 2002).

Acknowledgments

Thanks to Stephanie Voiland, my editor at Tyndale,
who used her talents and insight to carefully craft this project.

Scripture Index